Dorsality

CARY WOLFE, SERIES EDITOR

DORSALITY

Thinking Back
through Technology and Politics

David Wills

posthumanities 5

University of Minnesota Press

Minneapolis

London

Sections of chapters 1 and 2 were previously published in "Thinking Back: Towards Technology, via Dorsality," *Parallax* 32 (July–September 2004). An earlier version of chapter 4 was previously published as "A Line Drawn in the Ocean," *Social Identities* 7, no. 4 (December 2001), and as "Des lignes tracées dans l'océan ou la frontière arrivante," in *La démocratie à venir,* ed. Marie-Louise Mallet (Paris: Galilée, 2004). An earlier version of chapter 5 was previously published as "Full Dorsal: Derrida's Politics of Friendship," *Postmodern Culture* 15, no. 3 (2005), and as "En plein dos," in *Derrida: Pour les temps à venir,* ed. René Major (Paris: Éditions Stock, 2007).

Published by the University of Minnesota Press
111 Third Avenue South, Suite 290
Minneapolis, MN 55401-2520
http://www.upress.umn.edu

Library of Congress Cataloging-in-Publication Data
Wills, David, 1953–
    Dorsality : thinking back through technology and politics / David Wills.
        p.   cm. — (Posthumanities ; v. 5)
    Includes bibliographical references and index.
    ISBN 978-0-8166-5345-4 (hc : alk. paper) — ISBN 978-0-8166-5346-1 (pb : alk. paper)
    1. Technology—Philosophy. 2. Political science—Philosophy. I. Title.
    T14.W53 2008
    601—dc22   2008010197

Printed in the United States of America on acid-free paper
The University of Minnesota is an equal-opportunity educator and employer.

15   14   13   12   11   10   09   08   10 9 8 7 6 5 4 3 2 1

For Branka
behind everything, way ahead

Contents

Acknowledgments

My sincere thanks go to all those who assisted in the writing and publication of this book. Apart from the many friends and colleagues—too many to name—whose comments and suggestions were most welcome encouragements to its development, I wish to acknowledge those whose conference invitations gave me the opportunity to present material from, and versions of, a number of the book's chapters: Laurence Simmons, Michael Hanne, Robert Harvey, Ann Kaplan, Dragan Kujundžić, Paul Patton, Rosalind Diprose, Obrad Savić, Peter Goodrich, Nicholas Royle, Aron Vinegar, Jonathan Culler, Philip Lewis, Simon Morgan Wortham, Brigitte Weltman-Aron, Norbert Sclippa, Marie-Louise Mallet, and the sorely missed Jacques Derrida. Luis Correa-Díaz kindly told me about Frida Kahlo's *Broken Column*. I am also grateful for feedback provided by the students in my seminar class "Reversions of Technology and Ethics/Politics" at SUNY–Albany in spring 2007, with special thanks to David Parry for his authentic being-in-technology. Finally, thanks to Michael Naas for his generous reading; to Cary Wolfe, friend and series editor; and to Doug Armato, Adam Brunner, and the editing and production teams at the University of Minnesota Press.

Dorsality

1. The Dorsal Turn

THE ARGUMENTS MOBILIZED HERE, INDEED, THAT MOBILIZE themselves here, do so in the service of what might be called a "technological turn." I employ the contrived reflexivity of the syntagm "mobilize themselves" to emphasize the ineluctable effect of a certain mechanicity or automaticity. What mobilizes itself in the technological turn is a function of something that cannot but occur, has already occurred, occurs automatically, is itself already in the service of a machine. The technological turn describes the turn into a technology that was always there. The technological turn, therefore, cannot but occur. And cannot but occur as technological, for I will argue that the turn itself, the notion of the turn, implies a type of technologization. It is in order to explain something beyond the apparent syllogistic tautology of all that that I develop what follows.

For reasons that should become apparent in the analyses presented here—both their ethico-political and rhetorico-sexual emphases, as well as the set of permutations of the same—I shall presume in the first instance to deal with a turn that takes place with respect to the human as exemplar of the animate, to deal with a someone who turns. What turns will be presumed to be something human, some human thing, and the argument will be that in turning it turns into something technological, some technological thing. Therefore the turn is first of all an inflection, a bending, the movement of a limb that, as the Latin teaches us, is the sense of *articulation*. Within that logic, there is technology as soon as there are limbs, as soon as there is bending of those limbs, as soon as there is any articulation at all. As soon as there is articulation, the human has rounded the technological bend, the technological turn has occurred, and there is no more simple human. Which, for all intents and purposes, means there never was any simple human. I intend in the second instance that the technological turn, as inflection or articulation, be understood to begin well before the emergence of a limb. Although it is the limb that will determine the prospect of a relation to a tool, to what we call artifice in general, and so inaugurate and underwrite a conception of a human or an animate that becomes technologized by entering into a prosthetic articulation with whatever it fashions outside its own body, one might as well argue that the animate first articulates and so becomes technological in the self-division of a cell, in the self-generation of an amoeba.[1] Indeed, to the extent that the model of technology imposing its epistemological preeminence in our times is less the mechanical and increasingly the biotechnological, we should think technology beyond the confines of a traditional concept of a human-mechanical relation, as developmentally upstream from the articulation of a limb. We should think of a technology that grows, and of the *bios* in general as following the technological turn, as bending outside itself deep within itself.

For now, still figuring things according to the model of the human animal, of human animal articulation, as the articulation of limbs of a human biped, the turn would be the deviation that occurs—naturally, as it were—within the seemingly automatic advance of ambulation or locomotion. It turns as it walks. Technology as mechanicity is located—not for the first time but in a particularly explicit way, that is to say, as fundamental relation to the earth as exteriority—in the step. In walking, one, the human, any given biped, is with each step correcting its bearing, limping from one foot to the other, realigning its center of gravity, compensating for the disequilibrium of each movement, as it were turning one way then the other in order to advance. The particular importance of the privilege I am giving to the turn resides, therefore, in its sense of a departure that is also a detour, a deviation, a divergence into difference. We will imagine the human turning as it walks, deviating from its forward path in order, precisely, to move forward, advancing necessarily askew. To repeat: the turn is the deviation from itself by means of which the human, in being or "moving" simply human, is understood to become technological. And such a turn begins as soon as there is understood to be any human. The human is, from the point of view of this turn, understood to become technological as soon as it becomes human, to be always already turning that way.

For reasons that I will progressively enumerate and return to throughout the book, the "that way" of the turn will be interpreted, or work itself out, as a turning back, a turning to the back. Even if in turning one (the human) deviates from itself in the simplest or most minimal fashion, turns just a little to the left or right—say to correct its bearing—it turns, for all intents and purposes, *toward the back*. For my purposes and according to my interpretation, every deviation is a form of retroversion. This means that every turn is a type of turning around, movement toward the back, toward what is behind; in turning however gently to the right or to the left, indeed up or down, one is on the way toward the back. Any bending is a type of falling, or folding back, upon itself, with respect to itself. Any departure, however slight, from a pure and strict (and necessarily impossible to define) forward linearity makes reference to what is behind, raises that question, infects as it were that strict forward linearity of movement with a decelerating pull from behind and so implies or calls for a thinking of what is behind, a thinking of the back. Hence, as my title suggests, the turn I will deal with is a type of turning around or turning back, a turning from the back or from behind, a dorsal turn, a turning to or into *dorsality*. Dorsality will be a name for that which, from behind, from or in the back of the human, turns (it) into something technological, some technological thing.

In the first place, interpreting the technological turn in terms of the back, as dorsal, serves to emphasize the originary status of that turn: the human, in moving forward, in order to move forward, turns back to, and turns behind to, acknowledge the technological origin I have just been referring to. At a moment in which the human appears to be moving inexorably forward toward a biotechnological future, it is strategically important to recognize—to be *cognizant in return* of—the fact of a relation between *bios* and *tekhne* so complex and so historic that any presumption of the priority of one over the other can be sustained only by means of an appeal to a metaphysics of creation. I say "a metaphysics of creation" rather than a myth or even the concept of creation, which, by definition, cannot avoid the sense of artifice. Whereas creation is obviously artifice, a metaphysics of creation presumes a creation devoid of such contrivance and presumes to resolve the paradox of a divine and "natural" *tekhne* that would have preceded the *bios*. However, it is likely that rationalist or noncreationist descriptions of the evolutionary process are having unconscious recourse to another side of the same presumption whenever they privilege the organic to the extent of failing to acknowledge the becoming-technological of biological self-organization or self-programmation, whenever they ignore the originary mechanics at work in the evolution of the species. This is not to replace the organic with the mechanical but to argue against any rigorous purity of either. Making the case for an originary biotechnology would be an urgent imperative, prerequisite to a reconfiguration of the current terms of debate over the integrity of the human that so often has us paralyzed with anxiety at the prospect of our increasingly bioengineered future. Appeals to the integrity of the human, and the concomitant anxiety over presumed incursions of the machine within the human, are hardly limited to simplistic creationisms but can be found underpinning commonplace as well as philosophical conceptions of, to begin with, life and death, and they consistently provide the bases for ethical thinking in general. Indeed, how could we begin to conceive of an ethics of the mechanical? Ethical behavior, political "choice," free will, agency, indeed, the human itself are for us, by definition, representative of what breaks with mechanicity, automatism, or programming. Yet, according to my argument, the human breaks, or turns at the same time, into mechanicity, into automatism and programming. Hence I am not suggesting that we wholeheartedly endorse every biotechnological possibility, or that we stop resisting the presumptive assurance of a science that conceives of itself necessarily as human progress, especially when that science is increasingly employed in the service of an increasingly militarized commerce, or that we fail to engage in juridical attempts to wrestle with categories that are no longer adequate to the questions raised by certain conceptual quandaries, beginning with the issues of life and death or, for example, euthanasia, cloning, biodiversity, et cetera, but rather that we attempt to think it otherwise, that we investigate what shifts of terrain might occur once we take the technological turn back to a place behind where we traditionally presume it to have taken place, turning back around behind us from the start.

It also follows from what I have just outlined that the dorsal turn operates as a form, or forms, of resistance—what I shall later analyze as "dissidence"—resistance precisely to a technology that defines itself as straightforward, as straight and forward, straight-ahead linear advance, the totally concentrated confidence and pure technological fiat of an unwavering liftoff propelled by naked combustible force. We should reserve the right to *hold back*, not to presume that every technology is an advance. But we should at the same time remember the converse conservatism of the champions of unbridled progress, since their ideal and unstoppable technological force is presumed to be mustered and mastered by the human, to operate in the service of human will. That form of technicism or technologism would necessarily be the most powerful defender of the faith of the pretechnological integral human that discovers and controls everything it produces. Against it, we should maintain the dorsal chance, the dorsal as the chance of what cannot be *foreseen*, the surprise or accident that appears, at least, to come from behind, from out of range or outside the field of vision, challenging that technocratic faith or confidence and calling into question its control.

What comes from behind comes from beyond the simple perspective of the human and hence, from the point of view of perspective and of vision in general, it comes from another point of view, from outside the field of visual possibility. For the human, that means from behind. Although the human cannot necessarily see everything that comes from in front, *it necessarily cannot see anything that comes from behind, or at least not short of a turn.* Although it by no means controls the field of the frontal—for example, what is lateral and liminal—the dorsal necessarily escapes it. Now, the sense of a technology that comes from behind the human, unable to be seen or foreseen, would appear to contradict the definition of the technological as production or creation, as fabrication produced by hands manipulating matter within a visible field. What would be the meaning of a technology that the human had not produced in front of itself and in view of itself? It would mean first of all taking conceptual account of a technology whose effects exceed the strict conditions of its production, a technology that proliferates or mutates as the viral life that—for example, in information technologies—is the form and name it actually borrows. But more than that, it would mean again taking conceptual account of the extent to which, in increasingly explicit ways, technology defines and redefines the human and does so downstream from the point at which a given technological creation was brought into effect. It would therefore mean turning to see the technology of the human itself, inside itself, if you wish, in any case inaccessible or invisible from the perspective of an integral human gathered within its neatly prescribed limits or borders and gazing ahead into a controlled exteriority of the artifact.

A technology of the human itself, a technology that defines and so produces the human, cannot be part of the human self-image; it comes at the human from behind, is already at its back. Or indeed, *in* its back. The dorsal turn also refers, therefore, to the role played by the vertebral column in the constitution of the human. The figure or pose of our fundamental technological articulation and actualization—the point at which that emerges into visibility—is the upright stance. Anthropological accounts of the emergence of anthropoid species understandably have consistent recourse to that event, to a bending of the spine by straightening it, as a defining factor for the human. The discovery in 1959 of the *Zinjanthropus* fossil, along with his tools, meant that the criteria for hominization could be ascribed to a much earlier genus, the *Australopithecus,* than was previously thought. According to André Leroi-Gourhan, that genus was characterized by a relation between, on the one hand, the capacity for a widening cortical pan that results from a rebalancing of skull and jaw in the upright stance, and, on the other hand, the ability to split pebbles. The *Australopithecus* is the earliest known example of a brain freed from the suspension stresses of the skull, and although his brain, unlike his body, has hardly developed in comparison with the Neanderthal and beyond, he has begun making tools.

As Leroi-Gourhan describes it, it is as if "we" simultaneously made room for more brain, relieved that brain of some of its physical pressure, and freed our hands so as to be able to split pebbles on the way to producing tools; as if in standing upright the simian turned anthropoid and, in so doing, immediately turned technological. Leroi-Gourhan defines the human in terms of a technicity so fundamental as to be almost "zoological," as if an almost automatic technological outgrowth of the body occurred once the hand was freed from its motor function and once the face shortened and became independent of the cerebral part of the skull. He refers to the concept of tools as "a 'secretion' of the anthropoid's body and brain" such that "the Australanthropians . . . seem to have possessed their tools in much the same way as an animal has claws . . . as if their brains and their bodies had gradually exuded them . . . chopper and biface [tools] seem to form part of the skeleton, to be literally 'incorporated' in the living organism."[2]

There seems little doubt that a fundamental realignment of the human in its relation to technology occurs with the upright stance. The anthropoid "chooses" to give itself the prospect of tools and at the same time turns its back in a radical way on whatever is behind it. We know how it abandons the animal, refines the senses by downgrading smell and hearing, and reconfigures the knowable other within a frontal visual perspective, prioritizing a certain version of the *fore-seen* or *fore-seeable*. What is produced by that anthropoid, the technologies of tool use on the one hand, and language on the other, is henceforth presumed to occur within that frontal visual perspective of the knowable. That occurs in spite of the emphasis given, in terms of those technologies, to the surprise of discovery and of invention. Such discovery and invention are henceforth and consistently understood as being ahead, around the corner, or on the horizon of a forward progression. What is therefore being forgotten, I argue—perhaps until it is, or unless it be reawakened in the fear of some bioengineered monstrosity, some *retro*viral haunting—is the extent to which technology is, to begin with, literally in the back. It is in the human back as the spinal—or can we already say dorsal?—turn or adjustment, the primary or primal vertebral articulation that frees the hands to pick up stones and fashion tools, that redistributes the weight of the head and jaw to allow the brain to develop and the tongue to speak. From and in its beginning, back where it began, the human is therefore receiving a definition from a technologization of the body, in a becoming-prosthesis or a *becoming-dorsal*.

The dorsal turn refers, in the fourth place, to operations of reversal or reversibility as a fact of technology. This is most obvious in machine technology, where the basic articulation of, say, piston and connecting rod, implies an indifference concerning the direction in which the wheel is turned, forward or back. Now, that translates in the first instance to an indifference regarding spatial orientation: the machine is essentially always a spacecraft. The tool, for example, aspires to the conquest of outer space in the most literal sense of all those words by redefining our relation to what is outside us, our conceptions of the proximate and distant.[3] With the development of industrial machinery, that spatial relation will come to be more explicitly defined by speed, by a space-time relation that overwhelmingly implies forward motion, for we are not used to thinking speed in terms of reverse motion. But when it comes to the human machine, to technology in and of the space of the human (back), directional "indifference" comes back into play as a function of time, conceptions of soon and later, present and future. The relation to technology is, in more ways than have already been suggested, a complicated—even reversible or indifferent—relation to time. I shall discuss in the next chapter how that is brought into focus, and how technology thereby comes into perhaps unexpected focus, with respect to Being in the work of Heidegger. But for now let me emphasize that the invention of the technological relates to the past as much as to the future in this particular sense: it is a relation to past time and to the function of memory.

As readily as one accepts the status of artistic creation, as a paradigm for human production, in terms of a terrestrial afterlife—the desire to leave something behind—so might we insist that the artifact functions as archive and memory bank. And the same might be said of technological invention in general, for, as has often been pointed out, the word *tekhne* was used in Greek as much for what was produced as art as what was manufactured; it stands for the artisanal all the way from art to industry. Although the relation to memory and to archivation might not be immediately apparent in the case of a rudimentary tool, it can be understood that whatever is produced as nonorganic or "nonbiodegradable" remainder will necessarily constitute some form of memorial trace. And it is an obvious fact that artifactual technologies such as language, especially via writing, consist precisely in what Bernard Stiegler refers to as the exteriorization of memory, and that the contemporary technologies of information amount to a veritable "industrialization of memory."[4] If technology is a matter of exteriorization, of the human reaching outside itself (but, as was argued regarding corticalization and the upright stance, in a way that calls into question the integrity of any interiority), then it is also a matter of archivation: what is created outside the human remains as a matter of record and increasingly becomes the very record or archive, the artificial or exterior memory itself. The production of an artifact is the production of an archive; it means depositing in the present—in some "present"—an object, which, as it inserts and catalogs itself in the past, will become available for a future retrieval.

In reaching outside itself, the human therefore reaches both forward and back; in seeming to turn away from the past, it leaves the artificial trace that will have it forever referring back to that constructed past as the trace of its memory, as promise of artificial memory and promise or threat, eventually, of artificial intelligence. Memory might be called, after all, the first artificial intelligence, and it comes to be recognized explicitly as such once Freud discovers the unconscious like some self-produced biochip that controls (and derails), as if from behind, the conscious. The life of memory, its status as alive or dead, internal or external, real or artificial, draws the fault line along which the question of technology is still debated, from the desirability of "replacing" mental functions by machines (oral histories by writing, arithmetic by calculators, spelling by word processors, to begin with) all the way to nanoscientific cerebral implants and the manipulation of genetic memory systems.

Thus although the machine institutes a law of order that is like the artificial or artifactual version of life itself, a principle of creation or production to parallel organic regeneration—artists and artisans create inanimate "offspring," objects can be reproduced like the burgeoning spores of nature—it remains indifferent to that order, as it were unmotivated by it. That indifference derives from repetition itself, from repetition as automatism. It is the necessary structural possibility for memory, which is by definition a repetition designed to function automatically, to be "triggered," and to disrupt the forward momentum of time, perhaps simply interrupting the present by means of a single recollection, but potentially setting off a chain reaction of memories that multiply in reverse order. It is in terms of the disruptive repetition performed by memory that we can perhaps begin to understand a contrast between the reversibility inherent in machine technology and the more radical conquest of time that takes place in biotechnology, in a *genetic* engineering that disrupts the temporality not only of *re-production* but of *generation* itself. As I discuss in chapters 6 and 7, that technological disruption of temporality is what conditions the political as motor of change, and what provides the terms of reference and argues for a type of retro- or controversion as political strategy.

IN ITS GUISE of the technological, the dorsal therefore names, in a number of ways, what comes from behind to inhabit us as something other, some other thing, the other; an other beyond what can be conceived of within the perspective of our frontal relations. Not just an enemy, a wild animal, an avalanche, falling rock, or speeding train, and indeed not necessarily in the form of a threat—as we shall see, it could as easily be a caress—but also and even the known other to the extent that we allow it to fall back into the shadow, into the space of a type of faith or trust, of what is behind us. From that point of view, the dorsal might come to serve as the basis for an ethics beyond the programmable that would nevertheless function as an ethics of or for the technological, however counterintuitive that might seem. Not an ethics dictated by technology, or the nonsense of an ethics of the machine, but rather an ethics that takes account of the machine in the human, that deals with the form of unassimilable *inanimation* that inhabits the back of the human, an unassimilable otherness that participates in its functioning and so precisely yet paradoxically prevents its acting and responding from the presumption of what can be foreseen. Throughout the discussions and analyses that follow, I will try to point to the dorsal formations of such an ethics, in the first instance holding that it is only once one recognizes an originary technology, and a prosthetic human, hence a technology in the back, that one can begin to develop an ethos adequate to the challenges of the present age; and in the second instance, in more general terms, deriving whatever conceptual or philosophical advantage there is to be had from such a perspective, to let some sort of inventive difference emerge, some reversal or even perversion of a tradition that finds what comes from behind to be, as it were, beyond the *sinister,* farther out than left field, precisely out around back, the darkest version of what is untrusted and unknown, even if it is also recognized as the source of the most stimulating fantasy.

If the dorsal names the unseen, that is not the same as the invisible. But what is behind cannot be seen without a turning; knowing what is "in back" requires the compound artifice of a double mirror, hence an inverted narcissism. Short of that, it will come to us first of all through other senses: perhaps still sometimes through that of smell, from out of an animal past, but more likely through hearing, announcing itself in a whisper or a shout, in a rumble or a murmur; and more importantly still, through touch.[5] The back that relates to the back within us must do so by means of touch, and so it is that we will find the dorsal turn to refer necessarily to an erotic sensitization. What touches the back, even the surprise prod or slap of a friend or a stranger, implies an erotic relation, a version of sexuality, a version that raises simultaneously and undecidably the questions of sex and gender, of species, and of objects. A sexuality therefore that is not, at least not in the first instance, determined as hetero- or homosexual, as vaginal or anal, as human (or indeed animal) or prosthetic, not even as embracing or penetrating, but which implies before all else a coupling with otherness.

By means of dorsality, sexuality and human relations in general are marked by an extreme vulnerability, by the sort of passive trust that would be a condition of possibility for ethics in general. Such an ethics is defined in terms that are irrefutably animate: one can begin to be ethical only by respecting the most vulnerable forms of life, what, following Giorgio Agamben, might be termed "barest" life.[6] On the other hand, however, a dorsal sexuality also presupposes forms of coupling that are undeniably technological, not necessarily dependent on a type of mutual animate recognition, open instead to the anonymity, the namelessness or nonunique substitutability—indeed reversibility, as I have already suggested—the indifferent repetitivity that inaugurates the structure of the machine. Though the silent caress of a hand on the shoulder or a breathing on the nape seems precisely to be that of which the machine is incapable, in turning one's back, one cannot but invite an unassimilable unfamiliarity such as defines the inanimate. And although the machine would be similarly incapable of the unprogrammable surprise that turning one's back also invites, it signifies nevertheless endless inventivity and predicts both the unknown and, beyond that, the unknowable. The touch of the machine is, from behind, the caress from such a shadow.

The dorsal turn is also a turning back in the sense of a return, which also signals an original turning of the back, the senses of departure and abandonment. It is deployed along the axis that links home to exile, which, as we shall see, defines home as originary exile. In this way it should be understood as a function of the polis, of the city as political economization. Human organization could be said to become politics once the family depends on the construction of a house. That is to say that the house, paradoxically, not only consists of four walls to shelter and protect the family but also, necessarily, constitutes an appeal to an authority outside the house to respect and accredit those four walls. If the curfew or house arrest decrees the limit of political legitimacy, if an enforced clearing of the streets and closing of the doors implies both the imposition and the faltering of an absolute authority, if the state of siege prohibits public activism but provokes cellular resistance, requiring finally that the very doors it has closed be broken down, it is because political power has there encountered the paradox of the house: not just the problem of controlling whatever takes place in private, but the question of intervening across the line of definition of the political itself, namely, the walls of the house, contravening its own limit by stepping across the lines that demarcate it.

Although there is undoubtedly a politics of the family, the argument here is that there is no politics as long as there is only the family, no politics before the family installs the walls at its back that compose a house. Thus this means there is no politics without a certain technologization of the family, without the particular form of institutionalization that requires the construction represented by the house. This is not to contradict what I was saying earlier concerning the fact of technology beginning in the human, in its back. Nor is it incompatible with what, in a later chapter, I will define as the politicizing structure of the darkroom or recessive space within a house, in an attempt to account for how a figural domestic, or at least cameral, space is developed for the staging of certain paradoxes of politicization as the articulation of public and private, and of real and ideal. I am pointing here to a version of the corporeal technologization that "begins" in the back, whose extension into public space will necessitate the house; to how the form of human community that is the family finds its *erectilization* or verticalization in the construction of the house as something like the development of the family spine into its upright stance. By means of the house, the family does not just enter into a prosthetic relation with the inanimate in the same way as the individual does by clothing itself. Rather, it involves (and in the case of clothing also) a complex set of articulations whereby the family calls on a technology of construction, and so builds walls, to differentiate and negotiate its functions and relations both internally (different rooms for different purposes, some more solitary, others more communal) and externally (necessarily entering into a contractual relation with whatever form of social and political regulation takes place outside the house). In this latter sense, just as clothing is a negotiation and a negation of the body's own nudity, so the family—or the individual, for that matter—leaves home as soon as the house is built. By means of the house, the family is in fact leaving home, calling on and contracting with the external political sphere. That would be so even supposing the door were never opened; even though no one were ever to exit, there would nevertheless be the structural fact of this exile, and the enclosure of the house would define such an opening, an open opening to the outside. The house therefore means the externalization of its inhabitants, an externalization that ruptures the presumed internal integrity of whatever it houses. One is in exile at home, and the house is that to which one must permanently return.

The dorsal turn involves, finally, a turning back to language as primary technological system. Whereas the fact of language's technological status seems not to be in doubt, and is indeed made explicit by a Leroi-Gourhan, there is a sense, I maintain, in which language has not been theorized as technology in the same way as, say, machine, medical, or informatic technology. Stiegler, for example, emphasizes the relation of language to technology throughout *Technics and Time*, conjoining it to a nexus that includes corticalization, verticality, mobility, and time, all of which get concentrated on the question of speed. Yet whereas the other elements of that nexus are analyzed in terms of an evolving technology of self-acceleration, language is not subjected to the same examination and so remains, in the final analysis, instrumental to technology, simply words processed by that technology.[7]

What thus seems required is some accounting for what I would call the tropological speed of language, some sort of analysis of the technological logic of its operations beyond a simple mechanics of its syntax and semantics, and a conception of language and its rhetorical turns as high technology or technology of information, rather than a mute instrument for conveying information. Underlying the chapters of this book is the thesis that in order to elaborate an ethics, politics, or sexuality informed by technology, one cannot simply presume a language more or less adequate to the conceptual framework being developed; rather, one must seek to technologize language, or forms of discourse themselves. If the technology being employed to conceptualize an ethics, politics, or sexuality of technology is language, then that language must somehow be employed in a technological mode. For beyond the simplistic oppositions between text and world, thinking and acting, intellectual and political activity, and beyond the deconstruction of those oppositions, a technological time and speed remain to be enacted by language along the axis of politics and ethics, through the fault lines of sexuality. As long as a politics, ethics, and sexuality of technology are being "expressed through language," they can properly be conceived of, that is to say, only within the context and conduct of a technologized language, however much its sense remains to be developed.

The dorsal turn presumes a tropo-technological language, one determined by an originary turn and instantaneous deviation, one that is engaged as the technology of conceptualization, put into service within and throughout an elaboration of questions of politics, ethics, and sexuality, technologizing them noninstrumentally. Its two words—dorsal, turn—do not figure an idea of the concepts "back," "behind," or "from behind" as much as they make that turn, flip that switch, go back, swivel, at electronic speed, or reconnect disjunctively, change windows, access a countermemory, backload, at the speed of light. There is, as it were, no sense to them outside such a perspective, outside what they perform in technological terms. Beyond the perversity of a counterintuition or contravention, a willful contrariness, a destructive or creative desire to invert, the dorsal turn should be understood as enacting the shock of the technological shift itself, putting us where we are henceforth and probably have always been with respect to technology, behind, turned about, late, and bewildered, but nevertheless constrained, indeed shackled there, like Prometheus, bound from behind to the time of the Titans.

THROUGHOUT THE CHAPTERS that follow, a network of topoi will therefore come to be perversely, or *controversially* juxtaposed: the shadow and the machine, rhetoric and ethics or politics, the ocean and the house. My conceit is to articulate them and have them articulate successfully within the homogeneous thematic space of the dorsal. That necessarily produces a type of torsion, even a disarticulation with respect to the norms of logical exposition, but one that, I hope, remains within the framework of what we commonly understand as speculative thinking. As if it were a matter of saying: let's try it another way, the other way around. Imagine, try, at the risk of a crick in the neck, or a slipped mental disc, to see it from a (strictly speaking) impossible perspective, one that, however much it falls in the shadow of our everyday viewpoint, nevertheless is not entirely unknown to us, in fact intimately belongs to us, indeed constitutes the expansive scene and fecund scenarios of whatever happens behind our back.

Various chiasmatic relations obtain among the elements of that network. As I have already argued, in turning back we glimpse less the origin that we have left behind than the motor that propels us toward the future; less the organic integrality of our continuous evolution than the decision or disruption of a new, erectile relation to the earth that is also a gravitational shift and a sedentarization, rooting us to the inanimate even as we begin more, with a freer hand, to make of that inanimate the object of all our craft. It would be too simplistic to call our spinal cord *the* machine within us, in spite of how the idea resonates, for the mechanisms of the body are many and varied; but the upright stance definitely inaugurates a radically new relation of human to technological, and a radically new sense of how we conceive of and determine what is outside us in general and behind us in particular, a new definition of the dorsal. We henceforth cast, *automatically,* a different shadow, such as Nietzsche, along with Zarathustra, is required to reckon with, as I discuss in my final chapter. Only by negotiating the paradox of a technology that we produce, which therefore comes after us yet still lies before us as the unknown of pure invention, will we undo the reductive opposition, in favor of a series of operative differences, between frontal and dorsal. And only by inverting, or *controverting,* our presumption of a derivative, contrived technology, one under our control—at the crossroads of our greatest hopes and worst fears—in favor of a technology that is us and that we are through and through, will we adapt to the challenges that, with every step forward, we throw back at ourselves.

Nietzsche's shadow, as we shall see, startles the unsuspecting wanderer-philosopher and uses its longer legs to outrun a Zarathustra who seeks to flee it. However real it appears, it appears as a representational challenge to our modes of visibility, both anamorphosis and intermittence, projection and embodiment, doubling and insubstantiality. And however directly it speaks, it cannot present a new frontal enunciation but rather offers a version of dorsal obliquity, a calling to action and to account that requires a shift out of pure oppositionality into the controversions of nuance and figurality, out of confrontation or lockstep impulsion and into choreography.

As I have just explained, the enunciative or discursive apparatus in general seems to possess such a shadow in the form of what is called rhetoric. By means of it, language turns its back on any presumption of a homogeneous communicability, turning to and into tropological indirection and artifice. Yet the rhetorical space that opens behind language, as its immanent density and unsoundable reserve of complexity and power, is coextensive with what, on the one hand, constitutes the ethical and political subject, the subject of discourse that we are used to calling an "agent," and, on the other hand, allows for that agent to participate in any transformation of the real world. In the following chapter, I argue, with particular reference to Levinas and Althusser, that the call to ethical responsibility or the political interpellation presumes a turn that is a tropological realignment. One turns into a discursive relation that seems at first glance to be a simple communication—"Hey, you," calls the law; "Yes, here I am," responds the subject—but by so doing, one consents to a redirection that is also an indirection. By turning to become political, the subject is necessarily turning into a form of figuration, accepting a role. Not least because what calls and so constitutes the political subject, what makes her turn out of the imaginary and into the symbolic structure, from the policeman's whistle all the way to the complex machinery of the law and any number of other state apparatuses, is a form of technological surprise. In reacting or responding to that call, one turns into tropological space and into a cog within that discursive machinery. As my analyses attempt to explain, the friend, the lover, and the ethical subject are produced out of such an asymmetrical surprise; they mobilize the tropological dorsal force of such a surprise to have language function as rhetoric—a dramatic flourish in excess of the message, designed to catch off guard and off balance—as it were *before* it functions as communication. "Before" we hear the "Hey, you," we react to something as simple as its volume, but which represents the apostrophic, perhaps even adrenal, surfeit of what hails from out of the blue or out of the shadow, from out of dorsal inaccessibility or invisibility, shocking or surprising us into an instinctual repositioning or corporeal rectification "before" it calls us. It is as if our body turns to activate that tropological space before discourse comes to occupy that space, and as though the discourse of subjectification can only fix and define us—for example, as political agents—by transiting that same space of indirection. After all, interpellation, by definition, calls us not where we are but where it wants us to be, which also means that the constitution of the subject will resonate at the same time as a shadowy calling into question of the subject.

In chapter 6, the theatricality or representative scene of that tropological dramatization is analyzed in more detail, in order, first of all, for the definitions activated through the indirections of subjectification to

be understood to include the sexual. We would presume the sexual relation to function most ideally, or primarily, via a type of frontal symmetry,
but in fact, irrespective of the hetero- or homo-morphology of the bodies involved, the very morphology of sexual interaction, of its penetra-
tions, caresses, passivities, and so on, belies any perfect symmetry. We
do not need an extreme case such as Sade to convince us that sexuality
functions by means of its *versions*. But Sade's *Philosophy in the Bedroom*
brings into particular relief the coextensivity of the space of sexual tropologies (especially via the conjunction between anality and cruelty), and
the space of transformative political possibility, of revolutionary change.
Such change, my argument goes, cannot be effected without tropological
mediation: some idealized representation of an altered reality has to precede its implementation, or at least that is how political history, with its
programs and manifestos, has proceeded. Yet even for the real world to
be reproduced, it has to suffer the inversion figured by the photographic
darkroom; how much more so, therefore, the transformations of progress
and emancipation (as well as their more ominous converse or perverse
forms, fascism and enslavement). Although one may reach a point where
the tropological is no longer simply discursive or linguistic, where it is a
case of turning and transforming the matter of the world rather than the
matter of language—indeed, in order to effect such a transformation of
the world—one nonetheless relies on the darkness, chance, and unknown
of dorsal space. But this, I will attempt to demonstrate, is less because
when one undertakes to effect political change one cannot with certainty
predict or control the outcome, as the derailing of every revolution seems
to confirm, than because what I call the dorsal inversion is the condition
of possibility of the political itself, conceived of as the *realization* of a *representation*. Without it there is no *invention*—hence it is the poietic possibility in general—but because of it, whatever appears, is implemented,
or realized brings with it that very tropological structure. Without it also,
within the perspective of my final chapter, there is no politics of opposition, no resistance; but because of it, the con*front*ation of dissidence will
have to be reconfigured as *controversion*.

Final topos: the ocean, my con(tro)verse, reverse, or dorsal figure for
a natural technology, or a technological nature, converse with respect to
the Promethean fire that we normally identify as source of our inventions. Water functions as a counterpoint to fire in being more "directly"

harnessed to produce energy. In the Bremen lectures that I discuss in the following chapter, a certain diversion or interruption of the normal flow—a dam on the Rhine—haunts Heidegger as he imagines the natural elements bent to human instrumentality. Water, among all the four elements, bears the human in a type of passive and symbiotic relation from the time of our amniotic buoyancy in the womb, as a form of originary prosthesis. Fire, by contrast, is something our bodies cannot touch; air, similarly, is approachable only by means of complex contrivances; earth is closer to water in supporting or cradling the body; but only water itself both offers the particular supine repose of flotation and works as a medium of propulsion. We recline in the oceanic element as if in a fluid machine, one molded to our body and minutely tuned to the lunar clockwork, moving cyclically forward even as we lie back. Something of the paradox of how the fluid element holds us without housing us is, according to my analysis, encountered by Levinas.

Yet water can be as indiscriminately destructive as fire. To the extent that it rewrites boundaries and bears us far from home, the oceanic force is no respecter of identities; and of course it is, for the European imaginary, the antithesis of the continental landmass on the basis of which the modern concept of the nation-state developed. For all these reasons, it is the ocean, rather than the river or even the sea, that carries for me the rhetorical force of the fluid element, and the ocean that, in erasing the distinction between it and the sea, washes over every human identitarian horizon, creating an outer space within our atmospheric parameters, luring us in the direction of conquest, drift, and cataclysmic engulfment. In chapters 3 and 4, certain of those lures are exposed. They will attract again Zarathustra in chapter 7, and at the end of this volume, we will glimpse the philosopher who created him, mountain bound but with the force of that sea-becoming-ocean at his back.

When I am alone . . . what approaches me is not my being a little less myself, but rather something which is there "behind me," and which this "me" conceals in order to come into its own.

—MAURICE BLANCHOT, *The Space of Literature*

2. Facades of the Other Heidegger, Althusser, Levinas

THROUGHOUT HIS 1949 LECTURE "THE TURNING," HEIDEGGER elaborates the relation of technology to the question of Being that he had introduced with his notion of enframing *(Gestell)* in "The Question concerning Technology." In the latter essay, as is well known, he develops a distinction between the artifact that is produced via an ideology of causality and instrumentality, and that which is let come forth into presenc(ing). The distinction is not, however, that between artifact as *tekhne* and nature *(physis)*, for, as he clearly states:

Not only handcraft manufacture, not only artistic and poetical bringing into appearance . . . is a bringing forth, *poiesis. Physis* also, the arising of something from out of itself, is a bringing-forth, *poiesis. . . Techne* is the name not only for the activities and skills of the craftsman, but also for the arts of the mind and the fine arts. *Techne* belongs to bringing-forth, to *poiesis.*

Heidegger wants to draw attention, therefore, to a difference not between technology and the nontechnological but rather between instrumentality and the "realm of revealing": "Instrumentality is considered to be the fundamental characteristic of technology. If we inquire, step by step, into what technology, represented as means, actually is, then we shall arrive at revealing. The possibility of all productive manufacturing lies in revealing" ("The Question concerning Technology," 12). The conception of *poiesis* as revealing *(aletheuein)* works in the first instance to detract from the human as agent of production of the technological. Humanity does not, for Heidegger, guide technology before it. Indeed, the human who "challenges" to deliver for technology is himself already challenged in the same movement. This means that he is motivated and mobilized, as if from behind, and so *technologized* himself, becoming but a signifier within the technological chain. But in the second instance, the unconcealment of *aletheia* involves an irreducible element of surprise. In letting come forth as revealing, one does not produce whatever is foreseen by the program of that production so much as reveal "whatever does not bring itself forth and *does not yet lie here before us, whatever can look and turn out now one way and now another*" ("The Question concerning Technology," 13; italics mine). In technology as revealing, even as challenging or ordering revealing, there will necessarily be that turning to the unexpected, the turning that is the unexpected, the positioning that implies a repositioning, displacement, or turn, the gathering that is the placing, putting, or setting that Heidegger calls *Gestell*.

When he develops further the semantic and conceptual context of *Gestell* in "The Turning," Heidegger's interest appears to be elsewhere, to have itself taken a different turn. First, the essence of technology is displaced further from the realm of human activity. The discussion is no longer restricted to the context of a "human" turning, as a type of "choice"—albeit one that does not happen "exclusively *in* man, or decisively *through* man" ("The Question concerning Technology," 24)—between an instrumental technology that is challenged forth, and a poietic technology that is a revealing bringing-forth. Nor is it simply a turning from a Dasein with closed eyes, ears, and heart to one who is "everywhere already brought into the unconcealed" (19). The turning is now nothing less than the "turning about of the oblivion of Being into the truth of Being."[2]

Second, and more important for this discussion, whereas "The Question concerning Technology" already made explicit that the poietic producing that brings forth on the one hand, and the challenging ordering on the other, "are indeed fundamentally different . . . yet . . . related in their essence" (21), in "The Turning" Heidegger will produce from that analogous relation of difference a seemingly radical shift. As a result, Enframing will come to occupy a place of privilege within the ontological project as a whole, as it were trading places with Being. Enframing, previously the essence or "essencing" of technology, is now said to be "Being itself," and conversely Being is referred to as "the essence of technology" ("The Turning," 38). This is because, from or within the "danger" that the *Gestell*, as Being, is said to represent, Heidegger has drawn a notion of a turn and a "change" that allows for a chiasmatic or con*verse* relation, something like a directional interchangeability or interchangeable directionality between what we might traditionally call constituent elements, here Enframing and Being.

This chiasmatic conversion or turning takes place precisely as the division and diverging of sending or destining *(Geschick)*, in such as way as to emphasize, after the title of the essay itself, that what is most operative there is the turning itself: "That which has the character of destining moves, in itself, at any given time, toward a special moment that sends it into another destining, in which, however, it is not simply submerged or lost" ("The Turning," 37). Destining, as sending forward, gets diverted, turned aside or back. What is movement forward receives its impulsion from behind (is "sent") but remains susceptible, if not subject, to a type of transversal counterimpulse ("another sending") that will be the moment or force of ontological insight. For we are talking here not about a subject that moves, or even anything causal—"[Being] is not brought about by anything else nor does it itself bring anything about"—but rather about a version of Being that moves into Being, that "takes place so as to adapt itself" (44). We should understand it to mean less that the movement forward is subsequently diverted into an elsewhere than that the movement cannot begin unless it is structurally constituted by that sense of diversion; it moves forward *as* contrary or at least competing movement. Being might therefore be said to move forward as Enframing and vice versa; the essence of Being thus reads as coextensive with the essence of technology.

"The Turning" thus appears to be worlds apart from the reductive characterization of "the hopeless frenzy of unchained technology" that Heidegger refers to in his *Introduction to Metaphysics*.[3] For although this turning will continue to have explicit overtones of a danger turned into safekeeping, of a turning in that is a turning homeward, to the hearth if not to the earth, and a turning to the light and to (in)sight, or of an event *(Ereignis)* that is one of visual ownness *(eignende Eräugnis)*, it remains that what has been developed and exposed in the danger of this turning is nothing less than "the world com[e] to pass as world . . . the distant advent of the coming to presence of Being itself" ("The Turning," 43).

This relation of technology to Being recasts, while in a sense complementing it, the temporal exteriorization of the Dasein, its *ekstasis*, which informs Heidegger's thinking from the time of the "The Concept of Time" (1924), and especially in *Being and Time*. As Stiegler argues, the existential analytic of time, of the being marked as temporal that is the Dasein, promises "an analytic of the *prostheticity* whereby he exists and becomes embodied—of prostheticity as being his *already-there,* or of his *already-there* as being *essentially* prosthetic."[4] The time of the Dasein is the process of an individuation that also inscribes an incompleteness, nonaccomplishment, lack in being, or being-in-default, which for Stiegler amounts to a technologization and a prosthetization.

The Dasein is doubly, and differently, even "reversibly," in time. In its thrownness, its "already-there," it is projected or injected into a past that is not its own but which it must assume, which it follows: "In its factical Being, any Dasein is as it already was, and it is 'what' it already was. It *is* its past. . . . Its own past . . . is not something which *follows along after* Dasein, but something which already goes ahead of it."[5] The Dasein exists in, and exists as, this preexisting time machine; its authenticity will be derived from a recognition of that, a recognition of a forgetting that will have to be retraced, and an assumption of a forgetting, an originary "pastlessness." But conversely, the Dasein is also in a relation of default with respect to its *future* becoming. It becomes something only by means of the future anticipation of its own death. In Stiegler's words, "*Being and Time* will say that Dasein, as long as it exists, is not yet something. It cannot be grasped in its totality: it exceeds itself, and its end belongs to this excess—death."[6] The Dasein knows that it ends in death, that it exists with the anticipation of a being-toward-death, yet it cannot ever know that death in advance. And yet again, it can only experience its own death; it can only know death through its own experience of it—we can die for someone else, but nobody else can experience our death in our place. If, therefore, as I suggested earlier, technology as it relates to the human presupposes a type of *indifference* to time, it should now be clear that such an indifference is to be understood as an *in-différance,* that of a double and compounded *ekstasis,* whereby in being it stands outside itself, inhabiting the structure of the artificial. The Dasein is *in-différance* because, on the one hand, it defers to its end in its nonaccomplishment, holding in reserve its knowledge of that end, and on the other hand, because that end is its alone, the means by which it differentiates and individuates itself.[7]

But the time of the outside-of-itself that marks the Dasein merely reinforces the exteriorization of beings that takes place as soon as they are *in* time, an exteriorization that implies a technologization. Temporality is technological inasmuch as it is a, or *the,* fundamental form of exteriorization of the human memory: "The temporality of the human, which marks it off among other living beings, presupposes exteriorization and prostheticity: there is time only because memory is 'artificial.'"[8] When one juxtaposes the turning to the past and to the future that characterizes the Dasein in authenticating its relation to time, a "turning" that exteriorizes and so technologizes it, and the turning of the danger that figures the *Gestell* as essencing of technology and as authenticating the relation to Being, then the existential and ontological analytic appears to be articulated in the profoundest sense in and as the question of technology.

Heidegger's turning is sharp or abrupt, hairpin *(Kehre)*. It occurs in a flash, like lightning: "Will we see the lightning-flash of Being in the essence of technology?" he asks in concluding "The Turning" (49). If the model is drawn from nature, it is a nature distilled into pure energy, concentrated in the sudden discharge of that energy, a nature out of control. In the form of lightning, nature violently imposes its will; it opposes standing-reserve and confounds the challenging revealing of human technological instrumentality. Man can build dams on the Rhine to transform the energy of nature, but he has not yet learned to harness the lightning stroke. However, the change in or turn of nature represented by lightning can also be read as nature becoming unnatural, nature going against nature, turning against itself in the sense of an abundance turned into catastrophe, beneficence turned to pestilence. Nature thus reveals its own otherness and hence the possibility of its transformation. In the lightning flash, nature discloses a type of invention, like a big bang or the birth of a sun, and as it were issues an invitation to the invention of technics. Indeed, as a result, though man has yet to harness the lightning stroke, he has produced nuclear fission, the atomic bomb. But I am pointing here less to an idea of production become destruction than to the transformative turn itself whereby such a change takes place. The lightning turn would be the technological possibility itself as opening to the structure of countermotion or reversibility, to a nonnatural counterproduction.

Heidegger's turning is also, as I suggested earlier, something of a development of the semantic and conceptual context of *Gestell*. When he introduces the term in "The Question concerning Technology," Heidegger explicitly refers to the fact of mobilizing language in a particular way.[9] That, after all, is something he does systematically, since it is the very process of his thinking: "We dare to use this word in a sense that has been thoroughly unfamiliar up to now. . . . Words of a mature language are this misused.

Can anything be more strange? Surely not. Yet this strangeness is an old usage of thinking. And indeed thinkers accord with this usage precisely at the point where it is a matter of thinking that which is highest."[10]

He then reminds the reader of Plato's "daring use" of *eidos,* in contrast to which "the use of the word Gestell . . . which we now venture here, is almost harmless" (20). *Gestell* is coined as a term in the context of two other words, namely, *Gebirge,* the gathering of mountains that produces the mountain "range," and *Gemüt,* the gathering of emotions that produces a "disposition." In comparison with a natural gathering on the one hand and a human gathering on the other, *Gestell* will be the frameworking of what is set out, produced but in the same movement ordered into instrumental service. Yet it is nevertheless a gathering that, as we have seen, reaches all the way into the danger and turning of Being.

In "The Thing," the first in the group of four lectures that include "The Question concerning Technology" and "The Turning," a gathering that is perhaps even more ambitious or resonant than *Gestell* is described as *Das Gering.* Heidegger's essay takes an everyday familiar object, a technological or artisanal artifact, a jug, in order to explain that the essence of a thing cannot be reduced to its object status. Instead the container, and by extension the thing, comes progressively to be accounted for in terms of, on the one hand, the poured gift of water or wine that implies a marriage of sky and earth (rain from the sky received by the earth) and, on the other, the gift of a libation or sacrifice that relates mortals to the divinities. The jug contains, less than it outpours, what Heidegger calls the "simple singlefoldness [*Einfalt*] of the four [earth and sky, divinities and mortals]": "Our language denotes what a gathering is by an ancient word. That word is: thing [*Das Ding*]. . . . We are now thinking this word by way of the gathering-appropriating staying of the fourfold."[11] In the conclusion to the essay, the simple onefold of the four gathers in what he calls a mirroring or mirror-play *(Spiegel-Spiel),* and then a round-dance, ring, or ringing *(Gering)* that is both nestling and nimble *(gering):* "Whatever becomes a thing occurs out of the ringing of the world's mirror-play" ("The Thing," 179).

It would require a treatise on the entire work of Heidegger to analyze the version of the event *(Ereignis)* or the form of "appropriation" that he is elaborating here, something that, as he reminds the reader in "The Way to Language," he had been attempting for twenty-five years.[12] It matters most to me in this context that what is consistently being articulated in the gatherings of mountains *(Gebirge)* and feelings *(Gemüt),* and then in *Gestell* and *Gering,* what is being appropriated-expropriated amounts to a mobilization of language that I will not hesitate to call technological. In the first place, one could analyze the mirror-play and the ringing that produces the "thing" in terms of a downplaying of agency, human or divine, in favor of what might be called a will to artifice: the natural reflection of Narcissus in the pool becomes a mirroring that is also a playing, an acting out on a stage of abyssal representations; and the *ring*-around effusive dance implies also the decorative or contractual object worn on the finger, which, in its seeming simplicity, is one of the most befitting yet beguiling of human prostheses. But even more straightforwardly, language in general is giving itself over to its own type of mirror-play, to the repeated alliterative and assonant effects that are readily recognized as its poetic resource but which can as easily be understood as effects of mechanicity and automatism, language driving the thinking as it were, running on its own (and Heidegger is as conscious in "The Thing" as anywhere else of the reproach that "the understanding . . . that we are trying to reach may be based on the accidents of an etymological game" [172]).

We know that texts such as those of *On the Way to Language* make explicit Heidegger's own affinity for poetic language as the model of reflective thinking: "All reflective thinking is poetic, and all poetry in turn is a kind of thinking" *(On the Way,* 136). The way to language experienced qua language seems repeatedly to be a poetics conceived of, in the final analysis, as a type of dearticulated language, a reduction to the musical, itself reduced to the melodic. Appropriation, in its mode of saying, is said to speak "as the melodic mode, the song which says something in its singing" (135). This would appear to lie at the opposite end of the spectrum from a language conceived of as technology. Yet in the first instance, a speaking voice that speaks as melody, hence as a type of instrument, denatures itself even as it purports to revert to the animal, and becomes in a way purely technological. Would we, after all, be able to presume for the rhythmic—without which I doubt we can conceive of the melodic—the same sort of nontechnological, prearticulated naturality one understands to constitute the melodic? Would we not immediately identify in a music defined by rhythm an artificial externalization of the heartbeat, its exaggeration and perversion, its repetition become lifeless automation?[13]

But more specifically, in the context of Heidegger's work, one cannot avoid the fact that even though the way to language is supposed to lead to a detechnologized poetic speaking, here as elsewhere the way inevitably involves a shift or turn. Indeed, the constant return to the notion of a deviation operates as a type of reversal or dorsal impulse structuring the ontological project in general. First, one embarks on a path of questioning and finds it to be the wrong path: the essence of modern technology is nothing technological; or one sets out on the way to language only to find it "has become transformed along the way . . . it has shifted." Then, that reversing shift is a shift out of the human: modern technology does not reduce to human activity; or the transformation of language is a shift "from human activity . . . to the appropriating nature of language" (*On the Way*, 130). In fact, the movement proper to thinking, that which would allow us to understand the essence of technology, or allow language to exist as language, or things to appear as things, is "no mere shift of attitude" but a change from "one thinking to the other" that takes place by means of a "step back *[Schritt zurück]*" ("The Thing," 179). The step back has a general force throughout Heidegger's work of a return to, through, and as it were out the other side of the tradition, and it begins, no doubt, with the destruction of the history of ontology in *Being and Time*. In *The Question of Being* he tells Ernst Jünger that one can only overcome nihilism by entering into its essence and specifically by *turning back* to its origin: "The path of this entry *[Einkehr]* has the direction and manner of a going back *[Rückkehr]*. It does not, to be sure, mean a going backward to times lived through in the past in order to refresh them tentatively in an artificial form. The 'back' here designates the direction toward that locality (the oblivion of Being), from out of which metaphysics obtained and retains its origin" (103).

We have examined shifting in some detail via the *Gestell*, and indeed the example of Enframing is returned to in "The Way to Language" as a diversion into linguistic instrumentality that is a withdrawal of Appropriation, the means by which "all ordering finds itself challenged into calculative thinking" and "speaking turns into information": "Framing—the nature of modern technology holding sway in all directions—commandeers for its purposes a formalized language . . . and gradually abandons 'natural Language'" (*On the Way*, 132). It would therefore be something of a perversion of Heidegger's thinking to name the shift or turn "technological" when the shift to technology is described explicitly, in some instances at least, as an undesirable shift, a turn that means a withdrawal of Being.[14] Conversely, however, one might argue that, precisely to rescue Heidegger's thinking from a reductionist dismissal of technology, the model for the shift should be understood as something other than a fork in a forest path,[15] something like the technological reversibility I am referring to here. For language, capable of going the wrong way by reducing itself to information, is nevertheless "sent." And sending, as we have seen, means a passage via the danger of a radical lightning-flash turning. Thus even when Heidegger seems closest to a discourse of transcendent naturality, there nevertheless exists in his thinking this return to the destining switch at the origin, a sending that is a diverting, a natural that as it were precludes the human, or an inventing that as it were precludes the natural: "All *true language,* because assigned, sent, destined to man by the way-making movement of Saying, is in the nature of destiny. . . . There is no such thing as *a natural language of a human nature* occurring of itself, without a destiny."[16] The event or sending is precisely that oxymoronic *unprogrammable binary* of giving and holding back, unconcealing and withdrawing, appropriation and expropriation that can be read as the technological *retro-traverse* of the human I am calling the dorsal. Might it in fact be the case that the *Gestell* assumes the importance it does at this stage of Heidegger's thinking precisely because the thetic gathering he wants us to understand it to be, and even perhaps his sense of gathering in general, could not function without reference to a dangerous wholly otherness such as the technological represents? This is not just to affirm the tautology of a "radically endander[ing]" challenging represented by Enframing that is perilous for man, but to explain the coextensiveness of "ordering" and "saving power," on the one hand "block[ing] every view into the coming-to-pass of revealing," while on the other hand "let[ting] man endure," such that man can be saved only to the extent that he is endangered ("The Question concerning Technology," 33). The saving as much as the danger relies on a gathering that describes not just how mountains come to be ranges or how emotions add up to a disposition, or even how a circling becomes an alliance, but also what is gathered when unavoidable or undeflectable things are placed in our path such that we necessarily turn into otherness.

In the *Gestell,* as putting at the instrumental disposal of the human that technology is presumed to be, there would nevertheless be a gathering for, or by means of, a setting or placing that amounts to a displacement, or *exthesis,* that can be read as parallel to the *ekstatic* temporality of the Dasein. Thanks to the *Gestell,* the disposition of emotions or mountains carries with it the sense of a repositioning. Without that possibility of radical displacement, I would argue, without the possibility of what has to be understood somewhere somehow as a contrived or artificial turn-about that nevertheless functions beyond human handiwork or agency, the assembling or gathering of mountains or moods, or of the universal fourfold, risks falling back into an unexamined naturality or *physis.* Instead, thanks to an *exthetic* Enframing, the *physis* unconceals itself as *poiesis,* and thanks to the turning effect of the *Gestell,* gathering, as well as withdrawal, Appropriation, and Being themselves, come to be understood as articulated through the essence of technology.

A DIFFERENT TYPE of turning figures prominently in Althusser's account of the constitution of the political subject in "Ideology and Ideological State Apparatuses." It is described as both a reversal, a turning to a call come from behind, and a conversion, precisely a "one-hundred-and-eighty-degree physical conversion." This is the turn to ideology as personified by a policeman, a turn that responds to interpellation by the law: "*Interpellation* . . . can be imagined along the lines of the most commonplace everyday police (or other) hailing: 'Hey, you there!' . . . The hailed individual will turn round. By this mere one-hundred-and-eighty-degree physical conversion, he becomes a *subject.*"[17]

In Althusser's terms, the "individual" turns around in order to become a "subject." The individual becomes a subject by responding, by means of a turn, to the call and summons of ideology; he or she receives the status of subject in exchange for consenting to enter into an imaginary relation to the real conditions of existence.[18] Recognition of the policeman's hailing means accepting not only the repressive state apparatuses that he personifies (government, administration, army, police, courts, prisons), nor only the various ideological state apparatuses (religion, education, family, legal and political systems, unions, media, culture), but also the particular regime of misrecognition by which ideology holds sway. Yet conversely, however "eternal" it be, ideology does not simply preexist the subject but itself comes into existence by means of a subject that is "the constitutive

category of all ideology."[19] Indeed, Althusser insists that the scene of interpellation that he allegorizes in temporal terms functions rather as a chiasmatic relation that exists outside any temporal sequentiality: "Individuals
are always-already interpellated by ideology as subjects. . . . *Individuals are
always-already subjects*" ("Ideology," 176). What Michel Pêcheux calls the
"retroactive effect" of interpellation should therefore be understood less
as a delayed temporal effect than as an intersection of subject and ideology formations occurring in the space behind,[20] the hailed subject being
drawn back into *what he always already was* simultaneously as an eternal
ideology is constituted in him, by means of a paradoxical or chiasmatic
logic that I conceive of less as retro- than as dorsal.

It would be tempting for me to move directly to call the subject always
already turning around to ideology, to call it by virtue of that very turning a subject of technology. Indeed, in a rather straightforward sense, the
wheels of the repressive state apparatuses extend their impersonal and
automatic mechanistic connotations to the ideological state apparatuses
and to ideology in general as misrepresentation of the real conditions
of existence. Becoming a subject means becoming subject to a law that
operates inexorably, beyond control. It means being constituted through
a misrecognition, which in a sense means being constituted as divided:
the subject comes into being at least partially as something it doesn't recognize. Subjectivation means accepting the unassimilable foreignness of
that misrecognized self as part of oneself. Althusser's reference to the role
of the imaginary in securing the subject's consent, to the lure of a satisfying illusion or fiction, should not obscure the fact that, in the Marxist
terms of his analysis, it is a matter of being required to live the lie, or participate in the social formation that permits the reproduction of capitalist
conditions of production, to agree to continue to work in spite of being
exploited and alienated. As we shall shortly see, what therefore subsists
throughout the various versions of ideological functioning is quite clearly
the idea that the human is taken over by, or connects itself to a type of,
impersonal but material machine. Indeed, Althusser's insistence that "ideology has a material existence" conversely reinscribes a sense of materiality upon the imaginary, making of the *representation* of the imaginary
relation a type of technological artifice ("Ideology," 165). It might even be
ventured that the whole psychoanalytic theory of accession to the symbolic field—name of the father, language, mirror stage, et cetera—on

which Althusser's hypotheses depend, functions as a machinery of subjectivation. It would not be for nothing that Foucault, in recasting the constitution of the political subject in terms that seek to supersede both Althusserian and Lacanian models, often refers to "technologies of the self."[21]

However, without going so far as to assimilate ideology to technology or to reduce every speculative gesture to a type of prosthesis—which would nevertheless provide a figure for the contortion by means of which, from Descartes to Lacan, in order to turn into oneself, one is somehow required to turn outside oneself—we can analyze in more detail two aspects of Althusser's formulation that reinforce the reading being advanced here. The first is the matter of the turn itself, the specific figuration that Althusser gives to the scene of interpellation such that the individual is hailed not by something or someone visible, identifiable, or familiar, approaching from in front, but by an impersonal, unseen, and threatening voice calling from behind: "There are individuals walking along. Somewhere (*usually behind them*) the hail rings out" ("Ideology," 174; italics mine). Now, within Althusser's narrative schema, for the call to come from behind is entirely logical. In the first place—if we can fall back for a moment into the fiction of a temporal sequence—the individual "prior to" interpellation is not yet the subject and cannot yet know, anticipate, or *foresee* what will constitute it: "The theatre of consciousness . . . is observed from behind the scenes. . . . The subject is spoken *of,* the subject is spoken *to,* before the subject can say: 'I speak.'"[22] In the second place, interpellation falls on us as a law—here a policeman, but it could as easily be a god (the conversion of Saul of Tarsus into Paul resonates in the near background of Althusser's discourse)—that precedes us and inscribes us as always already guilty, so that without perceiving the precise address of the voice we hear, without seeing any hand pointing in our direction as the "you there" is proffered, our consciousness immediately becomes (guilty) conscience, causing us to turn and acknowledge that address.

Judith Butler pays close attention to the turn in her *Psychic Life of Power,* and Althusser's interpellation comes into focus as a prime example of subjectivation as subjection, following Hegel's unhappy consciousness and Nietzsche's bad conscience:

> The form this power [the external power that assumes a psychic form]
> takes is relentlessly marked by a figure of turning, a turning back upon

itself or even a turning on oneself. . . . The turn appears to function as a tropological inauguration of the subject, a founding moment whose onto- logical status remains permanently uncertain. . . Perhaps with the advent of this figure, we are no longer in the business of "giving an account of the formation of the subject." We are, rather, confronted with the tropological presumption made by any such explanation, one that facilitates the expla- nation but also marks its limit. The moment we seek to determine how power produces its subject, how the subject takes in the power by which it is inaugurated, we seem to enter this tropological quandary.[23]

Butler returns to this quandary a number of times, attempting to account for a subject whose origin is a turning, a subject that comes to be out of some sort of impersonality. This brings about a particularly abyssal "paradox of referentiality": in order to refer to a subject that has as yet no ontological status, one *turns* to the *tropic* or figurative resources of lan- guage, and the figure consistently lighted on is that of a *turn*: "Does sub- jection inaugurate tropology in some way or is the inaugurative work of tropes necessarily invoked when we try to account for the generation of the subject?" (*Psychic Life*, 4). In the case of Althusser, thinking the "'turn' as prior to subject formation" (107) calls into question both the narra- tive temporality of the event of interpellation (a policeman calls "Hey you!" [*Hé vous là-bas!*] and "you" turn around), something we have already noted, and its grammatical coherence (ascribing the name and place of a subject to something that does not yet exist as such), something the phi- losopher tried to solve summarily by distinguishing between pre-inter- pellated "individual" and the interpellated "subject." In the cases of Nietz- sche and Freud, Butler had found comparable narratives and comparable recourse to a tropological solution. Yet she appears to be satisfied that for Freud and Nietzsche the trope of turning back on oneself "is always and only *figured* as a bodily movement," and is one that "no body literally per- forms. . . . This relationship of reflexivity is always and only figured. . . . This figure makes no ontological claim" (68, 69).

That statement seems to contrast if not contradict the earlier acknowl- edgment of a tropological quandary, of a tropological inauguration of the subject whose ontological status is twice said to be "uncertain" (4). Indeed, Nietzsche is himself, as a result, turned against himself. In the context of the figure that "makes no ontological claim," we are told that "for Nietzsche, the writing of such figurations, and figuration in general, are part and parcel of the 'ideal and imaginative phenomena' which are the consequences of bad conscience" (69), whereas in a long footnote to the introductory discussion of the tropological quandary, Butler points out that for Nietzsche, "tropes are the stuff out of which literal and conceptual language emerges. Only through a kind of forgetfulness of the tropological status of language does something like customary language take hold" (201).

Although self-contradiction may have been one of Nietzsche's most consistent forms of tropic disabuse, something I attempt to reinterpret in my final chapter, one can read here something of a hesitation on Butler's part concerning the tropological quandary that she nevertheless espouses. How could one, indeed, ascribe a meaningful ontological status to a figure such as a turning, particularly one that occurs before subject formation? How can we conceive of a tropological inauguration of the subject? Yet that is precisely what the turning requires us to do. It requires us to conceive of the figure of a body that turns before any body turns (and in any case, a turning body by no means necessarily implies a formed subject); in other words, to conceive of a body and then a subject that are constituted tropologically or even rhetorically, by the very figure of the fact of a turn or the fact of the figure of a turn. This means in the first instance that the subject is formed by means of what we could call a knee-jerk response, as a function of some endocrinal or corporeal automaticity—Butler opines that a contracting radiator might do the job of hailing as well as any policeman (*Psychic Life*, 95–96)—and that just as articulation serves, in one sense at least, to define the human body, so turning will be the figure for the way in which something folds or divides on or in upon itself to become a subject. But it means in the second instance that the subject's relation to power is determined by the figure of a turn, by a tropology that is beyond or "before" any ideology or indeed any imaginary, a relation that would be figurative in a sense that has nothing to do with the idea of unreality. This would make the political subject indistinguishable from the rhetorical subject and, as should become clear in subsequent discussions, would point to a chiasmus of historical and discursive effects that exceed any integrity of either history or discourse, appearing rather as abyssal repetitions of that originary turning. For we should remember that the tropological configurations of the scene of subjectivation described by

Althusser by no means begin or end with the turning-in-response of the becoming-subject. The hailing itself has elements of another type of figurative turning, namely the apostrophe, rhetorical figure of digression and singular address like a "Hey you!" inserted into the flow of discourse. Thus when the policeman calls, the political that thereby comes to be, or comes to invest in subjectivation, does so by means of the apostrophic tropology of interpellation itself. Before there is a subject that turns, there is a turning back that is a turning-into-subjectivation. The subject is first formed as a subject by reference to what is behind or what comes from behind; that re-ference is precisely and literally a "bearing back." Second, the subject bears back to re-late to power; it turns to a power that is itself determined figuratively, mobilizing a tropological network or chiasmus that can never distill into a purity of the political subject.

The other aspect of Althusser's scene of interpellation that merits attention in the context of this discussion derives from his (as if) passing reference to "the practical *telecommunication* of hailings" in order to insist that "the one hailed always recognizes that it is really him who is being hailed." The subject-to-be cannot avoid being interpellated in this view, constitution as a subject is ineluctable, nothing escapes this law, hailings "hardly ever miss their man."[24] Yet we know that the subject-in-ideology falls prey to misrecognition. Something misses or is misdirected nevertheless. The manner in which the "Lacanian/Althusserian postulate of misrecognition" breaks open once exposed to telecommunication is astutely analyzed by Richard Dienst in his *Still Life in Real Time,* and the point comes back into clear focus in Thomas Keenan's *Fables of Responsibility.*[25] The word "telecommunication" reinforces the extent to which Althusser inscribes interpellation as a form of indirection or misdirection, for the hailings that are said to "hardly ever" miss their man necessarily have inscribed within them the structure of adestination, as Derrida calls it.[26] They are like the letter that *can*—always—*not arrive* and therefore *cannot arrive* to the extent that the possibility of nonarrival is inextricably lodged within it, comes to inhabit its very structure. "Practical telecommunication" means just that: there is no communication that is not a *tele*communication, no hailing that operates without a delay or a distancing; and because of that irreducible effect of distancing and delay, there is no telecommunication that *simply* arrives at its man: "When it has arrived, it is indeed the proof that it had to arrive, and arrive there, at its destination.—But before arriving, it is not destined." The hailing takes place across a telecommunicational void, without a guaranteed response, and the 180-degree physical conversion of the response—when it comes—is consequently seen in slow motion and with double takes, with a perceptual sweep through the lines of sight of other potential hailers before any response is given to the law. "At this level, ideology must be conceived of as a mass of sendings or a flow of representations whose force consists precisely in the fact that they are not perfectly destined, just as they are not centrally disseminated."[28]

From this point of view, interpellation depends explicitly on a technology, a telecommunication by means of which the voice of the policeman traverses the space of a suspense, falls into reliance upon some artificial contrivance in order to reach its man. And the turn, as a consequence, is a disjunctive turning, a turning into disjunction, taking place across a mechanical divide. However reduced that space and suspense are—Althusser's examples are the "verbal call or whistle [*coup de sifflet*]"[29]—however much this purports to be a vocal communication within the closed circuit of a phono-contiguousness, the structure of the technological has nevertheless inserted itself. For if the verbal call seems to issue from a nontechnologized human speaking subject (a supposition we would in any case reject in view of what has previously been argued concerning language's technological status), the whistle is indistinguishably human and mechanical, and indeed the French *coup de sifflet* specifies that in this case we are in fact talking about the little silver instrument of the policeman-referee and not a naturally produced sound. The same sense of a mechanized naturality will be reinforced in Althusser's example in "The Christian Religious Ideology," where God creates subjects who will be "his *mirrors*, his *reflections*": "We observe that the structure of all ideology, interpellating individuals as subjects in the name of a Unique and Absolute Subject is speculary, i.e., a mirror-structure, and doubly specularly: this mirror duplication is constitutive of ideology and ensures its functioning" ("Ideology," 180).

This is indeed a machinery of interpellation and an ideological treadmill that is being brought into play, one that will have the individual "submit freely to the commands of the Subject, i.e., in order that he shall (freely) accept his subjection." This "free" self-deliverance to subjection should be interpreted as an automatic response, an automatization of subjects as a result of which they will "work all by themselves [*marchent* tout seuls]" (182).

In "Ideology and Ideological State Apparatuses" Althusser makes only summary reference to the sense of ideology in Marx, noting the comparison that Marx makes, in *The German Ideology,* between ideology and dream, in order to advance the thesis that it has no history, which for Althusser means "*ideology is eternal,* exactly like the unconscious" (159–61). But, as Sarah Kofman shows, there is another precise visual model in Marx's text, namely, the camera obscura with its reversal of the image, such that in ideology "men and their circumstances appear upside down." Kofman—who notes that the mechanism of the camera obscura itself reversed Euclidean optical theory, according to which "it is from the eye that the luminous ray emanates"[31]—compares this reversal with how the turning table of *Capital* becomes a commodity by breaking the relation of producers to their labor, a relation referred to as a "physical relation between physical things" like "an actual passage of light from one thing to another, from the external object to the eye." The table, by contrast, is said to dance and to "stand on its head."[32] Kofman argues that in order to explain this upsetting or reversal of the order of things, Marx reverts in *Capital* to a religious analogy, as if "the metaphor of the camera obscura [were now] inadequate for speaking of ideological inversion." This occurs because Marx falls back on a *lumino*centrism as if to defend against the connotations of occultation, obscurity, and error that overshadow the mechanism of reversal taking place in the dark of the camera obscura.[33] I will take up the mechanisms of the camera obscura in detail in chapter 6. But consistent with the reading that I have been advancing here, it would have to be said that a certain technology of ideology has, at least figuratively, been irreversibly set in train. That technology appears, as if in the dark box, chamber, or *camera* that will be the forerunner of the very visual machination by which the real and the imaginary still act out their relations; it reappears via the market dance of the automaton table, taking the relations of production out of their reality into some fantasy that only a technology of special effects could create; and in both cases what occurs is a reversal, the reversibility that, as I have argued, is a specific fact of the machine. So whether ideology "begins" in the mechanism of interpellation or in the concealment of the camera obscura, it will have always begun by means of a technological turn.

"INTERPELLATION" is a word Levinas sometimes uses to describe the situation of the ethical subject, referring specifically to the role of language in the "immediateness" of the face-to-face: "The claim to know and to reach the other is realized in the relationship with the Other that is cast in the relation of language, where the essential is the interpellation, the vocative. . . . The interpellated one is called upon to speak."[34] The word recurs intermittently in the first part of *Totality and Infinity* and is reinforced in the 1987 preface written for the German edition.[35] Although developed in an altogether different context from Althusser's concerns, Levinas's sense of absolute responsibility before the other to some extent resonates with the interpellation described in "Ideology and Ideological State Apparatuses." This is so in straightforward terms because of a conceptual parallelism that automatically appears between the constitution of the political subject in Althusser and of the ethical subject in Levinas. Given the importance of Levinas's thinking for contemporary philosophy, and given his project of redirecting philosophy toward an "otherwise than being" that is fundamentally ethical—and by extension political—analysis of his work is something we would be at pains to avoid here. Yet that is even more so when one begins to consider how ideas of dorsality relate to the explicit priority he gives to the face. I shall first examine that in the context of the face, and of the face-to-face, as functions of visibility and reciprocity, and second analyze exteriority in general as a function of corporality, in order to underline what, for being explicit in Levinas, has particular resonance for this discussion: namely, that his ethical relation is anything but a reduction to the image of a symmetrical encounter.

As I have just suggested, the very use of the term "interpellation" helps Levinas to play down the effect of a reciprocal gaze in the face-to-face in favor of a linguistic relation: "We shall try to show that the relation *between* the same and the other—upon which we seem to impose such extraordinary conditions—is language" (*Totality and Infinity*, 39). By discoursing, or "conversing" as the English translation has it, one avoids exercising the panoramic gaze of objectivation, representation, and totalization. The face-to-face does not reduce to any idealistic idea of reciprocity or coexistence; rather, language and discourse are forms of "facial" expression that impose or retain at the same time an absolute separation, an exteriority, and the means of interpersonal communication: "The face of the Other at each moment destroys and overflows the plastic image it leaves me. . . . It *expresses itself.* . . . To approach the Other in conversation *[discours]* is to welcome his expression. . . . The relation with the Other, or Conversation, is a non-allergic relation, an ethical relation" (*Totality and Infinity*, 50–52). Such formulations are not without difficulty, and, as I discuss later, the emphases of *Otherwise than Being*, where "expression" gives way to "exposure" and discourse is reconfigured in terms of "saying," shed a different light on the questions raised here. But in *Totality and Infinity* at least, Levinas seems to want us to understand the face as expressing the Other "before" language, expressing without speaking—its nudity, its vulnerability—but doing that without allowing such nonlinguistic discourse to operate within an everyday regime of visuality. Hence:

Contrary to all the conditions for the visibility of objects, a being is not placed in the light of another but presents itself. . . The face is a living presence, it is expression. . . . The face speaks. The manifestation of the face is already discourse. . . . This presence, affirmed in the presence of the image as the focus of the gaze that is fixed on you, is said. . . . Signification is not an ideal essence or a relation open to intellectual intuition, thus still analogous to the sensation presented to the eye. It is preeminently the presence of exteriority. . . . Discourse is . . . an original relation with exterior being. (*Totality and Infinity*, 65–66)

This idea receives perhaps its most paradoxical formulation in the sentence "The eye does not shine; it speaks" (66). We have therefore to imagine a form of expression—where the emphasis, as the book's subtitle makes clear, is on exteriority, thus not some telepathy or communication of the soul—that takes place by means of the face and, since it doesn't reduce to the spoken, speaks through the eyes, but by the same token is not simply a question of the visible. As a result, it is as if Levinas's theory of the ethical relation were constantly relayed between the face, which first means the eyes, and speech, between visuality and discursivity. In the preface to his text, he writes: "Already *of itself* ethics is an 'optics'" (29), and, in contrast, much later, "To see the face is to speak of the world. Transcendence is not an optics, but the first ethical gesture" (174). While it might be tempting to read that as a contradiction, it should be understood as a necessary effect of the stresses of the new conceptual framework he is trying to develop. And yet it is on the basis of such an aporia that Levinas's work becomes susceptible to the type of "redirection" that I shall attempt hereafter.

The paradox of the eye that speaks will receive further clarification, or complication, in the importance Levinas gives to the immediacy of expression as a form of prediscursive or prelinguistic signification, a notion of sense "prior to my *Sinnbegung*": "The immediate is the interpellation. . . . The immediate is the face to face" (*Totality and Infinity*, 51–52). The presentation or self-expression of the face is, as it were, the first signifier, before any relation to a signified; it is rather what gives rise to signification. It is an immediacy or instantaneity such that there is no time or space for a differential play of signification, yet it somehow still takes place as a relation, a "presentation of the other to the same without the intermediary of any image or sign, solely by the expression of the face" (213). Speech itself, that which the mouth speaks rather than the eyes, "does not have the total transparence of the gaze directed upon the gaze, the absolute *frankness* of the face to face proffered at the bottom of all speech" (182). Given his emphasis on immediacy and frankness, Levinas will be drawn into a rather classic distrust of putatively indirect or nonimmediate speech, specifically rhetoric, which he denounces—referring to the *Phaedrus*—in no uncertain terms. Rhetoric means approaching the other obliquely (*de biais*) rather than frontally (*de face*), amounting as a result to a form of violence and injustice that is to be renounced in favor of the "justice" of "*this face to face approach, in conversation*" (71).

The word "justice" is put into play—by an effect of language that would presumably have to be understood as nonrhetorical, as involving no detour—with the word *droiture,* meaning "straightness," in obvious contradistinction to the word for "law" (*le droit*). *Droiture* is "straight(forward)ness" and by (nonrhetorical) extension a "frankness" or "sincerity," therefore a *directness* or *rectitude* rather than some form of obedience implying *rectification*: "Nothing is more direct than the face to face, which is straightforwardness [*droiture*] itself. . . . The Desire for exteriority has appeared to us to move . . . in Discourse, which in turn has presented itself as justice, in the uprightness [*droiture*] of the welcome made to the face" (*Totality and Infinity*, 78, 82). Yet this straightness or directness becomes problematic on two accounts. First because Levinas will describe the face-to-face relation not only as justice but variously as the interpersonal discourse we have already seen, as "religion" (40), which evokes the sense of a bond or link in the Latin *religere,* and as Desire and goodness (50). That implies, if nothing else, at least the *indirection* of forms of figuration or abstraction with respect to what we might call the literality of the face. However "straight" we might presume discourse, the link of religion, Desire, goodness, and justice to be, their connotative accumulation at the least broadens the sense of the face-to-face and opens space in which something like rhetorical detour might occur. It is perhaps not for nothing that the face in Levinas's French is resolutely *visage* rather than *figure.*[36]

Second, and more important, as I began by saying, the face-to-face is much less straightforward than the words suggest; it is anything but a simple reciprocity or symmetry. The other "remains infinitely transcendent, infinitely foreign" (*Totality and Infinity,* 194); he cannot therefore, short of a revelation such as Levinas assiduously refuses, appear in any straightforward manner. He resists both perception and apperception. In a section titled "The Asymmetry of the Interpersonal," Levinas refers to "the face with which the Other *turns* to me" (215; italics mine) and emphasizes again what has been developed from very early on, namely, the call to, or demand, indeed the command for responsibility, the interpellation that comes from a position of invisibility, from a "dimension of height." The alterity of the Other is ultimately that of the "Most-High" (34). Hence in the final analysis, the straightforwardness (*droiture*) of the relation to the other is in fact a turn, a curvature, indeed a "primary curvature": "The dimension of *height* in which the Other is placed is as it were the primary curvature [*courbure première*] of being" that makes my gaze toward him "incomparable" to that by which he "measures" me (86). The gazes are thus not comparable or compatible; they do not enjoy the straightness of reciprocity but are subject to curvature. The Other surprises me or, as Levinas prefers, *visits* me (indicating a further etymological drift by which presentation becomes a function less of *visuality* or *visibility* than of *hospitality*). The Other doesn't appear in front of me, facing me, so much as turn or incline itself toward me, summoning me as responsible from outside my consciousness or perception. It is precisely by means of such a "curvature of intersubjective space" that the face-to-face resists being reduced to vision, "goes further than vision":

The truth of being is not the *image* of being, the *idea* of its nature; it is the being situated in a subjective field which *deforms* vision, but precisely thus allows exteriority to state itself, entirely command and authority: entirely superiority. *This curvature of the intersubjective space inflects distance into elevation*; it does not falsify being but makes its first truth possible (*Totality and Infinity*, 290–21; italics mine)

In following Levinas at his word, a reading can therefore tend toward a formulation of the ethical relation that seems to directly oppose what he appears to posit: *a relation of the face to back*. The turn to the other, even if it is a turn upward (to the Most High), is a turn into the structure of otherness I call dorsality. If one is to understand fully Levinas's idea of a face defined by eyes that speak, that we hear from an elsewhere; if we are to seriously accredit his resistance to the visible and to vision as relations of objectification, in favor of visitation or what I will call "surprise"; if one is to give full force to the height or superiority by which the other preserves its separation as distance and inaccessibility "before" or "in spite of" becoming entreaty and command; if one is to support his refusal of transcendence; if we are to allow that other to be the absolute other, the foreigner, then we might more faithfully conceive of the other as coming from behind. The idea of a "face" that drops from a great height to stand before us, confront us, and stop us in our tracks cannot avoid falling into, and reducing to the regime of, visibility. Instead we are asked to imagine a face that "opens the primordial discourse" (*Totality and Infinity*, 201) and in that sense precedes us, is before us in the sense of being behind us, relates us to the infinite without our having time to turn around. The Other "exists" in that shadow of visibility or that blind spot of knowledge that no straight and forward facial orientation can perceive; in that sense it is behind the back.

A "face-to-back" relation also more powerfully connotes, I would argue, the nakedness, destitution, hunger, and vulnerability of which the other speaks in summoning us to the ethical. The nudity of the face is said to be defined by the fact of a turning: "The face has turned to me—and this is its very nudity" (*Totality and Infinity*, 75). Taking this again at its word, reading it by means of a literality that in one sense contradicts it but at the same time reinforces it, or perhaps unpacks it, we can understand that in order for me to hear the injunction (not to commit murder) that the eye speaks, for me to "see" the "nudity of the principle," namely, the "infinite resistance to murder . . . in the hard resistance of these eyes without protection—what is softest and most uncovered" (262), the face has to turn to me. That is to say I would have first not to see, then, following a turning, see the nudity of the face for what it is. Before the face turns, therefore, I would have to see its back, the back; I would have to see vulnerability at its most vulnerable, in the back. The logic of eyes that speak what is their softness and most uncovered by turning, outside a revelation whereby some veil would suddenly fall from them, is for me less the logic of eyes that show what is behind their surface than of eyes that show the back. The possibility of murder such as Levinas refers to is figured most forcefully in the utter defenselessness of the back—hence stabbing in the back is the ultimate treachery—in coming upon someone and reducing him to a dead object before even giving him the possibility of existing as a being with a face. The turning of the face is the "mechanism" by which the other comes into being as other and as prohibition against that murder. Hence although Levinas explicitly asks us to read both the possibility of, and the injunction against, murder in "the depths of defenceless eyes" (199), although he insists that it is "the straightforwardness of the face [that makes] murder possible and impossible" (262), I would argue that the nudity and destitution on which he places so much emphasis, nudity as principle, that is, as the vulnerability of the human to objectivation and extinction, is first, "before" being a nudity of the eyes—or necessarily also—a nudity of the body and of the back.[37]

This comes into clearer focus in Levinas's conception of the erotic relation, which "aims" precisely at the "frailty" of the Other, its "extreme fragility" or "vulnerability" (*Totality and Infinity*, 256), which he defines as feminine.[38] For the frailty and vulnerability, the nudity, of the feminine or erotic other to sustain its very eroticism, the face-to-face relation has to move from the face, and indeed "the feminine presents a face that goes beyond the face" (260). The feminine is an "inversion of the face" (262), and erotic nudity an "inverted signification [*une signification à rebours*]" (263). But the face remains the primary signifier; it is its nudity that allows for a lascivious apperception, which might suggest that the erotic inversion is a *perversion* of the face, although nothing in Levinas would seem to allow that interpretation. Everything points to the erotic as a privileged relation, especially once it gives rise, in the context of the concluding arguments of *Totality and Infinity,* to the possibility of fecundity and the child, through which being loses "the structure of an existent" and becomes "what is to be engendered" (266). And indeed, via the specifics of a relation ordained by the caress, and the status given to the feminine, one finds in the erotic the basis for the more fundamental calling into question of identity that Levinas will explore in *Otherwise than Being or Beyond Essence*. We might therefore argue that in order to preserve that privilege, the erotic inversion of the face, or the face beyond the face, should be made to resonate as a frailty and effeminization, indeed an eroticization of the back. Levinas allows that "the whole body—a hand or a curve of the shoulder—can express as the face" (*Totality and Infinity*, 262), suggesting, word for word, that the face beyond the face of the feminine and of the erotic moves, from the hand, up the arm to the shoulder and over it, to encompass the whole body and therefore include the back. Furthermore, he describes a "chastity and decency of the face" that "abides at the limit of the obscene yet repelled, but already close at hand and promising" (263), suggesting an erotics that functions as a decency at the limit of obscenity, forbidden but inviting. Any such erotic "solicitation" of the whole body will logically be led to inclusively promote, rather than exclude, what is behind: the back, the behind, and the dorsal relation. If the whole body can express as the face, if the erotic leads us beyond the face toward the obscene, promising what is offstage or off-limits, then the sense of the face has come to include the back and everything I am here intending within the idea of the dorsal.

In the erotic relation there is not just the tergiversation between eyes and mouth, between visage and discourse, that we have already noted, but a necessarily more distinct turn from the language of speech to that of the caress. The caress "solicits," "*searches*," "forages": "What the caress seeks is not situated in a perspective and in the light of the graspable" (*Totality and Infinity*, 257–58). Whereas the speech of the ethical relation already refused the panoramic reification performed by the visual, the caress goes further in avoiding objectification, allowing the feminine to exist in its inviolable violability, allowing the otherwise than being of something that "no longer has the status of an 'existent'" (259): "The face of the beloved . . . ceases to express, or, if one prefers, it expresses only this refusal to express, this end of discourse and decency, this abrupt interruption of the order of presences" (260). Such, and more—or rather less—is the form of subjectivity, "irreducible to consciousness and thematization," that Levinas will develop in his second major work, *Otherwise than Being*,[39] a subjectivity whose "disposition" or even "disposability"—terms I would offer to contrast with any idea of thetic or thematic "positionality," and to suggest Levinas's "substitution"—functions to reinforce the vulnerability or passivity that I am here calling "dorsal." For passivity—indeed, what I insist on interpreting as a dorsal passivity—marks a certain configuration of the subject beyond essence.

As I mentioned earlier, the relation determined by language of *Totality and Infinity* is understood differently in *Otherwise than Being* as "saying *[le Dire]*." Saying contrasts with both being (*être*) and the said (*le Dit*), but it also abandons the active force of an indicative verb in favor of the suspensive passivity of the infinitive: "*Saying* [means] *answering for the other* [répondre d'autrui]. . . . an extreme passivity . . . in the relationship with the other, and, paradoxically, in pure saying itself" (*Otherwise than Being*, 46–47; translation modified). Saying brings about an unlocking (*déverrouillement*) of communication that is also a "risky uncovering" of the self, a rupture in interiority and the "abandon of all shelter, exposure to traumas, vulnerability"; it means turning consciousness inside out as one would a jacket (48). Levinas defines the relation determined by saying, the medium of exposure to the other, as "proximity." But like the face-to-face, proximity is resolutely nonreciprocal, dehiscent, a break with synchrony (84–85). It is a contact different from the spatial relation of someone one can see or reach, hold or converse with, "in the reciprocity of handshakes, caresses, struggle, collaboration, commerce, conversation" (83). And it again reinforces the passivity of a type of corporeal anxiety before the other who comes so close as to become "incarnation," a word we should understand in the sense of "ingrowing," like a toenail.

In the terms of this more generalized bodily stress, the emphasis given to the face and eyes in *Totality and Infinity* is therefore displaced in favor of the skin, of an "immediacy of a skin and a face, a skin which is always a modification of a face, a face that is weighted down with a skin" (*Otherwise than Being*, 85). The face is still required to function outside visual manifestation or phenomenality—"It escapes representation; it is the very collapse of phenomenality. . . . Non-phenomenon because less than a phenomenon" (88)—and if it still impresses by virtue of its nakedness, that nudity is no longer the same sort of docile vulnerability of the child or animal; it is rather a nudity of the face that shows its wear and tear: "The disclosing of a face is nudity, non-form, abandon of self, ageing, dying, more naked than nudity. It is poverty, skin with wrinkles" (88). Indeed, the face will also be turned, as it were inside out, changed for the worse, rendered "obscene," "altered." Levinas reinforces in a footnote the erotic force of those terms, referring again to the "extreme turnings about [*retournements*] of a face" by means of erotic alterity (89, 192n).

Thus the physical, indeed corporal terms in which subjectivity is called into question in *Otherwise than Being* could not be more explicit:

> The subject is not *in itself*, at home with itself, such that it would dissimulate itself in its wounds and its exile, understood as *acts* of wounding or exiling itself. Its bending back upon itself [*recroquevillement*] is a turning inside out. Its being "turned to another" is this being turned inside out. . . . Here exposure has a sense radically different from thematization. . . . exposure in response to . . . [this ellipsis Levinas's] being at the question before any interrogation, any problem, without clothing, without a shell to protect oneself, stripped to the core. . . . a denuding beyond the skin . . . denuding to death, being as a vulnerability. . . . This being torn from oneself in the core of one's unity, this absolute non-coinciding, this diachrony of the instant, signifies in the form of one-penetrated-by-the-other. The pain, this underside of skin, is a nudity more naked than all destitution. . . . The subjectivity of a subject is vulnerability, exposure to affection, sensibility, a passivity more passive still than any passivity, an irrecuperable time, an unassemblable diachrony of patience, an exposedness always to be exposed the more. (49–50)

As this lengthy parsing reveals, the repetition of such formulations is relentless: ipseity "fold[s] back upon" itself (110), oneself "recurs" within itself, is "incarnated" (109), gets twisted or folded back over itself in its skin. The subjectivity that is otherwise also falls back on itself in temporal terms, as if backing up to a nonexistent origin; Levinas will term it both "anachronous," an anterior older than the a priori, and "anarchic," "*delayed* behind [*en retard*] its present moment" (101), and instead of the self-reflection of consciousness, he will speak of what comes to pass prior to or on the "hither side [*en-deçà*] of one's own nuclear unity" (92). On at least three occasions, Levinas's preferred term for the corporeal recurrence of the self within itself, translated as "backed up against itself," is *acculé*, which more literally suggests a body that is turned inside out by turning back to front; or a body that folds back upon itself to the extent that its front gets pressed against its back(side), a body that, in a sense, becomes dorsal.[40]

Now, Levinas systematically proffers the being for the other of maternity as the "ultimate sense of this vulnerability" (108). In one paragraph, it heads an impressive appositional list—"maternity, vulnerability, responsibility, proximity, contact"—of what constitutes sensibility (76). Clearly, evocations of tightened skin relate in an important sense to that particularly female form of incarnation, ingrowth, or "gestation of the other in the same" (75), and maternity represents for Levinas an obvious case, perhaps the paradigm, of the giving to and for the other that means nourishing, clothing, and lodging in the visceral sense of bread snatched from one's mouth, what for him constitutes the substitution, persecution, and being hostage of the ultimate exposure of the self. A pregnant woman is passive hostage to the guest-fetus in that sense, a substitution that "operates in the entrails of the self" (196).[41]

However, as I have been reading it here, there remains a generalization of the corporeal whose figures do not always reduce to the maternal and which, in going beyond the face at the same time as avoiding interiority, necessarily gets enacted as a contortion of, or inversion upon, the figure of the body. Indeed, at times it seems as if what is being described could be interchangeably a pregnant mother or a concentration camp victim. Thus, to the extent that we can talk about an "image" of this subject, there seems little doubt that the other who previously disarmed and then commanded with the docile eloquence of its eyes has become some form of naked, contorted self with a stretched skin huddled in a corner:

The oneness without any duality of oneself [is] from the first backed up against itself [acculé à soi], up against a wall, or twisted over itself in its skin [tordu sur soi dans sa peau]. . . . The ego . . . is in itself like one is in one's skin, that is, already in a tight spot [à l'étroit], ill at ease in one's own skin. . . . Backed up against itself, in itself because without recourse to anything, in itself like in its skin, the self in its skin both is exposed to the exterior . . . and obsessed by the others in this naked exposure.[42]

This subject is less one that waits for the other to turn its naked eyes toward it than one that shades its eyes or turns its head and body to protect a subjectivity that, however, remains, exposed. Or it is a subject whose front has been hollowed out from within or from behind so that it is a wrinkled and sagging skin devoid of the flesh and substance that would give it form, whose bread has been snatched from its mouth and whose body has been taken over, a body twisted and contorted in extreme passive exposure and therefore necessarily understood as a body that has, in some way, turned to offer its back.

In the 1984 essay "Peace and Proximity," Levinas emphasizes the "nudity of pure exposure" and the "face as the extreme precariousness of the other" by quoting from a scene in Vassili Grossman's *Life and Fate* where a woman waiting in line "can see only the backs of others." Grossman writes: "[She] had never thought that the human back could be so expressive. . . . Persons approaching the counter had a particular way of craning their neck and back, their raised shoulders . . . seemed to cry, sob, and scream."[43] Clearly, then, the face can be the back; at the outside the shoulder blades can speak as eloquently as the eyes. But what is perhaps more interesting is the fact that Levinas's commentary on the quotation from *Life and Fate* says something different: not that the face can be the back, but rather that "the face is not . . . exclusively a human face." Now while that could also be a way of saying that the face might be not the human face but the human back, it opens the possibility, literally at least—and because he does not elaborate, the idea is left to resonate—that the ethical relation may not be a human relation at all but a relation to the nonhuman other.[44]

A VULNERABILITY understood specifically as passivity, such as informs the arguments of *Otherwise than Being*, refers less (than in *Totality and Infinity*) to the idea of the other stopping us in our tracks; less, I think it is fair to say, of a frontal relation that will always risk implying a confrontation between two entities. Instead the emphasis of Levinas's second major volume is the "defeat of the ego's identity" by means of "vulnerability, exposure to outrage, to wounding, passivity more passive than all patience, passivity of the accusative form, trauma of accusation suffered by a hostage." At the outside the ego is effaced to the extent of being a "hostage who substitutes himself for the others" (*Otherwise than Being*, 15). The ethical relation as recognition of the other thus cedes to the radical passivity of this substitution for the other, a passivity that is said to be *"more passive still than the passivity of matter"* (113–14; italics mine). In pursuing this question through one more of its turns, both in concert and in a certain torsion with Levinas, we will be led to consider the stakes of interpreting the passivity that is more passive than matter as an inertness, not to say inanimateness, of the human.

One encounters a different configuration of the body and the feminine from that just analyzed—whether it is maternal or simply uxorial is not made explicit—in the second part of *Totality and Infinity,* "Interiority and Economy." There, it is as if Levinas steps back from the ethical relation to develop something of a phenomenology of alterity in everyday life. He ends the section by returning to the question of the face-to-face and of the absolutely other, but only after having first considered how one relates to more familiar others, with specific emphasis on the otherness that is articulated, both inside and out, and in strangely paradoxical ways, by the walls of a house.

Stating that "the things we live from are not tools, nor even implements, in the Heideggerian sense" (*Totality and Infinity,* 110), Levinas argues for a relation to one's immediate environment determined precisely by the fact of living in it (*vivre de . . .*) and enjoying it (*jouir de . . .*). There is no strictly utilitarian adoption of an instrument of technology without that instrument's functioning also as a form of enjoyment; for that reason, even utensils come to us adorned or embellished. Our use of such things is related to our love or enjoyment of life, such as that experienced in eating, such as produces in us "the very pulsation [*frisson,* "shiver"] of the I" (113). The world as other is experienced not as a world of represented objects but as what Levinas calls the "element," an enjoyed and lived-in world that as it were precedes the known world. The lived-in world is an interior, a milieu that one basks or bathes in, and whose constituents, unlike movable objects (*meubles,* "furniture"), cannot be possessed; it exists as a sort of natural or amniotic commonwealth, with explicit connotations of liquidity: "the wave that engulfs and submerges and drowns—an incessant movement of afflux without respite" (135). Yet at the same time, this element exists in a chiasmatic relation with the domicile: the domicile holds back the flow of the liquid element, functioning as a form of resistance to it; but then it is from out of the domicile ("the primary appropriation") that one plunges back into the element.

The house is therefore the negation of the general economy of a universal interior, which would have us bathing in a boundless lived-in and enjoyed ocean, in favor of the restricted economy of an appropriated interior, on the basis of which interiority itself comes to be understood:

> To tell the truth the element has no side [face] at all. . . . One is steeped in it [on y baigne]; I am always within the element. Man has overcome the elements only by surmounting this interiority without issue by the domicile, which confers upon him an extraterritoriality. . . . Man plunges into the elemental from the domicile, the primary appropriation. . . . He is *within* what he possesses, such that we shall be able to say that the domicile, condition for all property, renders the inner life possible. The I is at home with itself. Through the home our relation with space as distance is substituted for the simple "bathing in the element." But the adequate relation with the element is precisely bathing. (*Totality and Infinity*, 131–32)

To the extent that "objects" are directed toward, or subordinated to, the enjoyment of living—furniture, house, food, clothing; bread, fire, cigarette, but also the cigarette lighter, the fork—they remain within that sense of the elemental and reconstitute its general economy: "To enjoy without utility, in pure loss, gratuitously, without referring to anything else, in pure expenditure—this is the human" (133). But as I read it, that form and sense of enjoyment, that type of liquefaction of more or less solid objects, which thereby return to the element, relies again on the interior solidification constituted by the body as sensible or sensitive being. Indeed, as we shall see, it relies on a particular body defined by a particular sensibility. And it relies in turn on the archetypal, architectural, and artificial form of solidification that is the house. It is the house that interrupts the element and defines interiority; it is thanks to the house that a body coalesces within it, as a result of which the I comes to be constituted as an at-home-with-itself that is then able to relate to the element. Thus, although man supposedly exists prior to appropriating the domicile, we have to assume that at that point he exists as indistinguishable from the element, that he is still swimming within it, for it is the domicile that renders inner life possible and allows the I to be at home with itself; not just in the sense of allowing the I to be in its house, but in the sense of allowing the I to be precisely by being defined as an I that is housed within itself. From that point of view, the I does not exist without the conception of the house; the house exists and is constructed, as it were, prior to the formation of the I.

In his desire to distinguish between the consciousness of a Dasein that "is never hungry" (*Totality and Infinity*, 134), or between a biological or sociological person, and the I that enjoys, in attempting to develop a form of being that distinguishes itself from an ontological interiority, Levinas has recourse to a conception of the house as fabricated or constructed medium of interiorization (and exteriorization), to a technological economy whose terms will resound, by extension, all the way through the face to the hollowed-out skin and exposed back beyond essence that we have just been examining. This is not to say he could have done otherwise once he set out to write an "essay on exteriority," once he sought to reject the objectifying and totalizing gaze in favor of a relation to otherness as relation to the infinite. Once speech as effect of consciousness is replaced by eyes that speak, and once the face that is those eyes is more radically desubstantialized as wrinkled skin turned inside out and become hostage, the dissolution has to stop somewhere. For an ethical relation to exist, something must be concretized within the infinite sufficient to relate to it. The candidates for arresting such a dissolution are not too numerous: soul, mind, body—all of those have their own problems and their own philosophical history. Levinas opts, in his language, for versions of the corporeal, but to the extent that the body consistently bears the figure of being, it suffers serious maltreatment in his work. My argument, which puts the body and domicile of *Totality and Infinity* into play with the maternal or persecuted body of *Otherwise than Being*, is this: in order to hold up at all, in the final analysis, the body, the separate being, or any interiority more generally, as figure of what is otherwise, has to read as a type of house.

Let us follow summarily Levinas's exposition in the pages leading to and including the section on the dwelling in *Totality and Infinity*. Sensibility is the way of being in the element; it "establishes a relation with a pure quality *without support,* with the element. . . . The sensitive being, the body, *concretizes* this way of being" (136; italics mine). The body functions therefore as a form of support in a milieu where such support is lacking, and it does so by means of its solidity, by means of a concretization. The body is not only what bathes in the element but "what *dwells [demeure]*,"

(137). Its concretization is therefore that of the house, not just something that dwells in the sense of staying still, but also something that functions within an interior space. In parallel, the lack of security provided by enjoyment "provokes" a movement of individuation, the "production of a being that is *born,* that breaks the tranquil eternity of its seminal or uterine existence to enclose itself in a person, who in living from the world lives at home with itself" (147). The movement of individuation is therefore the construction of a house, the fabrication of a separated being described precisely as one "whose door to the outside must . . . be at the same time open and closed" (148). The separate being staves off insecurity about the future by assembling itself *(se recueillir),* thanks to representations such as "are produced concretely as *habitation in a dwelling* or a house" (150; translation modified).[45]

What, then, is the status of this house, we will want to know, with respect to the enjoyment whose flow it would have interrupted, and the representations, possessions, and movables that are produced within it? How will it fall on one side or the other of the life that is for living in and enjoying, and the life that requires recourse to utilitarian objects, and by extension to work outside the house? Indeed, Levinas begins by situating the house on the side of utility: "Habitation can be interpreted as the utilization of an 'implement' among 'implements.' The home would serve for habitation as the hammer for driving in a nail" (*Totality and Infinity,* 152). But the home nevertheless comes to occupy a "privileged place" within the category of objects that are defined by their being the means to various ends, or as "finalities," and its privilege derives from the paradox of its being not "the end of human activity but . . . its condition, and in this sense its commencement" (152). It is literally thanks to the house, on condition of it, therefore, that the separate being is formed and becomes a consciousness that produces representations. But this is not, Levinas clearly explains, because a house magically brings the separate being into being; not because, once a house exists, beings are separated from one another by its walls. Rather, the house is what defines separation and recollection *(receuillement),* representations and possessions, by "concretizing" them: interiority in general is "concretely *accomplished* by the home" (154). The house is therefore required to be *in* the world of objects without being *of* it; objects, including buildings themselves, are produced "out of *[à partir de],* starting from a dwelling" (151). The house occupies this strikingly transcendent position as initiator of a series of which it is not a part, namely, the series of constructed objects, the series of the becoming technological.

If the house seems thus to be redeemed from the world of objects to which, according to the logic of construction and fabrication, and of artificial and inanimate, it should belong, if it manages to give rise on the one side to recollection and intimacy, indeed a certain "warmth" or "gentleness" of intimacy, and on the other side to labor and representation, separation and alienation, it is because there is lodged within it a particular type of body. For the body, as we have seen, functions like a house; it concretizes or solidifies the sensitive being, so preventing it from being drowned in the element. But one has to presume that that body as separate being, to the extent that it is separate and constitutes a subjectivity, risks being an object such as depends on the house for its existence, such as "takes refuge empirically" in the house (154). Any such body or subjectivity would, like the concretized house, have also to be redeemed from the world of objects; its concreteness would have to be softened, its "roughnesses" smoothed over. That is achieved by having the house inhabited by a privileged or at least a prioritized inhabitant, an "inhabitant that inhabits it before every inhabitant" (157). In its defining instance, the house is thus inhabited less by the concreteness of a separate being than by the softness (*douceur*) of a feminine body: "The woman is the condition for recollection, the interiority of the Home, and inhabitation" (155). The feminine, consistently referred to as softness or sweetness, as welcoming and hospitable, infuses the body and the solidity of the separate being with a new becoming-fluid, creating as it were a new element. But "infuses" is probably not the best word, for according to the logic that gives primacy to the house as concretization of recollection, as becoming solid of what is separate, the soft body of the feminine would have to be built from the outside in. The woman is a soft house built within the house; her softness relies on a secondary, derivative deconcretization that depends on the first intimacy or "primary concretization" of the house itself (153): she is like plasticine within walls of concrete. The logical order of the events as developed here by Levinas, or the *evenemential* order of Levinasian logic, is not that one first meets a sweet, soft feminine and builds a house with or for her, but that one first establishes the concretized interiority of the at home and then sweetens or softens it with a woman. The way to the other is indeed through the woman, but before that, it passes through the (half-open) door of the house.

Once the feminine is installed as elemental soft center of the house, objects will more easily fall outside it, into an alienated world of labor, where the hand will come to mime the visual panoramic grasp of consciousness and begin to discover the world by taking possession of it. But the house itself is preserved from that impulse, precisely thanks to the feminine: "The home [*maison*] that founds possession is not a possession in the same sense as the movable goods it can collect and keep. It is possessed because it . . . is hospitable for its proprietor. This refers us to its essential interiority, and to the inhabitant that inhabits it before every inhabitant, the welcoming one par excellence, welcoming in itself—the feminine being" (157; translation modified). Starting from the house, one falls out of the redemptive softness of the feminine as well as out of the element; one gets instead into the business of possession as acquisition, stretching forth a hand that variously snatches, blindly grasps, tears up, crushes, or kneads, in a "rigorously economic movement of seizure"; one becomes involved in a labor whose "primary intention is this acquisition" (159–60). As we shall see in conclusion, the grasping of the hand has its own form of redemption, one that is of particular interest to us and to the question of what Levinas explicitly refers to, in an extremely rare instance, as "technique." But in the pages that follow his description of the house as site of the feminine, the emphasis remains on a world of separated objects that are seized on both as objects of consciousness and as acquired possessions, snatched from the outside and brought back inside. And throughout Levinas's analysis, the means by which those operations are articulated, the means by which, both outside and inside—all the way outside to products falling from the assembly line, and all the way inside to the feminine body (and no doubt inside her body to the house constituted by the womb, although that is not explicit here)—the separate functions as separate, owes its definition and constitution to the house itself, "at the limit of interiority and exteriority . . . at the frontier of interiority" (162, 153). This is no minor role for a component within an essay on exteriority. It suggests that infinity as much as totality relies on a separation that operates by virtue of a construction, that the other begins at the point at which there is building.

For the other is indeed the logical end point of Levinas's analysis. The house that enables separation also enables the relation to the other, experienced first as a relation to the feminine. The economy of the interior is also an *oecumenia,* a sharing of inhabitable space, the space of an other who is revealed not as a threat but as a gentle welcoming.[46] Thus it seems not to be exaggerating to claim that even the ethical relation, the first face of the face-to-face, is produced within the house, thanks to the house, as house and therefore as technology; that the house is the technological extraterritoriality on the basis of which the face will become possible. The house resists the element and so produces interiority, that of the I at home with itself, but also extraterritoriality; and then the primary inhabitant of the house, similarly produced by it, its first interior facade, is a soft feminine face, the first other who softens the blow of such an encounter with alterity:

But the interiority of the home is *made of* extraterritoriality. . . . This extraterritoriality has a positive side. It is produced in the gentleness [*douceur,* "softness"] or warmth of intimacy. . . . The Other precisely reveals himself in his alterity not as a shock negating the I, but as the *primordial phenomenon of gentleness.* . . . The welcoming of the face is peaceable from the first. . . . *This peaceable welcome is produced primordially in the gentleness of the feminine face.* (150; italics mine)

Thus the feminine serves not only to soften the concretized house but to give it a face, to distinguish it once again from the objects one goes out to work on and grasp in a "violence" that is "applied to what is faceless" (160). She serves to bring the house closer to the elemental that it nevertheless interrupts (an elemental that does not, of course, have a face either but, by virtue of its liquidity, might be understood as having something of the softness of the feminine). By extension, one can understand otherness itself, in its wholly otherness, with all the asymmetry that we have seen, all the way to the Most High, as functioning with the force Levinas gives it at the center of his ethics precisely because it has first been tempered by the softness of the feminine face. The soft and unprotected eyes that, in the face of the other, say, "You can, but must not, kill," would logically be understood as the return of the feminine softness of the first face found, or the face first found in the home. But, let us repeat, "in the home" here means literally produced by the house. For if we previously saw those eyes as turning toward us as if they had first shown us the back, here it is a matter of the face of the other that constitutes the ethical relation being found back in and in the back of the house, as discreet space within the house, there where the serious inhabiting gets done: "The relation with the Other . . . welcomes me in the Home, the discreet presence of the Feminine. . . . The 'vision' of the face as face is a certain mode of sojourning in a home" (170, 172). We can say that if the feminine is the first other, the soft other that prepares us for the haughty absolute other, it is because the house is the first face, one side of which is washed by the elemental and the other required to define the hard edge of separateness. It is because the house is there to effect exteriority (and interiority) itself, in the strange sort of paradoxical or tautological relation that we have seen with respect to the body and to the feminine, that there is exteriority.

From this point of view, "Interiority and Economy" reads as the elaboration of the idea that because a house is built, because there is that technology, interiority can be defined. And exteriority also; and, by extension, infinity. For the way of living in a house, the inhabiting of it in fact has the somewhat provisional status of a sojourn or a visit. The house is constructed in order to have its doors opened; even inhabiting is for Levinas a form of exile or *errance*. The "concrete and initial fact" of the house "coincides" with a desire for the transcendent, and ultimately exterior, other (172), such that in showing us her face, the feminine is also showing us the door. Or perhaps she is doing something more radical still; perhaps by inhabiting the house and figuring the other, she is stretching its walls and hollowing it out in the same way that the subject gets distended in *Otherwise than Being,* making it a naked and vulnerable house, no shelter at all finally, the pure passive exposure of a type of facade. A facade, however, is not nothing. I do not use the term here in the sense of a fake face; the facade is rather a pure face, the pure sur*face* that is the face, like the sagging skin of a hollowed-out face. If the facade is a face without depth, it is by no means a face without a back. It is precisely a face that is most closely related to its back, nothing but face and back, a face propped up by its back, a face become dorsal.

Strictly speaking, the house has no face; however privileged an implement it is, it remains too much of an object to have a face. But we can now
understand how, by virtue of the pivotal role it plays in the articulation of
Levinas's ethics, the house is something from whose facade the face can
never be separated. In this way, it stands or is built behind that ethics, as
a type of backbone; without it, that ethics could probably not be launched
forth.

TWO OBSERVATIONS to conclude. First, if the hand dedicated to labor
and to the acquisition of possessions is to be in any way distinguished
from the automatic movements of a machine, it will be thanks to another
softening—not related to the feminine—whereby grasping always
remains a type of groping, whereby it fails to eliminate uncertainty: "The
hand ventures forth and catches hold of its goal with an inevitable share
of *chance* or of mischance, since it can miss its try. The hand is by essence
groping [*tâtonnement*]." In a rare reference to technics, Levinas goes on
to say that "groping is not a technically imperfect action, but the condition for all technique. . . . The body as possibility of a hand—and its whole
corporeity can be substituted for the hand—exists in the virtuality of
this movement betaking itself toward the tool" (167). Apart from the fact
that this logic repeats the whole economy that we have just seen, with
the hand representing the body and functioning as a house—hard but
also soft, grasping but also groping, determined to possess but subject
to chance, implanted as separate being out in the world but remaining at
home with itself in that world—it also says that technology as invention
retains something of the accident, that however much it is about production and control, about snatching at nature and gaining the upper hand
(*emprise*), it arrives through a type of blindness or groping in the dark.
Technology thus retains something of the unseeable or unforeseeable
other; our relation to it has something of the structure of our relation to
the absolute other. If it never shows us a face or speaks to us through its
eyes, that is because it exists to some extent outside our vision and our
grasp. But it also means, conversely, that the other that is encountered
as it were by chance, outside visibility, and turns to show itself as if first
showing its back, enabling its eyes to speak thanks to some special effect,

retains something of technology; that what was hidden from us before we encountered the other, and what remains out of sight and out of the encounter once the eyes begin to speak, is that very technology in the back.

We can understand an incompletely human, technologized, even an inert or inanimate other, as either a perversion or a consecration of Levinas's ethics. In the first place, it obstructs the path to theological transcendence such as he was often at pains to resist, and reinforces his avowed atheism.[47] It also reinforces his deconstruction of the subject that we have examined in some detail. But perhaps thinking a type of *inanimation*—not simply inert matter—before or behind the human is the ultimate ethical challenge, forcing us to realize that we are not completely human and can never become so. Perhaps an ethics that presumed an originary nonhuman would be the beginning of a rethinking not just of relations between the animate and inanimate and between Homo sapiens and technology, but also of everything that we understand as experience of the inhuman, at that point to which every ethics seems to lead us and which is our everyday despair. Levinas's eyes that speak give us a human that is most human in its becoming-feminine, becoming-child, or becoming-animal. The back behind those eyes that I am calling the dorsal gestures toward a human that is most human not as a contradiction of the becoming-feminine, becoming-child, or becoming-animal—for it is all of those—but as a compounding of them with an equally pathetic becoming-technological.

Second observation: Levinas's writing might be said to come in waves, with each consecutive idea washing over the presumed solidity of the previous formulation. Derrida has referred to it as being deployed "with the infinite insistence of waves on a beach: return and repetition, always, of the same wave against the same shore, in which, however, as each turn recapitulates itself, it also infinitely renews and enriches itself."[48] This would determine it, on the one hand, as a writing that functions within its own element, to use Levinasian terms, having us bathe in the ideas, feed on them, live in them, and enjoy them rather than represent them to our consciousness or treat them as movables or possessions. It might also account for some of the changing perspectives of terms and formulations, such as have enabled my reading to develop out of the torsions of his text, and enable me to exert certain logical stresses upon it. On the other hand, his writing does not reduce to something wishy-washy but coagulates around certain key assertions: philosophy as ethics, Being as an interpersonal relation, the other as originary responsibility, and so on. Those are the ideas in which Levinas's thinking dwells; they perhaps even account for its feminine face within such a dwelling. But they account for something of its foreign face also, for however French Levinas's language might be, it often reads as though it were in exile from itself. The house in which his thinking dwells is open to the possibility of an *errance* and an exile. That opening is, as we have seen, the opening to the other that occurs already in the house and determines the house as production of the ethical; in the terms of what I am developing here, it inscribes within his language and his writing an ethical dimension. Similarly, however, it means that Levinas's language is constantly breaking, like a wave or liquid element, against its technological dimension. To the extent that it can solidify at all, and in the terms of what he says about the house as concretization, it breaks *as* the technological. In using language and in building a house, we are unavoidably in technology. In order for language to be able to signify the way that Levinas would have it do, both as thesis and as *alterization,* it has to dwell on one side and the other of the hollowed-out facade of the house, and to be in technology as never before.

Behind. Perhaps there is someone.

—JAMES JOYCE, *Ulysses*

3. No One Home Homer, Joyce, Broch

THE STRESSED AND DISTENDED SUBJECT IN LEVINAS FINDS its echo and, as I have argued, its condition of possibility in a house that is similarly an "abandon of all shelter, exposure to traumas, vulnerability." A house that creates an interiority for the formation of a subject, but only to thereafter ease that subject (via the feminine) into—and finally expose it more radically to—relations with the outside element, with the space of labor and alienation, and with the other. This is a house that exists on the frontier between interiority and exteriority, a house that is finally nothing more than that frontier, what I have called a facade, not just a front wall with nothing behind it but a wall that is both front and back, whose front is in its back and whose back is in its front. And a house inhabited by a sojourner, someone passing through, one that no sooner constitutes itself at home with itself than it externalizes itself to encounter the other, living therefore in a state of exile and *errance*, exiled both within itself and with respect to its home, crouching naked turned inside out and back to the wall in utter exposure.

If we follow Lévi-Strauss, we have been at least limping back home and away from home from the beginning, limping back at our beginnings. To the extent that we are like Oedipus of the swollen foot, our originary self emerges podiatrically challenged, bodily impaired, and undecided which way the way home lies. We have one foot caught in the earth that would have produced us as we struggle to reconcile that conception of our origin with an idea of human sexual (re)generation. Lévi-Strauss's famous structuralist analysis of versions of the Oedipus myth, concluding that "the myth has to do with the inability, for a culture which holds the belief that mankind is autochthonous . . . to find a satisfactory transition between this theory and the knowledge that human beings are actually born from the union of man and woman,"[1] demonstrates the paradoxical bind into which we are inevitably led when we found our concepts of identity on some impossible coincidence of blood and soil, mother-womb and father-land. Freud was acknowledging, rather than resolving, that paradox when, in "The Uncanny," or in *Civilization and Its Discontents,* he referred to the house "as a substitute for the mother's womb, the first lodging, for which in all likelihood man still longs."[2] In his view, the womb as place of consanguineous origin is inseparable from the house as connection to the earth or paternal soil. But that inseparability should also be understood as a structural commonality. I read Freud—perhaps in spite of himself—as saying less that the womb precedes the house that comes to replace it, leading to the nostalgia that has us looking for it, striving to get back to it all through our lives, than that *there is no notion of the womb without the notion of the house,* and vice versa. We always already imagine ourselves in a safe haven that we are always already constructing for ourselves, rooting ourselves at the same time to the complementary but also contradictory origins of blood and soil; and more than that, we cannot reconcile that contradiction except by some form of contrivance—a genealogy, an Oedipal myth, or later an Oedipal complex, for example—by introducing into our supposed natural origin some form of artificiality.

I permit myself this interpretation in consideration, especially, of the context of Freud's reference to the womb as house in *Civilization and Its Discontents.* The allusion occurs in the paragraph preceding the famous statement that "man has, as it were, become a kind of prosthetic God" (38–39). The technological civilization in the form of prostheses that man has attached to himself begins with "tools, the gaining of control over fire and the construction of dwellings" (37), and goes on to include "ships and aircraft . . . spectacles . . . the telescope . . . microscope . . . camera . . . gramophone disc . . . telephone . . . writing" (37–38), and finally "the dwelling-house . . . substitute for the mother's womb" just mentioned (38). In other words, the road back to the natural origin or womb leads via a continuum comprising various prosthetic constructions or artificial contrivances, with no structural distinction being made in Freud's schema—read literally—between prosthetic supplements to the human and natural occurrences of that human. According to the taxonomic logic or coherence of Freud's list, the child in the womb would be a prosthetic attachment to its mother, and indeed the womb itself would be a prosthetic attachment, a house built within that same mother. The child, or humankind in general, would thus be born into exile with respect to its own naturality, always already a prosthesis, always already biotechnological.

The search for some homogeneous origin, which finds us stumbling across the limping Oedipus, also leads to an encounter with another mythological figure. We meet someone who is more explicitly a father of us all, namely, Hephaestus (Vulcan), that other lame hero who shuffles through our beginnings. One of the children of Zeus and Hera, or else Hera's parthenogenetic son, Hephaestus is the god of fire and the limping blacksmith, patron to smiths and weavers alike, and craftsman supreme. Zeus's thunderbolts, Athena's aegis, Eros's arrows, Helios's chariot or golden bowl, Achilles' armor, Harmonia's necklace, and Oenopion's underground house (or womb within the soil) are all Hephaestus's creations. Married to Aphrodite, who was cuckolding him with his brother, he constructed an elaborate net above her bed to catch her in flagrante delicto. Ardently desiring Athena, who came to visit him in his forge, he tried to force himself on her and ejaculated on her thigh as she tore herself from him. She wiped his sperm away with some wool and threw it onto the ground, thereby impregnating Mother Earth. He is sometimes confused with Prometheus, the creator of humankind, and in any case is inextricably linked with Prometheus's story. It is Hephaestus who is called on to bind Prometheus with chains when he steals fire and gives it to humans; and Hephaestus again who, on Zeus's orders, crafts woman (Pandora) out of clay as a Greek gift for Prometheus's brother Epimetheus. Like Eve, Pandora is held responsible for the original transgression of opening the forbidden box and setting loose the ills of humankind.

The Hephaestus myth repeats elements of the Oedipal contradiction exposed by Lévi-Strauss but at the same time gives us a different perspective on it. Although my brief résumé hardly amounts to a structural analysis, it points to various instances of confusion among autochthonous, parthenogenetic, and sexual reproductive origins for humankind. But at the same time, it emphasizes doubt about not just how we came to be produced but also whether we came to be produced, that is to say whether we were constructed or generated, whether we conceive of our origins as organic or technological. When it comes to woman, at least the Pandora fashioned by Hephaestus, the mother of us all and the bearer of our womb-home is explicitly understood as technological production, as artistic production or technological artifice. As we are conceived within such a home and connected to its lifeblood, we are at the same time born or produced into the nonnatural dwelling place that, in the myth, woman is represented as. That is, however human we become, we do not for all that shake off the mythological heritage of artificial creation: our first room is a womb of clay. The home back behind us all is an artificial construct. Indeed, returning to Oedipus, what haunts that myth, especially as it is developed by Freud, is another, more abstract confusion of natural with unnatural, precisely the paradox of a fall out of the natural into unnatural relations, the supposedly monstrous perversions of natural relations that are infanticide, incest, and parricide.

The confusions of Hephaestus and the fall of Oedipus can be said to be brought about by a fiction and within a literature, first within the framework of mythology and second—in the case of Oedipus, at least—via the hermeneutics of the Sphinx's riddles. Once that mythology gets narrativized as the literature proper of Homer or Virgil, the originary paradox of the home seems to have faded into a sublimated background. Indeed, in the discourses of origin and identity, and exile and homecoming, that have become the stuff of so much literature and, quite obviously, the causes of so much bloodshed, the home as place of origin is consistently yet indiscriminately conceived of as the source of blood or the repository of soil. Within that model, exile is a state of nostalgia and of an incomplete and impossible mourning, and all literature is a type of odyssey, a homecoming. And furthermore, irrespective of whether the narrative literature that we are reading is explicitly a tale of exile and homecoming—but we would have to ask whether any other literature is possible—we consistently read it that way, we necessarily read narrative within the teleological structure of a homecoming; we read it to the end in order to get home. We approach literature as an enigma to be solved so that we can find our way home, even if that means we are coming home to find our way into bed with Mother. Nothing will stop us, neither lotus nor ambrosia, neither Poseidon nor the Cyclops, neither Calypso nor Circe, neither the Sirens nor Nausicaa; from this point of view, we have only one mission in life and in reading. The only irresistible, and irresistibly natural, call seems to be that of an end to exile.

It would be precisely to resist that logic, based as it is on repression of otherness—the nonnative, the nonnatural, the nonsingular—that I am constructing an argument here for the origin as prosthetic and the home as place of originary exile into the nonorganic or technological. I say "construct" or "make that argument" precisely against the seeming naturality of all our myths, histories, and stories of homecoming, in order to emphasize that from the beginning we were in the process of such constructions. If we agree with Freud about repression, then we cannot ignore the fact that a strange paradox is in play here. That is, we believe or desire home to be a homogeneous space, that of the self in its ownness or *property*. The suggestion that it would be otherwise, that home would be inhabited by foreignness, gets repressed. Yet if repression is understood as the sending back of something prior, then that repression of the foreignness of home assigns to that foreignness a home "more" originary than home or the origin itself, more at home than home itself, safely at home before we came there. If nostalgia for home means unconsciously seeking to return to the womb, then by indulging that nostalgia and in the process repressing whatever impedes that return, we are, by this same logic, assigning what is repressed to a more originary space, the space of a prior home; we are repressing a "more prior" nostalgia, what we would have to impossibly call a nostalgia for exile. It would seem that we cannot conceive of the home as homogeneous origin without also conceiving of the heterogeneity that threatens that home from the outside, the heterogeneity that we must immediately repress, thereby accrediting it as prior to the origin itself.

Once it is a question of the desire for home as a desire to return to the womb, this paradox goes beyond the complications that derive from conceiving the unconscious in topographical terms, beyond the generalities or specifics of processes of condensation understood as cohabitation and displacement understood as removal or *déménagement* (moving house); or else it brings those complications into specific focus. For the uncanniness of a neurotic relation to the female genitals, our discomfort before the entrance "to the former *Heim* [home] of all human beings, to the place where each one of us lived once upon a time and in the beginning," works to disclose an uncanniness in the very theory of repression. As Freud explains, "what was once *heimisch*, familiar," becomes *unheimlich*, where "the prefix *'un'* is the token of repression." We thus repress what is homely about our first home (the womb) once we begin to live in homes that, for being further removed from the origin, should be considered less homely. But thanks to repression, the priorities get reversed, and the first home becomes uncanny. We become neurotic about it while still desiring it. Yet we have to understand the repressed homeliness of the first home to be thereby relegated to a space impossibly "prior" to the womb and impossibly more natural than that womb; or else *we have to imagine a desire to return to a first home that was never natural and always already invaded by foreignness;* we have to imagine an originary *Unheimlichkeit.* Hence the prefix "un-" of the *unheimlich* and the uncanny, once it is attached to the home and once it evokes the womb, does not simply betoken the repression Freud refers to without also calling into question the homogeneous status of the home itself, of any home, beginning with the womb. Once there is repression, it would seem, there is no first or natural home, and returning there means confronting the arrayed forces of uncanniness and foreignness that are our very hearth and heritage. Our neurosis before the uncanniness or unhomeliness of our original home is indeed, in these terms, an Oedipal neurosis, an unresolved contradiction, but a contradiction concerning less our reproductive or autochthonous origins than what constitutes the home or the origin itself. We will have limped all the way from the beginning and as far as parricide and incest without ever resolving that contradiction and without ever leaving home and the contradiction of that home.

However much the exile dreams of the lost home as idealized homogeneity, the space of an amniotic contentment, his narrative—at least in the paradigmatic version that is the *Odyssey*—inevitably inscribes hesitation along the path that leads back there. The fact that obstacles to return keep cropping up, that an Odysseus finds himself time after time in yet another spot of bother, is not without an element of parapraxis, such that as he returns, the repressed desire for exile returns with him. Examples of this are not restricted to the obvious cases where he makes things harder for himself, such as the insults thrown at the Cyclops as he and his men flee. Indeed, we should understand the whole mechanism of seduction that generates the narrative—and finds its most extreme form only, not its definition, in the charms and solicitations of Calypso or Nausicaa—as opening, and as operating within, the space of that desire for exile. Without it, there would be no narrative, nothing more than "I left, I returned." Indeed, not even that, for the seduction begins as a desire to leave in the first place. It is at work within and beyond ideas of duty, military obligation, and so on, as enticement within and beyond any necessity to leave,

as the exotico-libidinal *economy* of the home itself, the law or administration of the house *(oikos/nemein)* defined as management of an interior vis-à-vis an exterior. And it continues through every obstacle, side-
step, dalliance, delay, or relay that plots the course back to that home,
making the exile's progress, like the pilgrim's progress, a narrative trajectory that comes to be defined precisely by its deviations, however much it
involves constant repetition of the ideology and teleology of the straight
and narrow.

According to my hypothesis of prosthesis, the tentative framework I
am constructing here, the *Odyssey* is to be read that way. To do so means
less to impose a modern concept of desire on a classical hero ruled by the
fates and the gods—to ascribe an unconscious will to a fated Odysseus
such that he constantly slips into parapraxis as he wends his way back and
disavows his proper desire for Penelope with the improper distractions of
the exotic—than it would mean interpreting the acts of the gods, their
discord, jealousies, rivalries, and Oedipal dramas, precisely as that complicated desire to which Odysseus finds himself subject, understanding
fully how incompatible is the behavior of the deities with any originary
or promised domesticated or domiciled homogeneity. Odysseus will have
a hard time getting home because the gods cannot get their act together;
or to put it differently, mythology's inability to reconcile itself at its very
source—say, in the case of the *Odyssey,* Athena's dispute with Poseidon—means that there is no undisturbed domestic space from which to
set out and to which to return. The deific oversight of Odysseus's wanderings, the economic basis for the events and mishaps that befall him, is
riven in its conception by deviance and deviousness, as well as counter-
feit and contrivance, such that there cannot be any direct route back to a
space of the proper or the contained, the native or the natural.

If a certain narrative home or point of departure can be presumed to
reside in the opening lines of the epic, then it is telling in more ways than
one—as we shall later see in some detail—that the Muse is exhorted to
"launch out on [Odysseus's] story" by "start[ing] from where you will,"
by "sing[ing] for our time too."[3] It clearly means renouncing any ultimate
beginning, starting out from a point of exile both with respect to the
narrative itself—*in medias res,* not at its beginning but anywhere—and
with respect to the narration—starting at a then that is also a now ("for
our time too"). Beginning a story in that sense means connecting to a

narrative machine that is already on and running, and of course the Muse is that timeless poetic force whose voice and power bring into operation the punctual effects of a particular narrative instance. In the instance in question, starting out from where the Muse wills will take us directly into the heart of exile, namely, to the middle of Odysseus's absence and sojourn, in Ogygia. There, well fucked and fed, Odysseus is vaguely content by night although wrenchingly nostalgic by day. When Calypso puts it to him, he has to agree that she has it all over Penelope for beauty and stature, to say nothing of staying power. Yet the yearning is inexorable: "Nevertheless I long—I pine, all my days—to travel home and see the dawn of my return" (159), and so he spurns her invitation to stay and be immortal and resumes his journey, seeming therefore to define the journey solely as an Odyssey, an inevitable and necessary return home from exile.

On the other hand, as I have suggested, every part of that journey can also be interpreted as a further movement into exile; as long as he despairs of reaching Ithaca, and as long as the gods or his own susceptibilities create obstacles for him, Odysseus is in fact being driven further from his destination. The seeming relentless force of his desire for home, what appears from one perspective to be a natural impulsion or propulsion toward his goal, cannot efface the empirical weight of his remaining away: the *Odyssey* is the story of an exiling. By recounting what both prevents and allows Odysseus to return home, the narrative persistently reinscribes the distances from home that it purports to reduce. If the narrative finally gets him back to Ithaca, it is thanks to the obstacles or milestones he has passed in the form of the monsters and machinations that determine that very narrative. Monsters and machinations of the gods' creation, the motors of each episode function within the opening to otherness that keeps the hero bound, and the reader spellbound, by the logic of the exotic, a logic that is also that of a world beyond his control and that of every phantasmatic production to which his imagination can lay claim. Veritable *dei ex machina*, whether of redemption or perdition, those monsters and machinations are the forces of whatever remains out of reach of the mortal, of whatever, by crossing the path of the human, lays at our feet the mechanisms—superanimate or inanimate, it matters little—of exorbitant invention. The *Odyssey* thus becomes a type of retracing of what we might call a "technological departure." The technological departure is figured most explicitly by Odysseus's donning his armor to leave home and join Agamemnon, but that explicit exile into a world of military technology is simply a particularly striking moment within a structure that we enter—and so take leave of our purely natural selves—at least as early as the moment we step out of the womb. At least as early as that, we begin to arm ourselves against the outside and the foreign; we find ourselves required to negotiate with difference to establish identities and sovereignties; we become engaged in prosthetic relations with the technological (clothing, furniture, implements). After that, any return home will involve our relating back to that structure of the departure, as departure into the technological, and any Odyssey will reinforce that negation of the idealized homogeneity of our place of origin. Each step back will reinforce how far and how irremediably we have strayed, no matter how close we presume we have come to being back home.

In the case of Odysseus, however, and this is the point I want to reinforce above all else, there exists another striking form of technological departure, namely, his talent for telling tales, his predilection for narrative fiction. The *Odyssey* has as its protagonist and central narrative motor a "great teller of tales" (211), who is unbeatable for "all-round craft and guile" (296), a "man of craft" who represents as "hard labor" the need to tell his story (187). The *Odyssey* therefore opens within itself a seemingly limitless space of fiction, and it does so from its first line, as it sets out to sing the song or tell the tale of "the man of twists and turns" (77). We have to understand those twists and turns in terms not only of Odysseus's being "driven time and again off course," as the second line states, not only of his deviating in the sense of being forced into detours as he seeks to set sail straight for home, but also of the tropological deviations that, as the book makes clear, are his stock and trade. The first adjective applied to Odysseus in that very first line is *polytropos,* which we might be forgiven for transliterating as "polytropic" or "polytropological." He is one who, irrespective of risking losing his way home, turns by his very character into the space of rhetoric.[4]

No one makes this more explicit (in Robert Fagles's translation at least, but more about the Greek etymologies shortly) than Athena herself, Odysseus's guardian goddess, when she reveals herself to him upon his landing back in Ithaca and after he, dissimulating more than ever, has explained to her "with a winging word . . . not with a word of truth" how he came to be there (294):

Any man—any god who met you—would have to be
some champion lying cheat to get past *you*
for all-round craft and guile! You terrible man,
foxy, ingenious, never tired of twists and tricks—
so, not even here, on native soil, would you give up
those wily tales that warm the cockles of your heart!
Come, enough of this now. We're both old hands
at the arts of intrigue. Here among mortal men
you're far the best at tactics, spinning yarns. (296)

Athena is here emphasizing what has become obvious in the four preceding books (9–12), namely, that as Odysseus recounts the narratives
that constitute the epic, which have become the archetypal narratives of
Western culture, he is also constructing and reconstructing his autobiography. After doing it for the Phaeacians, and then for Athena, he will do it
also for Eumaeus the swineherd and the Suitors, all the way home, all the
way to Penelope's bed. As Athena also emphasizes, not even his native soil
calls him to a more authentic account. From this point of view, Odysseus
constructs his identity as the fiction of an exile and the exile of a fiction
even as he is supposedly returning to his true and only home.

It is not exaggerating to compare Odysseus's narrative constructions,
his literary craft, with the technological cunning of Hephaestus. First
called *polytropos,* as we have just seen, he is also *polyphron, poikilometis,*
and then consistently *polymechanos,* words that refer to different types
of ingeniousness or inventiveness, which, in the last case following the
English cognate, we can understand as specifically technological. Another
frequent epithet for Odysseus, *polymetis,* is in fact also applied to Hephaestus in the *Iliad* (21.355),[5] and indeed the latter's web or trap *[dolos]*
invented to snare his adulterous wife is the root for the word Odysseus
will use to describe himself when in book 9 he finally reveals his identity
to Alcinous and the Phaeacians (212 [9.19]). I am Odysseus, he says in
effect, crafty, as adept as Hephaestus when it comes to invention, capable
of setting the most elaborate trap, of spinning the most intricate fictive
web, of forging whatever snare will work for me. Odysseus's narrative constructions function thus within the same technological semantic framework as Hephaestus's creations.

Now, once the central character of the *Odyssey* is described in this way as an inventor of fiction, and given that the center of the narrative opens to develop his elaborate tales, it becomes difficult to prevent a type of mirroring narrative effect from being woven throughout, and in a sense from "corrupting" the whole epic. For although, after recounting his story to the Phaeacians, Odysseus maintains that the tale has been told clearly and so should not be repeated word for word, or, as he says, "mythologized [*mythologeuein*]" (285 [12.453]), there is in his own version a circularity that ripples all the way back to the beginning. His abbreviated résumé told on the previous day (book 7) leads more or less straight from Calypso to Nausicaa, and the full-blown version (books 9–12) comes full circle back to "Ogygia, Calypso's island" (285), which is where the reader finds Odysseus at the beginning of book 5, although he has of course been announced as languishing there within the first twenty lines of book 1. That is to say, although the crafty spinner of yarns ostensibly weaves his narrative web once and once only, in the center of the epic, the structure of that narrative will have been opened and repeated at least three other times starting from the beginning of the book. And what I am suggesting, in the final analysis, is that as much as one presumes the Muse to fulfill the function of mistress-narrator, one can as well understand Odysseus to be putting his words into the mouth of the daughter of Zeus from the beginning, to be mythologizing a tale with no single creative origin, contriving to generate the entire myth. The exhortation of the opening line—"Sing to me of the man, Muse, the man of twists and turns" (77)—is just that, an invitation that comes from an absent and unidentified narrator and can be read as receiving no response. The *Odyssey*, like the *Iliad* ("Rage—Goddess, sing the rage. . . . Begin, Muse, when the two first clashed . . . what god drove them?" [77]), calls to the Muse, but its narrative voice never explicitly interrupts the homogeneity of that call, inscribing the whole epic, therefore, within it. Although it all functions, no doubt, within an accepted schema of narrative conventions, and although the Greek has its own system and subtleties of voice, mood, and tense, there is nevertheless an empirical sense in which the utterer of the invitation to sing continues to narrate the whole text. We do not explicitly know that the Muse replies to the invitation made to her by recounting the tale, but we nevertheless read an entire tale recounted by a narrator omnipotent enough to speak for and of the gods as well as for and of Odysseus. This means on the one hand that the space of narrative fiction has been opened by a transcendental Muse who is spoken without speaking, silently singing, generating the whole narrative from behind the scenes, refraining from sullying herself by performing utterances on the same level as the Homeric narrator. However, it also means, according to my argument, that the Muse is no lesser or greater an inventor than Odysseus himself, that the structure she inscribes is indistinguishable from that opened by the hero as craftsman and as teller of tales: what opens the text is a technological structure whose concentric ripple effect flows from the center of the epic out to its narratological edges.

From the first line, therefore, narrator, Muse, and a *polytropic* Odysseus are arrayed in a type of apposition that folds their functions one within the other within the abyss of technotropological space, that of the fictive song or narrative introduced by the first imperative—*ennepe*—tell, recount, invent a fiction, make something (up) (77 [1.1]). Odysseus's first exile, that of the first line, is his departure into that technotropological space, into the twists and turns of his own invention. On the one hand, it makes him omnipotent like the narrator or puts him on the same level as the goddess or Muse, but on the other, it is a departure from the pure humanity *[aner]* of the first word, an exiling of the pure human into the mechanics of language and more precisely into the technics of storytelling.

The closer he gets back to home, it seems, the more consistently Odysseus wanders, or flees, into that exile, reinventing himself, his origins, and his narrative for successive, and progressively more native, interlocutors. For although those encounters—with Eumaeus, with Telemachus, with the suitors, with Eurycleia and Penelope—obey a classic logic of homecoming as restoration of identity and revelation of truth, one can also read in them a persistent and even reinforced thematics of what I have called originary exile, as if the heightened sentiment of separation that is felt the closer one approaches home were understood to mean that there is no home from which the sense of exile can completely be banished. One can identify among Odysseus's interlocutors various relations to the fact of exile and interpret these inhabitants of his native land as constituting anything but a homogeneous autochthony. Telemachus, for example, suffers a minor version of his father's exile: a stranger in his own house, stalked by enemies, forced to travel on a sacred mission. In returning, he repeatedly explains—to Theoclymenus (335), to Eumaeus (339), to Odysseus (342)—how his home is no longer his to enjoy. Even the suitors themselves are forced, by their persistence and by Penelope's resistance, into a type of limbo, as if exiled into some antechamber of unfulfilled desire.

Exile is an explicit existential fact for the swineherd Eumaeus, "a man who's weathered many blows and wandered many miles" (332), whose contentment in the service of Odysseus's father supposedly compensates for his abduction—"much as I grieve for [my parents], much as I long to lay my eyes on them, set foot on the old soil, it's longing for [Odysseus] that wrings my heart." Separated first from "the house where [he] was born," he now must endure the heartbreak of losing the adoptive home represented by his new master, Odysseus, who will "never come home again. Never" (306). Eumaeus has built "with his own hands" a "high-walled, broad and large" farmstead with a stockade and sties for his master's swine (301–2), but he sleeps outside ("not his style to bed indoors" [318]). One could perhaps hypothesize that it is such an experience of dwelling or nondwelling, of constructing homes and identities, coupled with his inconsolable nostalgia for the lost master of his house, that leads him to reject Odysseus's fictive story—"who are *you*, I ask you, to lie for no good reason? . . . don't spellbound me with lies" (313)—however much he remains blind to his master's true story.

Penelope suffers the form of house arrest imposed on her by first her husband's, then her son's, departure, and by her suitors, so she remains closeted away with her loom. But the mythological history tells us that she is already an exile, her marriage to Odysseus having required her to abandon her native Sparta. Though the *Odyssey* alludes only in the most subtle terms to any potential infidelity (her seductive powers, her preference for Amphinomus), according to archaic accounts, Penelope's reluctance to leave Sparta and follow her husband gave rise, alternately, to her legendary demurring modesty or to her vengeful cuckolding of Odysseus for his nonrespect of matrilocal custom.[6] But above all, as the epic makes abundantly plain, Penelope experiences her husband's absence as an experience of waiting that mirrors his exile to the extent of her inventing the technological complement to his storytelling, yoking herself to her loom in a cyclical labor of creating and undoing, weaving and unweaving a series of different webs from the same yarn, just as Odysseus spins and respins his narrative identity for the appropriate local consumption. Penelope and Odysseus spin their yarns in tandem, and the literal home and origin of such a common vocabulary for their occupations are perhaps forever lost. Is Penelope's fundamental yarn the robe she creates from her loom or the narrative she recounts to her suitors to account for it? Is Odysseus's yarn the series of episodic adventures that tell of his exploits and wanderings or the exile itself that they structure and constitute? We cannot tell whether Penelope's or Odysseus's spinning is the more metaphorical staging of their respective predicaments, whether her weaving is an allegory of her being pursued or the actual text and tissue of her waiting; whether his tales are allegories of the threats of danger and exile or the substance and live matter of his longing and nostalgia. What we can conclude, I am arguing, is that one and the other share the common structural space of the technotropological, inventing and reinventing, spinning limitlessly thanks to the loom or to the machine of narrative possibility that is also the mechanics of a type of exile; that they are both suspended within that rhetorical drift, shuttling across the warp and woof of a space within the origin that keeps them occupied home or away, away even at home.

Odysseus's ultimate return is in any case not the resolution it should be, neither for him nor for her. Beyond Penelope's entrapment in the fictive web, such that she needs a lot of convincing before she will believe in the truth of his return, we know—because we have been told in one of Odysseus's identity-constructing stories—that no sooner is he home than he must set out again in fulfillment of Tiresias's prophecy, in an endless effort to placate Poseidon, god of the sea. For what defines exile in the final analysis, at least according to the paradigm that the *Odyssey* establishes, is less wandering, or settling far from home, than seafaring, a commitment to the ocean as what denies the possibility of home, the absence of a terra firma, Mother Earth, or fatherland. Odysseus's particular form of shuttling and drifting means he is condemned to sailing: if the epic begins in the *medias res* of Calypso's Ogygia, it is because it is an island that is hardly even an island, an island whose name means "Ocean," according to Graves (*The Greek Myths*, 2:368); and it will finish only when Odysseus has exhausted every drop of the sea and come across a people who mistake an oar for a winnow; or beyond that still, down on the beach and facing the sea from whence his death will emerge as he is felled by a stingray spear. The *Odyssey* ends beyond its own borders, in the no-man's-land of a limitless narrative meander that is the prophesied future of everything that will happen after the return to Ithaca and to Penelope, a veritable narrative ocean to come. Such a meander transforms what is presumed to be the Odyssean logic of voyage, and of the narrative that depends on it, determined by exodus and return: "We are children of the exodus, the Hebrew exodus, the Odyssean exodus. . . . We are children of exiles, children of meanderings. The exodus gives up its place, steps aside, and goes off course, it becomes a meandering."[7]

I will argue in my next chapter that the ocean both defines and confounds the sense of home as national identity, inscribing the latter as a founding fiction whose attempt at literality—drawing the line, defining the border—is problematized by its own rhetorical excess. Here we are confronted by such an ocean of excess, by a sort of boundless narrative impulse—new storms, new shipwrecks, new islands, new adventures—that is presented as the antithesis of the security and fidelity of the home fires but always risks becoming an end in itself. This means that the Greek archipelagoes, for being the cradle of Western civilization, nevertheless constitute the fraying edges of the woven tissue of a continental Europe, but also, more to the point in the context of Homer, that the home of narrative is the ocean because it is the possibility of an endless exile and that, seen from the high seas, home becomes imaginary and fictive, a mirage of desire and memory that gives way to the siren call or "nautical murmur" of an endless displacement,[8] settling into story after story, dwelling finally in the wide diegetic watery expanse.

Such then, is my hypothesis of prosthesis, the hypothesis of a technotropology defining an originary exile in the first line of our archetypal narrative experience of it. In a sense, of course, a polytropic or polytechnic Odysseus exists only in that narrative; he is possible only as fiction. To believe in him as one who wants to stay away, as talking himself out of coming home, would amount, as Athena has suggested to Odysseus, to the exiling of truth, its departure from home, its endless detours through the "twists and tricks" of storytelling, such twists and tricks as home itself would, precisely, have no more need of. "Not even here, on native soil, would you give up those wily tales," she remonstrates (296). Native soil has no need of wily tales, home no need of fiction. Indeed, the naturalist or organicist model whereby everything grows from an original soil might simply be reinforced by the countervalence of a fictive or technological corruption of it that I am describing here. Yet what if literary production itself were to be considered the model for any creation whatsoever? What if, "before" any act of creation or procreation, before any domestication via the womb or the earth, before any Earth Mother or Uranus, any Rangi or Papa, any Zeus or Hera, there were only the fiction of the same? What if the origin could only ever be conceived (of) in the form of such a construction, if the originary home were the possibility of a concept, a technotropological hypo-prosthesis that is the opening to inventing, to thinking and to fiction? What if in order to venture anything whatsoever, anywheresoever, one had to begin in that technological, rhetorical, and fictive spacing, in the spacing of a displacement that necessarily meant a movement into exile, and a wandering without hope of any final return?

SOME SORT of confirmation or affirmation of the idea of an originary fictive exile or deracination can be derived from the fate of the *Odyssey* throughout Western literary history, the fact of its being exported into so many different versions. No sooner was the epic established as the home for our narratives than it was destined to wander, beginning with Virgil and leading all the way to Joyce and beyond. Two examples will serve here to outline the figures and extent of that drift: Broch's *Der Tod des Vergil* (The Death of Virgil) and Joyce's *Ulysses*. Many reasons could be adduced for privileging Broch and Joyce, or these two novels by them, as paradigms for the nonoriginary exile of fiction: their being culminating points of a high modernism that revolutionized narrative prose (for George Steiner, *The Death of Virgil* represents "the only fiction to move any distance inward from Joyce");[9] their nontranslated publication-in-exile (*Ulysses* in Paris, *Der Tod des Vergil* in the United States); the intersecting points of the paths to exile of the authors themselves (Joyce fleeing Paris for Zurich, Broch out of Austria, with Joyce's help, to America). At the risk of imposing a reductive logic on these immense works, I shall nevertheless exploit a limited number of elements within them to bring into more contemporary focus the technotropological departure that is set in train in the *Odyssey*, staging in stark terms the respective exilings of author, narration, and narrative itself, and threatening to loosen the secure moorings of the political scene itself.

One states the obvious by holding that the narrative center or origin of *Ulysses* leaves home before Leopold Bloom does, and that she or it is somewhere other than in its own bed, and perhaps even all at sea, by the end of the novel. But well before that, the sun is already setting, "the last glow of all too fleeting day linger[ing] lovingly on sea and strand,"[10] when Bloom comes upon Gerty MacDowell and friends in the Nausicaa chapter. The reader has encountered significant examples of narrative dissipation, but nothing concentrated in quite the same way as the phantasmatic crossover that begins to occur once Bloom throws the ball toward Cissy Caffrey only to see it roll back down the slope and come to rest between Gerty's thighs. One witnesses a type of telepathy of the interior monologue during the scene of mutual arousal and fireworks; we can identify a voice belonging to Gerty different from one belonging to Bloom, but we cannot be sure that Bloom isn't projecting or inventing Gerty's voice, for example, speaking her desire in order to "rationalize" or confirm his own. In retrospect this can be understood as having prepared the reader for Molly's definitive appropriation of the narrative voice in the final chapter, and Gerty's voice of feminine desires certainly foreshadows Molly's.

At the end of Nausicaa, still bathing in his onanistic afterglow ("O! Exhausted that female has me"), Bloom is distracted by items of jetsam as he moves off along the strand: "Never know what you find. Bottle with story of a treasure in it thrown from a wreck. Parcels post. Children always want to throw things in the sea. Trust? Bread cast on the waters. What's this? Bit of stick" (381). The stick in question becomes the "wooden pen" with which Bloom writes his famous incomplete "I AM A" before erasing the letters with his shoe and flinging the writing instrument away. Now, in a text characterized by what is traditionally called stream-of-consciousness narration, the moment when a or the principal character utters the words "I am a" has to be considered highly relevant. Indeed, that fragment ranks in the secondary literature with Breen's "U. P." postcard as the primary unsolved enigma of *Ulysses*. But whether Bloom intends to write something like "I AM A naughty boy," or "I AM About to . . . ," he cannot avoid explicitly performing here as a first-person narrator. His fragment is not spoken but written, is not conversation but inscription, not just written in a private letter but exposed publicly, and although he calls it "a message for her," it is also admitted to be something that "might remain." Furthermore, only the reader sees or reads these words; no other character from the novel does. One might therefore take this fragment, inscribed in the center of the novel, to be its beginning, to be the opening words from a narrator-writer saying, "I AM A man telling the story of my day in Dublin on Thursday, June 16, 1904." Thus when (back inside his head once again, "writing" in *Ulysses* rather than in the sand in *Ulysses*) Bloom gives "No room" as the first explicit reason for abandoning his writing, he does complete his sentence by "writing," or otherwise uttering, that not even the infinite sandy expanse could hold the narrative of that day, not to mention of his desire: "I. . . . AM. A. [¶] No room" is exactly what the text says, and we can read it, in spite of its punctual and paragraphic discontinuity, as "I AM A narrator without enough room." His second reason is "Hopeless thing sand. Nothing grows in it. All fades," which suggests a "no time" to complement the "no room."

In other words, Bloom's aborted scriptural endeavor, however fragmentary it may be, does convey the complete sense of something like "I AM A failed writer" or "I AM An incomplete narrator." He is clearly less than the omnipotent creator who utters simply "I am (that I am)"; his "I am a" is much more indefinite than that. However much his narrative eye transmigrates, it never becomes that of a god. Nor is he as prophetic or sibylline as another, related to the first, who wrote in the sand when faced with questions about an adulterous woman. Both versions or generations of God are evoked by Bloom's utterance and action here.[11] But as we know, nothing in the following five chapters of *Ulysses* will give to his ephemeral sentence any more definitive meaning, yet much in them will confirm it as an avowal of a type of narratorial impotence.[12] We cannot be sure that when Bloom flings his wooden pen away he throws it in the direction of the sea, like a child or a castaway, his instrument like bread cast on the waters, food for limitless fictive thought or possibility. But wherever he throws this rudimentary writing machine, the chances are good that the sea will reclaim it, that it will be wrecked between some Scylla and Charybdis of narrative choices as surely as the fragment itself is lost in the sea of signification.

We also know that Bloom has cast bread or at least cake on the waters on another occasion ("the day I threw that stale cake out of the Erin's King picked it up in the wake fifty yards astern" [152]). He mentions it in the Lestrygonians chapter as he throws away the throwaway he has just been given, instead of throwing himself, off O'Connell Bridge: "He threw down among them [the gulls] a crumpled paper ball. Elijah thirtytwo feet per sec is com." The narrator's wooden pen "flungaway" of the Nausicaa chapter can easily be put into the context of this earlier throwaway that is acknowledged as providing an important strand of narrative coherence for the novel. Referred to first in chapter 8, its progress down the river charted throughout the Wandering Rocks chapter ("a skiff, a crumpled throwaway, Elijah is coming" [227], "a skiff, a crumpled throwaway, rocked on the ferry-wash, Elijah is coming" [240], "Elijah, skiff, light crumpled throwaway" [249]), the leaflet Bloom has been given by the somber young YMCA man (151) receives its full narrative contextualization in the penultimate chapter. There it is confirmed, as we have progressively learned throughout the novel, that when Bloom told Bantam Lyons that he could have his newspaper since he was about to throw it away, Lyons understood Bloom to be giving him a tip for a bet on the horse of the same name (Throwaway), which indeed won the Gold Cup at odds of twenty to one earlier in the day. In the Cyclops chapter, the citizen, in his nationalist and anti-Semitic rant, will have reproached Bloom for slyly cashing in on the winning horse at his expense, or at least for not buying a round to celebrate his success.

Bloom both gives and receives a throwaway, therefore: on one trajectory, the sense of his everyday throwaway syntax about disposing of a newspaper becomes fixed in a horse's proper name; on another, intersecting trajectory, a throwaway tract promoting a prophet's proper name is taken and treated for what it is (what, in the mind of its distributor, it should not be), committed to the waters and by extension to the waves. It is doubtful that one could add anything of critical note to this throwaway, an exegetical chestnut whose significance has been tabulated all the way down to CliffsNotes. But its trajectories are those of the hermeneutic stakes themselves, like anything an author throws at the reader and at the same time throws away, like bread for gulls or crumbs from the writing man's table: either it finds its way, against outside odds, to the winning post of interpretive certitude, or it follows a line of flux or flight, bobbing through eddy, rapids, and wake, out to sea; or both. It takes the narrative rupture marked by the flingaway stick into a more radical network of fictive structuration: whereas there we saw a Bloom take control as first-person narrator, however briefly or fragmentarily, before renouncing the task, here he produces an utterance that is immediately deformed and snatched away from him by another character who will pass it on to another, and so on, so that it comes back to haunt him in a scene where he narrowly escapes physical violence; or on the other hand, he receives a text whose message concerning Elijah is too hot to handle or only has the value of a piece of refuse, which remains "unheeded" even by gulls and floats away. This is the adestinational trifurcation of a single signifier—throw away/Throwaway/throwaway—at least in its spoken form, and each form of it has a different status within the narratological framework: protagonist's conversational fragment within third-person narration, textual fragment in protagonist's newspaper (remaining invisible to reader and, presumably, to protagonist), third-person narrator's word for textual object placed in protagonist's hand.[13] The throwaway is less about narrative origin and control than about the far more complex and vexed question of the destination and limits of textual signification in general, but it demonstrates how in *Ulysses*, thanks to so-called stream-of-consciousness narration, those two effects become intertwined. We no longer have a coherent or homogeneous narrative voice directing the outflow of signifying elements; indeed, narratorial effects get caught up within the vagaries of signification in general. Thus when Bloom flings away his wooden pen after writing "I am a," the reader is cast back to the Bloom who, about to throw away his newspaper, has it intercepted by Bantam Lyons. In the earlier case, Bloom effectively says, "I am a . . . bout to throw it away," to a Lyons who picks up on something and runs with it; in the Nausicaa episode, he writes "I am a . . ." for a reader who must also pick up on it and run with it. But in each case, for being identifiable and limitable—to the name of a horse, to any supposition one can imagine—the complement to the phrase is at the same time thrown out of reach, committed to the waves. Narratorial voice, and finally signification in general, are thrown away in *Ulysses* to the extent of being cast away, castaways as in Mallarmé's *Throw of the Dice*, shipwrecked, like Ulysses or Odysseus, far from home.

Waves are in evidence at the beginning of *Ulysses*, where Buck Mulligan refers to the sea as "our great sweet mother" (5), and the sea calls duplicitously to Stephen at the end of chapter 1 (23). Waves are there toward the middle, when the sirens pass a seashell from ear to ear, "her ear too . . . a shell. . . . The sea they think they hear" (281). And they are very much there at the end, with Molly's soliloquy like the sound of the sea in a shell, memories of life on a rock gateway to the world's oceans, and the final encounter on Howth Head or Gibraltar or both, as though she were throwing herself back into it ("O that awful deepdown torrent O and the sea the sea" [783]), the flux of her affirmative desire streaming into powerful tides of fictional possibility.

But the sea in *Ulysses* is also related to certain national and nationalist beachheads. Gibraltar is the European outpost of an "English" empire that is called "the sea's ruler" (30), the "overseas or halfseasover empire" referred to again (73) before coming under more serious scrutiny once the citizen finds his stride in Cyclops ("We have our greater Ireland beyond the sea" [329]). At important moments in the novel, an Irish nation, language, or identity is put into relief against a sprawling transoceanic English hegemony. Early on, Haines, an Englishman, "thinks we ought to speak Irish in Ireland" (14). When Edward VII appears in the Circe chapter, Stephen says he has "no king [him]self for the moment." However, he is no simple nationalist, and rather than die for his country, he says, "Let my country die for me" (591). Later he intones a similar reversal of Bloom's cliché that both brain and brawn belong to Ireland, saying, "Ireland must be important because it belongs to me" (645). Bloom's sensitivity to questions of patriotism no doubt stems from his being a Jew, and indeed, from Mr. Deasy's claim that "England is in the hands of the jews" (33) to the ravings of the citizen, certain characters persistently pose the question of national allegiance in terms of racial or religious identity and purity. Ireland appears, in the context of the debate in Cyclops, as an island sandwiched between an imperial Britain and a continental Europe, which have conspired together to commingle and dilute each other, even and especially with Jews.

The citizen's solution is simple and time-honored: "It'd be an act of God to take hold of a fellow the like of that and throw him in the bloody sea" (338). For it is important to remember that Bloom's presumed offense, apart from or because of being Jewish, is to have made a killing on Throwaway and kept silent about it. His innocent two throwaway words spoken to Bantam Lyons thus become sufficient cause for his being threatened with a fate similar to the YMCA man's throwaway (thrown into the river and last seen heading out to sea). Bloom himself will, if the citizen or God has his way, end up being thrown into the sea, completely cast away. Now while that might presage the narratorial fate that we read in his flinging away the wooden pen, being thrown into the sea would definitely, in this context and by his own first attempt at a definition, signify his loss of nationhood, for, says Bloom, "a nation is the same people living in the same place" (331). That naive definition exposes him to ridicule, and he subsequently qualifies his definition with "or also living in different places," then claims Ireland is his nation because he was born there, although he "belong[s] to a race too . . . that is hated and persecuted" (332). When he is told to stand up to the injustice he has just denounced, he says that "force, hatred, history, all that" are no use, and claims that everyone knows that love is really life. Then he makes his first exit, escaping unscathed. But his logic is all at sea.

THE THROWAWAY—element and operation of signification within a work of fiction—is, like the castaway, in exile, at a loss for home and country. Bloom's unsettled national status intersects with the question of authorship that is Stephen's subject in Scylla and Charybdis (chapter 9). Perhaps unable to prove "by algebra that Shakespeare's ghost is Hamlet's grandfather" (28), he nevertheless makes questions of fidelity and paternity (related to shipwreck and storms [195]) a focus of literary understanding and concludes, among other things, that "a father . . . is a necessary evil. . . . Paternity may be a legal fiction" (207). Whether Stephen thereby makes orphans of us all may remain open to question, but as long as there is debate over the authorship or proprietorship of a work of art, then the paternity of fiction is indeed a fiction. Such a debate is put onstage by Hermann Broch from the moment he makes Virgil the central character of *The Death of Virgil,* and even more explicitly once Virgil's desire to burn the *Aeneid* at the end of his life, as well as Augustus's frustrating of that desire, becomes that novel's central event. Virgil, historical figure and author of the *Aeneid,* is exiled into Broch's work of fiction. Virgil's role as author is brought into focus, but by the same token he steps out of a certain structure of authorship to become Broch's fictional character. In that fiction—however much it remains an imitation of the facts of history—Virgil returns from a type of exile to die, and rather than suffer his work's own exile, watching it being "borne away" by Augustus's slaves like "the remains of a child, of a life," and so live on in a type of purgatory, he wants it to die with him.[14] Virgil does not want his work to become such a "borneaway"; instead he wants to take the *Aeneid* home with him to his death.

The showdown that takes place between the dying Virgil and the triumphant Augustus is set against the background of imperial Rome, whose founding the *Aeneid* celebrates, establishing a mythological becoming that shuttles between Aeneas and the emperor, whose political importance I discuss shortly.[15] But of course, Virgil's *Aeneid* as founding myth of Rome already represents something of an exiling of Homer's *Odyssey* on which the later epic is modeled, and which it overturns. The parallels between the two texts are too fecund to be enumerated here: for mnemonic purposes, Odysseus/Aeneas, Athena/Venus, Calypso/Dido, Tiresias/Anchises, the suitors/Turnus. But the most dramatic reversal that occurs between Homer and Virgil, brought into sharp focus in Broch's novel, is the existence of a written text, and it is on that basis that the debate over its status—genesis, edition, ownership, heritage—takes place. Such a debate could not have taken place had not the *Odyssey* and Odysseus within it been already, always already, drifting uncontrollably away from home, that is to say, were the narrative not to be readable against itself, as it were in reverse, were home not to be read as exile and the return home as but steps toward the origin of that exile, the origin as exile. That is to say on one simple level, as I have been repeating here, that the possibility of fiction is the necessity of exile understood as abandonment of the economy of immutable self-enclosed truth. That universal fictionalizing, before the "existence" of any historical event or persons themselves, makes what we call a historical novel possible; it is what allows Publius Vergilius Maro, author of the *Aeneid*, to emigrate as a character into a novel by Hermann Broch. What is specific to Broch's novel, functioning within that universal structure, is among other things the staging, via Virgil's deathbed argument with Caesar, of the very question of the fate of a text in the context of its author's death, the right or ability of that text to migrate as unfinished draft into the hands of editors and into an imperial position within the canon, or, on the other hand, to be burned. And more specifically still, how the fate of such an epic text, such an act of literature and of literary history, is to be compared with the acts and legacy of the head of the Roman Empire.

History records that the Virgil who, having fallen ill while traveling in Greece and Asia Minor in order to revise his epic, and returns with Augustus to die in Brindisi in 19 BCE, has suffered at least the threat of dispossession of his land following the defeat of Brutus and Cassius at Philippi.

Broch restricts himself to the last eighteen hours of Virgil's life, beginning with the landing at Brindisi, and from the first pages the reader is introduced to one whom destiny had not allowed "to be free from staying nor free to stay at home" (13). Though the poet has returned to die on native soil, his regret, paradoxically, concerns his having left, and his remaining absent from, a still more native spiritual homeland: "Fled now the hope that the hallowed and serene sky of Homer would favor the completion of the Aeneid. . . . Fled the hope ever to be allowed to enter the Ionian land" (12). Exile and homecoming are the massively overwhelming motifs of *The Death of Virgil* from the opening passage describing the arrival of the fleet at Brundisium, through the paragraphic invocations at the end of chapter 2 (208–20), to the title of the final chapter. The protagonist is "a rover . . . an errant through the passions of the inner life and the passions of the world, a lodger in his own life" (13). The return to the homeland is endlessly invoked yet seems endlessly frustrated: Virgil hears voices that remind him of "the familiar-strange breath of a long since vanished homeland" (67); homecoming is described as "irretrievable" (210). As a result, the novel is redolent with an inassuageable nostalgia, "the yearning of one who was and always must be only a lodger" (19).

Home is also consistently feminine: it can take the classic maternal form of "an undiscoverably remote motherly once" (58) or function as a constructed masculine womb that the hero longs for, hoping to return "into the dark cavern which has been built in myself like a homestead I no longer know [hoffend . . . heimkehren zu können . . . heimzukehren in das dunkle Gewölbe, das in mir errichtet ist wie eine Heimstatt, die ich nicht mehr kenne]" (68/73). Or it can be represented as the phantasm of Virgil's lost wife Plotia, called an "undiscoverable homeland" (297), but nevertheless "home to me, the home to which I come back and enter [Heimat bist du mir, in die ich heimkehrend eindringe]" (300/320). But home is also the native soil: "man's existence avails him nothing until he breathes his native air, returning to the earth [heimkehrend zur Erde]" (17), and Virgil's nostalgia is that of a peasant's son for "his earth-bound, earth-bent, always earthly longing" (36), a yearning for "the primal humus [Ur-humus] of being" (37/40), a need to "go back into the humus of the beginning [in den Humus des Anfangs zurückkehren]" (420/451).

As the fevered Virgil's visions and hallucinations of regressive journeys into the animal and vegetal make clear, however, and as the entire novel recounts, the only really original native soil is death. It is precisely "the poetic power of death" that has acquired the "privileges of domicile" for him (82). One returns home to die; Virgil's last voyage is to another world. The only complete return from exile is into death, yet death is the very voyage from which one never returns; it remains the ultimate oceanic exile. As he lands at Brindisi, Virgil is setting sail on that other voyage and yearning also, therefore, "for the sea . . . the sea in its tritonic-immeasurable reality [tritonisch-unermessliche Wirklichkeit]" (227/243). Indeed, the final homecoming of chapter 4 begins with a detailed description of that journey and that exile as a sea voyage.

In spite of its complexities and paradoxes, there is nothing particularly unusual about the nexus of competing versions of home that *The Death of Virgil* develops. As I have been suggesting from the beginning of this chapter, they are the timeless commonplaces of our mythologies and of our literatures. Hence we will not be surprised to find textual production and the work of the poet implicated within that nexus and similarly fractured by its paradoxes. In coming home, Virgil remonstrates with himself for leaving, for leaving the country for the city, and by extension the life of a peasant for his career as a poet: "this erring path which had led him from his native fields to the metropolis, from the work of his hands to self-deceptive rhetoric" (142). Or rather, for a career as an artist or *littérateur*, for there is presumed to be a natural poetry of the soil that finds itself corrupted by an urban promiscuity: "Most perjuring . . . was he whose foot had estranged [entwöhnt] itself from the earth and touched nothing but pavements, the man who no longer tilled and no longer sowed" (144/156). Artistic perjuring involves an estrangement of art "into vulgarity and there where vulgarity is at its worst, into literarity!" (142). Poetry is reduced thereby to a "vulgar, urban literarity" (150). No doubt the plebian vulgarity (Pöbelhaftigkeit) of literature, for being associated with the people, does not, in a prefeudal sensibility, connote any solidarity with the peasant, but it remains difficult to understand how an art that "descend[s] step by step, penetrating deeper and deeper through the inner thickets of [the soul's] being" (139), can still retain a link to the tilled soil.

The Death of Virgil provides two prolonged versions of the debate over the purpose of art: first, in Virgil's feverish final night in chapter 2, and second in the discussions with those who will become his literary heirs and editors of the *Aeneid,* Lucius and Plotius, discussions that frame Virgil's debate with Augustus in chapter 3. Art has to choose between a truth that is its own beauty—"the self-perceptive finding and proclaiming of truth . . . the disclosure of the divine through the self-perceptive knowledge of the individual soul" (139, 140)—and a beauty that exists "for its own sake," which attacks art "at its very roots," substituting "the empty form for the true content . . . the merely beautiful for the perceptive truth," an "intoxication with empty forms and empty words," the art "reduced to un-art *[Un-kunst],* and poetry to mere literarity" already mentioned (140–41/152). Virgil finds himself guilty of this un-art and so seeks to redeem himself by destroying the *Aeneid.* It will be left to Lucius and Plotius, and then Caesar, to convince him otherwise.

What keeps art art, Virgil argues, what keeps it down to earth and at home in the country instead of walking city streets or abstracting itself into "a mere sham-artistic, decorative adornment of life *[als die bloss schmückende Lebenszier der Unkunst]*" (343/366), is reality: "High above the law of beauty, high above the law of the artist . . . there was the law of reality. . . . I have made my poems, abortive words. . . . I thought them to be real, and they are only beautiful" (249, 258). Thus a type of *literality* seems to be opposed to *literarity.* However, "all that art has is metaphor" (327), it is by definition a departure from literality into tropological space; platitude haunts it as much as sham does. Hence poetry cannot come home to reality, in any finality, any more than could the exile. Art's journey home will falter in the same way that Virgil's does, wandering further and further, "compelling the soul to reveal level after level of her reality . . . descending step by step, penetrating deeper and deeper," gradually approaching a darkness that nevertheless remains "unattainable" (139). The "verse's meaning" is not found either in the earth or indeed in the poem, but is something "that [rises] beyond it," representing a "full reality" that is "unachievable" (243).

From this point of view, death again looms as the only way into that full reality, the only homely reality, the only end to the exiling of language. In the center of his debate with Augustus, Virgil describes the return of language to its roots in terms that uncannily mirror his own voyage home to death. There is no life without a tropological departure, no origin for it and no end to it other than death: "Life was to be grasped only in metaphor. . . . The chain of metaphor was endless and death alone was without metaphor. . . . Language could regain its native simplicity from death alone, as if there lay the birthplace of earth's simple language, the most earthly and yet the most divine of symbols: in all human language death smiled" (357). Un-art or sham literary art may be disparaged as the reduction of truth to beauty, but conversely, an art come back to basics or to its "native simplicity," the return of language to its birthplace and humble origins, means its death. According to Virgil's logic, death is the only reality: all the rest is metaphor, exile into rhetorical space, wandering on a tropological ocean.

We know, of course, that an Orphic task for the poet is as old as the myth itself: "Poetry [is] the strangest of human occupations, the only one dedicated to the knowledge of death" (81). Virgil more than once compares his task to that of Orpheus (157, 327) and figures a competition of desire between Plotia and his slave and lover Alexis in Orphic terms just before Caesar enters in chapter 3 (291–303). Indeed, the question of turning around becomes climactic in the last voyage of the final pages. The relation of poetry to death is emphasized in the debate with Augustus, and when Caesar asks Virgil whether the goal of his poetry is the understanding of life, he responds that it is the "understanding of death" and hears his own statement "as if springing from a state of illumination," "a re-found, re-recognized homecoming enlightenment [*wie ein Wiederfinden, wie ein Wiedererkennen, wie eine heimkehrende Erleuchtung]*" (321/342–43). "Only he who is able to perceive death is also able to perceive life" (325), he later maintains; such is "the goal of all genuine poetry" (326). The reference to death as the end of metaphor just quoted is a reformulation of the same insistence.

But understanding death as the poetic task is not the same as destroying the poem before one dies, consigning the work to death at the same time as its author. When Virgil resolves to burn the *Aeneid*, he explains it as a means to avoid the "ghastliness of [an] eternal earthly death" such as writers like Homer are condemned to, the purgatory of their orphaned and exiled work that continues to function like "a death that must endure until the last line of their writings be tilled out of human memory, until there was no human mouth to recite their verses" (247). By burning the *Aeneid,* Virgil will short-circuit that type of limbo. We can understand this as an insistence on a type of mortality for the work that derives from its being a product of human vanity, of "self-idolatry and . . . greed for recognition" (141), and so not deserving to survive; or as recognition of the structural insufficiencies of any text, of which the unfinished status of the *Aeneid* is but a case in point; or as obedience to a logic of sacrifice such as Virgil explains to Caesar: "Since I could not consecrate my whole life to sacrifice as you have done yours, I must designate my work for this purpose" (386). But whether it represents euthanasia or sacrifice, we should not confuse Virgil's linking of his work to his life, in death, as a simple reinforcement of authorial ownership; or at least we should see him as taking that idea to its logical conclusion. In its classical appurtenance, Virgil's sense of necessary but impossible homecoming for both author and text rejects the post-Renaissance presumption that a text returns to its author, so that, by surviving, the poem will be able to permanently resurrect the poet; the presumption that the author is kept alive by means of a text that outlives him, for which he remains the persistent anchor, its ultimate home or mooring. Instead both are presumed to return to the earth and to a death that is itself understood to reside at both the origin and the end of life. In this, Virgil—or perhaps Broch—is close to Blanchot, for whom Orpheus "carr[ies] the work beyond what assures it . . . by forgetting the work, seduced by a desire that comes to him from the night, and that is linked to night as to its origin."[16] Death as the final tropological leveler, as that which is without metaphor, an end to rhetorical detours, also comes backs to meet the death that gives rise to such departures in the first place, the death that is the birthplace of language, the rupture at the beginning that produces or is an originary exile.

However pertinent those somewhat local questions or problems of literature might be to a thematics of exile, it is finally the relation that is established between works of art and political actions that raises Virgil's debate with Augustus to another plane of interest. When Caesar comes to take away the *Aeneid* before Virgil can have it burned, the argument devolves upon comparisons between control over what he has produced as a man of state and what Virgil has produced as a man of letters. Broch, whose novel was conceived when he was imprisoned by the Nazis following the Anschluss, and published in 1945,[17] obviously had a specific political configuration before him as he wrote. Virgil's disparaging of an "urban" art for its "affiliation with the mob [*Pöbelhaftigkeit*]" (141), constant references to the "herd," his insistence that art not be reduced to serving the state (334), and his reproach to Caesar for indulging the people's "intoxication with blood" (384) are no doubt to be understood in the context of fascism. But nothing encourages a simple reading of *The Death of Virgil* as allegory, and even if it were that, the transposition to the Augustan Empire remains an irreducible recontextualization that poses the political questions within a certain transhistoricality. We cannot not read them as Roman questions, but we also cannot not read them as reaching, migrating, or being exiled beyond Rome.

Who has right of ownership over what is produced in the domains of politics and art, Virgil and Caesar ask, and they thereby raise the questions of distinctions between word and deed, on the one hand, and of agency in general, on the other. Caesar argues that the *Aeneid* is public property, whereas Virgil replies that he wrote it for himself, in seclusion, and so may dispose of it as he pleases (311–12). Caesar retorts that the poem amounts to a collaborative effort, that the people of Rome are glorified in it, and that as portions of it have been circulated and admired, Virgil has received at least the feedback represented by such admiration: "It is no longer your work, it is the work of all of us, indeed in one sense we have all labored at it" (313). Burning the work would be akin to Caesar's trying to undo the facts of history: "Can I, on my side, set Egypt free . . . strip Germania of troops . . . renounce the Peace of Rome?" (311). Virgil concedes that the state can be considered a work of art but suggests that it can undergo revisions by a politician's successors, whereas "for me there is no successor" (315). Both agree that the Rome created by Augustus functions as a symbol or emblem of the Roman spirit in parallel to the way in which poetry functions by means of metaphor (354–55), but whereas Virgil will follow metaphor to death, as we have already seen, Caesar wants to come back to a reality that endures beyond symbol (359). Although the argument is resolved on the level of personal friendship and animosity, with Virgil renouncing his plan, the stakes raised by the debate are in fact difficult to back away from: a Virgil who burns his work is comparable on one level—but poles apart when it comes to measuring the consequences—to a Nero who burns his Rome, and a poem can be revised by others just as a state can. But conversely, the producer of a political or ethical deed does not control that deed throughout its life—presuming we could determine the limits of such a thing—nor does he control it at its beginning, any more than the poet controls the meaning of a work she produces. How we might reformulate consequences and responsibilities in the light of that fact is something I return to in my final chapter, but what is already clear in terms of the structures of an originary exile that I have traced all the way from mythological beginnings to the operations of fiction and this comparison between literature and politics is less that no one produces anything or commits any act that can be traced back to him and for which he might therefore be responsible than that the meaning of that act comes to be constituted in the shifts and detours that it borrows in being enacted, and without which it would not amount to an act, in the tropological divergences and substitutions that constitute it.

An eerie staging of that takes place during Caesar's debate with Virgil, where the facts of succession have been raised and the question of ownership thereby brought to a head. Caesar is exasperated, turns his back, and stares out the window. Virgil has spent half of the previous chapter at the same window (95–162), in a trancelike meditation that precedes the passage that will conclude with the idea of burning the *Aeneid* (178), and immediately before Augustus enters the room, Virgil has been imagining Alexis dreaming at the same window (301). As he looks at Augustus, his imagination puts Alexis in Caesar's place:

> Then all became calm and silent. Augustus stood there at the window, narrow and quite slender, a mortal with a mortal body divided into members, wrapped in a toga, thus he stood there against the light from the window, a narrow human back, covered in the draped folds of a toga, and suddenly one no longer noticed whether a front view *[Vonderseite]* existed, even less if there was a countenance *[Gesicht]* . . . least of all whither its glances strayed. Was it not Alexis who had stood there not long since on the selfsame spot? But yes, it had been Alexis, childishly slim and with an almost touching beauty, almost like a son. . . . He had stood there with averted face . . . dreaming out into the dreaming landscape . . . and for him . . . the fauns . . . had danced their measures. . . . For him, the landscape, moved to its very core by the dance, had opened out . . . the whole creation unto its final borders, moving in the dance of desire. . . . However, nothing of all this was now to be seen. (316–17/337–38)

Caesar is here starkly contrasted with Alexis. Whereas the imagined Alexis brings the whole world outside the window to life, the real Caesar's "stubborn onesidedness . . . severity . . . obduracy" means that "nothing of all this was now to be seen." Whereas the desiring imagination of Alexis is inspired by an "incessant in-and-outflowing of desire which was full of recognition," Augustus inspires only a "strangely desireless . . . almost disapproving attachment . . . a bond irrelevant and strange." And whereas Alexis causes things to be "woven into one great aspect," Caesar's aspect is "utterly severed . . . cut off because of [his] stubborn onesidedness" (317). Augustus is like the castrating father, or threatening son, who turns his back in anger, exiles himself from the affection of the other, and continues to fill the place of an appropriating desire, staying always just out of reach and leading the other on a maddening odyssey to satisfy an insatiable superego; one always *must* but never *can* get back to such a point of departure.

Virgil substitutes for Augustus another type of son, who is observed desiring in his own right—"enveloped in perceptive desire, himself desiring" (317)—and through his desire bringing a whole world to life. The trope of succession has been radically altered by a dorsal relation, one that begins with Caesar's willful turning away, by his turning his back, but thereby opens the possibility of a substitution that derives from "no longer notic[ing] whether a front view existed, even less if there was a countenance, graced with the power to see" (316). By turning his back, Caesar is deprived of a face or front and so can assume the identity of another. Alexis is identified and takes Caesar's place but "willingly" or "spontaneously" puts that identity to work in the service of a world beyond it, a world that will necessarily succeed and transform the original Alexis (even as it is transformed by him). Indeed, when Alexis reappears in a vision later in the novel, he will only be "visible . . . insofar as he was recognizable from his back [von hinten]" (411/442). Here he "averts" his face as if with resentment against Virgil and therefore emerges into the Oedipal trap, but he is immediately seen to have been "dreaming out into the dreaming landscape [hatte er hinausgeträumt ins Landschaftsträumende]," causing it to open out and causing him also to become part of the "trembling flow" (316–17).

We can begin to see in this movement an ethics—and, in view of our previous discussion, a politics—that functions beyond the face by virtue of allowing the other to be other even to the extent of being unrecognizable, indeed to be another who freely desires. In this way, what one imagines or produces lives on, not by giving back in a frozen economy of reciprocality, not by demonstrating what it owes to whoever or whatever has produced it, but rather by turning its back, and by being suffered to turn its back and so to open out a whole new perspective of tropological possibility. All this takes place on the diaphanous threshold of the house, at the point where the voyaging out begins, no longer conceived of as an exile that depends on that economy of leaving and returning, indeed of interiority and exteriority ("dreaming out into the dreaming landscape"), but rather as an originary departure or leaving that is here called desire.[18] And it takes place via a type of technoprosthetic becoming of the body—"a mortal body divided into members . . . a narrow human back, covered in the draped folds of a toga *[eine schmale Menschenrückseite mit schrägen Togafalten darüber]*," whose limbs, clothing, and house are the very articulations by which it comes to life and which it brings to life by this form of departure, turning its back and stepping out, vesting itself in, and accommodating itself to, a limitless world.

Whether he recognizes it or not, Virgil is, for me, home at this moment. He is home at the moment at which the neuroses of completion, of succession, of possession, the whole appropriative and Oedipal bind within which he is forever caught vis-à-vis Augustus, cedes its place to a dance of desire. When Virgil's imagination substitutes Alexis for Caesar, he opens the whole creation moving in the dance of desire. It is as if Virgil engendered all that without moving an inch: he is suddenly everywhere and at home. He can die knowing he lives still, not in any simple sense of the work he will leave after him, but knowing the vital force of a life of desire. This is the opening to fiction beyond narrative, perhaps something we would have to call the opening to poetry, but a poetry beyond the intractable commerce with death that Virgil seems to define it as.

In this homecoming, or myth of origins, a back emerges out of the silence and calm and proceeds to disembody itself to the extent of losing its face and its identity, ceding them to another. As a result, the world is brought to life. Thanks to this front-to-back relation, a frozen image of controlling power is transformed into a free flow of creative desire. Another form of interrelation develops, as applicable to the interhuman as to the relation of the human to the nonhuman, to what it produces and what produces it. What produces—or what is behind—sees without foreseeing what it produces, without seeing what face that offers to the future and to the world; it supports without shaping any final form. What is produced—or what is in front—remembers without the hindsight of indebtedness, faces its own unknown becoming, and waits for the contact of the familiar while presuming that that can only still arrive in the form of surprise.

Homecoming in *The Death of Virgil* is most often *Heimkehr* or *heimkehren*, consistently involving a turning that evokes Heidegger's danger. The journey home is dogged by the fate that haunts Orpheus, and at one point Virgil calls to Plotia as his "homecoming, turning home without turning back *[Heimkunft ohne Rückkunft]*" (295/315). Virgil's wager is to get home before he dies, but like Odysseus, the closer he approaches, the more he feels the breath of a vengeful Poseidon on his neck. At the end of the Proteus chapter of *Ulysses,* Stephen Daedalus, masturbating by the sea, looks back over his shoulder as though he were being watched by someone similarly castrating: "Behind. Perhaps there is someone. He turned his face over a shoulder, rere regardant." He sees something quite different: "Moving through the air high spars of a threemaster . . . homing, upstream, silently moving, a silent ship" (51). The ship is not someone but something, "homing" like a cognizant or prescient machine, a silent home on the waves heading home, less to turn in once arrived there than to turn home itself around by bringing the voyage back to it, rigging home ready to sail once more.

(Turn around, go back!)
Breathe breathe breathe deeply,
And I was seething, breathing deeply

—DAVID BOWIE, "Width of a Circle"

4. A Line Drawn in the Ocean Exodus, Freud, Rimbaud

Joyce's 1904 three-master homes to Dublin, back to what were called the British Isles, even if the island in question was home to an Ireland that often and justifiably marked itself as recalcitrantly non-British. The ships home nevertheless to a type of or piece of Europe. In my experience, for what it is worth, there existed a rich mythology of six-month ocean crossings in three-masters or similar that brought "my people" to their new home,[1] but our strongest sense of voyaging, since the beginning of the twentieth century at least, was that of leaving the South Pacific to return to the European motherland, back to the British Isles (even if we were partly Irish). From our new home at the other end of the earth, we voyaged in order to home, just like Joyce's three-master, to Dublin or London.[2]

Home is what we presume to find behind us, abiding there as the place of our origin and the marker of our identity. But as we saw in the preceding chapter, at least one of our mythological origins tells us that we never really know how we began, and at least one of our narrative origins has us coping with troubled seas in the way of the way home. In the discussion that follows, that sea, or rather some more boundless version of it, will figure as what both determines and confounds identity and difference, and as what functions as nondiscriminating nostalgia for a fusional identity on the one hand, and the lure of exoticist difference on the other.

Before leaving my South Pacific "European" island home to cross the ocean and *experience Europe for the first time*, I read some Rimbaud. In fact, once I arrived there, I realized, in terms I return to later in this chapter, that before crossing that ocean, I had not read him at all. But that fact had nothing—nothing in the sense of everything—to do with Europe. It no doubt had much to do with what appeared as the mind-numbing inanity of the paragons of excellence of French literary scholarship, second only to the mind-numbing inanity of the paragons of excellence of Anglo-American literary scholarship, whose commentaries on the poems filled the pages of my Garnier edition of Rimbaud's works and served as some-thing of a basis for my reading of him. I remember looking at those com-mentaries at the time and thinking, my oh my, is this the best they can do, and resolving not to read anything but the poems themselves. Once I got to Europe, I thought, shit, oh dear, this *is* the best they can do. Look-ing again at all that over thirty years later, I am not sure what to think. But such a glance back recommends itself as central to the network of concepts I call the dorsal.

My slip into the personal is here determined by more than one exi-gency. First, simply to "locate" myself within the context and thematics of an ocean that, in this chapter, serves explicitly to interrogate the grounds of national, psychic, and textual identity. Second, to return to a question that has, in many ways, provoked every effort of thinking and writing I have been engaged in, a question that derives from my primary disci-pline of literary analysis, and from a formative experience within that dis-cipline, namely, analysis of the poetry of Rimbaud. That question is: what is the status of commentary on a work of literature? Commentary comes from after or from behind to put a new face on the work it refers to; it rewrites the natural or creative function as a techno-rhetorical one; and it ruptures the self-identity of the work, exiling it and exposing it to oce-anic drift.[3] By extension, and by implication, the discussion that follows is also something of a commentary—of questionable status, since giving the subject its due would require a whole other analysis—on current his-toricist approaches to literature inasmuch as they presume a nonliterary literal before and after the textual, and which, in certain versions of the form I shall call, by contrast and in shorthand, "transatlanticist," cross the ocean to better ignore it.

Rimbaud, as well as learned commentary on his poems, will therefore be my point of reference in sketching out a logic of European identity with respect to the ocean such as is opened up by what we take to be the first narratives of the West, Homer and Virgil, and continued all the way to Joyce and beyond. But the trajectory will this time begin with Moses and include Freud. In Homer, the ocean served as vehicle for Odysseus's techno-tropological departure, the context for his fictional meanderings, the guarantor of his exile. In analyses that move from the Red Sea to the oceanic feeling and the drunken boat, from the founding of a nation to the jettisoning of religious sentiment and to a baptism in the phantasmagoric swill, the ocean will here surge in the back- and not so background as the paradox of a *natural technology,* a *pretechnological technology,* or *technological différance.* Limitless oceanic water, as the energetic force of an essence of technology—which, as we have noted, Heidegger, for all his insistence on poiesis, did not seem to recognize until it came to a dam on the Rhine and an instrumental harnessing of fluid force—is the figure here for what drives technology, and it does so before, behind, and beyond any human production or invention. As we shall see with Moses, an oceanic force held back and then released gives rise to, but also problematizes, a technology of identification that takes place as the inscription of a border; with Freud, an oceanic force is rejected in favor of the machinery of Oedipal relations and of the law; and with Rimbaud, an oceanic force thrust onto the shoals attempts to fix poetic signification on the dry ground of its sources of reference. If the figure of the human technological being was earlier represented by the upright stance, then the ocean would seem to defy it and to brook nothing but the supine, to be the necessarily destructive force that sweeps everything before it, horizontally; but it is precisely the aim of human technology, at least in the high-technological age that is ours, to return to a seamless fluidity of the machine and its environment, to be, as it were, invisible, nanotechnological, infinitesimal intervention, silent and unassuming as the ocean; we should imagine our future selves bathing or floating in technology as in Levinas's element, buoyed by an automatic ocean that effortlessly supports us, has us in it flat on our backs. But we should also understand the risk of overturning that comes from whatever technology unleashes, coming always from behind us, capable of landing us flat on our face.

My aim in this chapter is thus to develop further the rhetorico-technological, what I have previously called the techno-tropological, turn that makes for a particular configuration and a particular politicization of identity. This draws on the presumption that functions never further removed than the near background of this book's argument, namely, that any rupture within the plenitude of a self-enclosed intact human identity opens the space of the technological or even the inanimate, and that such a rupture is in evidence well before or behind where common sense or tradition would locate it, back in the beginning that I am calling the dorsal. In chapter 2 certain realignments of ethical relations recommended themselves once the face-to-face was understood to imply and even require the back, and once the extreme exposure of the subject was seen to fall back on the wall of the house in order to preserve and even define its interiority. In this chapter, I am interested in outlining a series of originary articulations of the rhetorical and the political, beginning with that which regulates but problematizes the formation of national identity. As we shall see on the one hand, as if we didn't know, this version of identity is heavily overwrought by a rhetorical machinery, by mechanisms of inscription and erasure; its origin is technological in that sense. On the other hand, to the extent that the assertion of national sovereignty is a founding political instance, whatever relations are cemented in that moment will continue to function all the way through whatever we call the political and in some sense will continue to define that political.

The figure of the ocean that returns in these pages can also function, paradoxically, as a form of banality, something like a rhetoric of the literal, nothing more than the idea of waves or walls of water, breakers on the sand, the repetition of commonplaces, a terrestrial or telluric self-evidence that will have us doubting, by the end, whether anything has been said or changed at all. Yet within the time it takes to read these pages, within the space of its discourse, other commonplaces will have been perpetuated, with little if anything being said or changing, covered by the rising waters of a banal repetition: the Israeli occupation of the West Bank and Gaza, and the Anglo-American occupation of Iraq, will have ground more lives down to the bone, Kosovo or Macedonia will have continued to simmer close to the boil, perhaps a body will have been lifted high by the hands of mourners as if delivered from earth to sky, not to mention that in Africa more scores will have died of starvation and other scores of AIDS, and in America the 3,600 men and women on death row will have inched that much closer toward the front of their queue. All that happens without anything being said, and yet it is the hyperbolic defiance and figure of impotence of everything we say and do.

It is banal and commonplace enough to assert that the discourses of the proper, of blood and soil, that organize everything from race, naming, and identity to nationhood, frontiers, nationalism, and genocide are caught in the paradox between literality and rhetoric. As is every discourse, especially one calling itself a banality, posited thereby on a notion of the proper, the degree zero of self-evidence. But those discourses of blood and soil provide a particularly striking case of the paradox: the very blood and soil that are held to be the essences of literality itself—watch it flow, feel it in your hands or under your nails, nothing could be more basic, nothing represents more incontrovertibly the very life that constitutes us—also serve as the basis for the most egregious rhetorical excesses. Because a certain European mythology and rhetoric of the soil operates in conjunction or in contrast with the sea or ocean, analysis of that contrast will uncover, *en abyme,* to say the least, the impossible opposition between literal and rhetorical, what is also the impossible opposition between rhetoric itself and the blood and soil without which, or without a conception of which, there could be no Europe. If the ocean represents a type of European unconscious, it does so not just because we are finally talking, through all its manifold and violent reconfigurations, about a series of contiguous countries forming a continental landmass that is ultimately able to constitute itself, somewhere, in opposition to the ocean. We are not just talking about how that is performed by a continent in contrast to how it is performed by an island (in this respect, note the rich history, all the way from the colonial experience mentioned earlier to weighing vegetables metrically and the euro, in terms of which the British Isles, already in contrast with Ireland, do or do not belong to Europe). Rather, if the ocean represents a type of European unconscious, it is not just because of geography, geology, and topography, but also because it is in that ocean, wherever or whatever it may be, that the solid security, the terra firma of the literal, the possibility of an operative distinction between literal and rhetorical, falls into something of an abyss.

In seeking to establish the frontiers of Europe, something that we have been doing for a long time and in a sense structures much of what we do whenever we discourse on history, politics, and religion, whenever we discourse *tout court*—inasmuch as our discourse is caught in the history, politics, and religion that circulate within the awkward limits of a changing Europe—we are brought to the realization that drawing the limit or frontier is a rhetorical act, a legislative performance that renders problematic any secure geographic, political, or religious delimitation. It is a rhetorical act because it represents a tropo-topological inscription upon nature, making a river or a coastline a political frontier or drawing an artificial boundary. And because of that, it relies on further discursive rhetoric concerning politics, history, and rights of inheritance to legitimate the primary inscription. Much as we might name and characterize Africa, the nondemocratic, or the Islamic, as the opposite outside or foreign limits of a domestic and familiar Europe, we are confounded in attempts to identify and singularize the frontier between the two terms of that opposition, to say where Africa, the nondemocratic, or the Islamic begins vis-à-vis that supposed same and familiar Europe. In our confounding, we end up disfiguring and truncating the very Europe and the very identity we thought we were protecting. Hence the ocean examined here appears finally to be less the limitless expanse on the other side of Europe than the very confounding of a separation, an ocean of a line redrawn as it is drawn in an event of (non)discrimination that both enables discourse itself and inscribes the relation between discourse and the acts we Europeans call history and politics. It is both the line drawn like some fundamental literal utterance and the series of discursive or historico-political acts superimposed wave after wave upon it.

IN THE BOOK of Exodus a series of events of distinction, delimitation, and discrimination give birth to the Jewish nation, its rooting somewhere within mythological or geographic borders that remain a matter of bloody dispute to this day. Without a doubt, those borders also remain, ideologically and mythologically, to some extent geographically, in any case geopolitically, the disputed borders of Europe. Among the events described in Exodus are, in the first place, God's holocaustic elimination of the Egyptians' firstborn, the discriminating yet indiscriminate divine slaughter that draws the line between races and within seniorities while crossing the border between classes and species in order to better and more indiscriminately destroy, "from the firstborn of Pharaoh that sat on his throne unto the firstborn of the captive that was in the dungeon; and all the firstborn of cattle."[6] Later, in the second place, there is the complicated institution of the law with its precise prescriptions and proscriptions. Between expurgation and legislation there occurs the exodus or flight that names this second piece of the Pentateuch itself. That exodus is in turn marked by the crossing of the Red Sea, an event that is itself marked by the mark, the trait *en retrait* par excellence, that is Moses's or God's dividing of the very sea:

And Moses stretched out his hand over the sea; and the Lord caused the sea to go back by a strong east wind all that night, and made the sea dry land, and the waters were divided. And the children of Israel went into the midst of the sea upon the dry ground: and the waters were a wall unto them on their right hand, and on their left. And the Egyptians pursued, and went in after them to the midst of the sea, even all Pharaoh's horses, his chariots, and his horsemen. . . . And the Lord said unto Moses, Stretch out thine hand over the sea, that the waters may come again upon the Egyptians, upon their chariots, and upon their horsemen. And Moses stretched forth his hand over the sea, and the sea returned. . . . And the waters returned, and covered the chariots, and the horsemen, and all the host of Pharaoh that came into the sea after them; there remained not so much as one of them. But the children of Israel walked upon dry land in the midst of the sea; and the waters were a wall unto them on their right hand, and on their left. (Exodus 14:21–23, 26–29)

Territorialization, in the form of the Israelites' exodus or reterritorialization, is here described as the cataclysmic break from an Egyptian past that will allow the elect to journey unencumbered toward the promised land. And that break is defined precisely as the discrimination of land with respect to the sea, the dividing of the sea to produce dry land that is also a further discrimination of the Egyptians vis-à-vis the children of Israel, allowing for the indiscriminate annihilation of the former. The cross-species hecatomb of "the horse and his rider" thus matches the extermination of the firstborn sons and cattle of the tenth plague. The sea divides to give the land priority and to anoint the children of Israel as the survivors on land. It withdraws, disavows itself, cedes to the dry land under it, becomes a wall protecting and defining that dry land, discriminating itself from it, but then returns to its usual business of confounding all in utter destruction. This elemental event of territorialization is marked also by the inscription of a divine and bellicose rhetoric, a rhetoric describing a strategy whereby an aggressive response will be provoked so as to provide the pretext for a successful military subjugation. God's words here could not be more topically, or typically, those of the nationalist or imperialist strategies of all time, a matter of inciting or interpreting an act in order to define it as an aggression, so as to legitimate one's own expansionism: "I will harden the hearts of the Egyptians," he tells Moses, "and they shall follow them: and I will get me honour upon Pharaoh, and upon all his host, upon his chariots, and upon his horsemen. And the Egyptians shall know that I am the Lord, when I have gotten me honour upon Pharaoh, upon his chariots, and upon his horsemen" (Exodus 14:17–18). The New English Version says: "I will make Pharaoh obstinate, and he will pursue them, so that I may win glory for myself at the expense of Pharaoh and all his army." I'll set them up, says God, goad them into stepping over the line, so that I can unleash on them my superior firepower, or rather water power.

Yet God's particular brand of warmongering bravado is not the only rhetoric that comes into play. The massacre of the Egyptian army becomes the occasion for something like the first national anthem, the first musical festivity recorded in the Bible, the dithyrambic outpouring and overflowing by which the blessings of past occasions become the celebration of a present geopolitical fiat and a future imperialist mission:

> Then sang Moses and the children of Israel this song unto the Lord, and spake, saying, I will sing unto the Lord, for he hath triumphed gloriously: the horse and his rider hath he thrown into the sea. . . . The Lord is a man of war: the Lord is his name. Pharaoh's chariots and his host hath he cast into the sea: his chosen captains also are drowned in the Red sea. The depths have covered them: they sank into the bottom as a stone. Thy right hand, O Lord, is become glorious in power: thy right hand, O Lord, hath dashed in pieces the enemy. And in the greatness of thine excellency thou hast overthrown them that rose up against thee: thou sentest forth thy wrath, which consumed them as stubble. And with the blast of thy nostrils the waters were gathered together, the floods stood upright as an heap, and the depths were congealed in the heart of the sea. . . . The people shall hear, and be afraid: sorrow shall take hold on the inhabitants of Palestina. Then the dukes of Edom shall be amazed; the mighty men of Moab, trembling shall take hold upon them; all the inhabitants of Canaan shall melt away. Fear and dread shall fall upon them. . . . And Miriam the prophetess, the sister of Aaron, took a timbrel in her hand; and all the women went out after her with timbrels and with dances. And Miriam answered them, Sing ye to the Lord, for he hath triumphed gloriously; the horse and his rider hath he thrown into the sea. (Exodus 15:1–8, 14–16, 20–21)

No doubt Miriam jingles her bells and struts her stuff because she is swept into this spontaneous revel of deliverance. But we should note the precise narratological disposition of the text, the fact of its being a sequence that is also a circle, whereby the call of Moses and the children of Israel receives a response from Miriam, who breaks off with the women, second-lining, singing the same song. It means that without a doubt it is a rhetorical wave that sweeps over her; it is the song itself as much as the subject of the song that has her repeating an orgiastic mantra, singing and dancing the celebration of this military triumph of Jahve the "man of war," his consigning of Egyptian horse and rider to a watery grave.

The God and Moses who divide the sea to create a terrestrial passage subsequently set about conquering territory. The sea has closed behind them to engulf the Egyptians, but it is as if they will bring it with them, their hidden weapon of mass destruction whose undiscriminating power sweeps all before it. Knowing how to divide it, they will unleash it as leveler and neutralizer against any chosen opposing force; and as long as they can harness it, the better to unleash it, they will prevail. For the sea represents on the one hand the secret weapon that is a warrior God on "our" side, but on the other hand, in banal and prosaic terms, it is nothing more nor less than that rhetorical effusion. It is the indiscriminate and uncontrollable force of a bellicose rhetoric that functions by means of repetition, a mantra of God and right intoned with oceanic intensity. We should hear the deadly force of the sea as the song of a warrior God, via the lyrical force of poetry and tambourine, the animistic impetus of inspired cadence and dancing women. The sea divides to produce the land through which the children of Israel are able to flee, but when it closes again indiscriminately on the Egyptians, its vapors overtake those same fleeing children, anointing them as future community and at the same time intoxicating them, binding Miriam and all of them through song and dance in the consummate plenitude of an oceanic feeling.

The event of religion as institution of the law, which soon follows the passage through the Red Sea, looks very much like an event of dry land. The law comes down from the mountain, from that pinnacle of clarity and distinction, drawing cut-and-dried lines in the sand: Do this, don't do that. Yet, as we have just seen, the originary mythological line drawn in the sand, the dividing line, is in fact a line drawn in the sea, perhaps even in the ocean. Its distinguishing force is accompanied by an undiscriminating and overwhelming one that will follow it everywhere. In instituting religion, the religion that will give rise to Europe, in walking on the dry land that will define Europe in one of its most important and increasingly problematic senses, we, inasmuch as we are children of Israel, to the extent that we function as their sectarian inheritors, will have turned our back on the sea. We will instead have climbed Mount Sinai. But the ocean comes back. The law gets retrofitted to the carnival, as Patočka has argued concerning European religion in his *Heretical Essays on the Philosophy of History*, which Derrida reads in *The Gift of Death*. In Patočka's view, just as Plato tries to deliver philosophy from the thaumaturgical tradition but retains some form of demonic mystery, so the Christian religion, as a practice of responsibility that is not yet understood as such by Europe, brings with it the ripples turning to waves of the *mysterium tremendum*.[7]

IT IS SURELY such a thaumaturgical religious effect that Romain Rolland is alluding to when he writes to Freud in December 1927 after the publication of *The Future of an Illusion*, speaking of "a peculiar feeling, which [Rolland] himself is never without, which he finds confirmed by many others, and which he may suppose is present in millions of people." This feeling causes Freud "no small difficulty"—a difficulty that perhaps even surges within him—precisely because he never felt it, as explained in the opening pages of *Civilization and Its Discontents*:

> It is a feeling which [Rolland] would like to call a sensation of "eternity," a feeling as of something limitless, unbounded—as it were "oceanic" . . . one may, he thinks, call oneself religious on the basis of this oceanic feeling alone, even if one rejects every belief and every illusion.
>
> The views expressed by the friend whom I so much honour . . . caused me no small difficulty. I cannot discover this "oceanic" feeling in myself.[8]

Freud doubts very much whether the oceanic feeling works the way Rolland describes: "whether it is being correctly interpreted and whether it ought to be regarded as the *fons et origo* of the whole need for religion . . . what claim this feeling has to be regarded as the source of religious needs . . . does not seem compelling" (12, 19). For Freud, religion is better understood as a form of paternalism, a function of the law and of the father, shades of the superego: "The derivation of religious needs from the infant's helplessness and the longing for the father aroused by it seems . . . incontrovertible." The oceanic feeling, on the other hand, would be a regression, the persistence of a primary "ego-feeling" that seeks the "restoration of limitless narcissism" (19).

There is room for reading Freud's reluctance to conceive of religion in terms of the oceanic feeling as itself a form of repression, a reluctance to recognize the extent to which the ocean of thaumaturgy coexists with the mountain of the law. As I have argued before, the serious problem in *Civilization and Its Discontents* is one of accommodation, of finding room, of configuring psychic space vis-à-vis temporal progression.[9] Hence the telling example of Rome that Freud uses, telling for us here especially in terms of the institution of an imperial Europe, inasmuch as the Romans donned first the political, and eventually the religious, mantle of conquest that was mythically inscribed by Moses's parting of the waters. If one were looking for a "truly" European and Christian Mount Sinai, Rome would present itself as a particularly viable candidate. Thus it is that, still in the first chapter of *Civilization and Its Discontents*, in aid of figuring out the oceanic feeling quandary and the development of the ego, in order to understand the topography of psychic space, Freud invites us to imagine a Rome whose successive architectural layers continue to coexist in their pristine form within the same space, rather than being constructed one on the ruins of the other. Within this imagining, or imaginary, Rome is repeatedly a citadel and a rampart, a bridgehead or a beachhead: the Palatine, the Septimontium, castle of Sant'Angelo, Pantheon, Santa Maria sopra Minerva. That is of course a self-evidence; Rome is not Venice. But Freud is talking about something that is anything but self-evident, and thus the preference for Rome as an example and a paradigm that excludes the possibility of accommodating the sea, as the example and the paradigm that in defining Europe excludes or represses the sea, should not be dismissed as insignificant. It suggests that a thematic continuity exists between the founding ancient moment of the law and the modern moment of its undermining by the unconscious; that in spite of the subversive force of a psyche driven by the unconscious as resistance to the law, a new, monumental, or elevated form of law is being imposed over the ruins of the old. In this sense the internal psychic mechanism, for which the successive architectural Roman monuments serve as a model, is itself a new architecture or architectonic that inhabits the same structure as the Mosaic law even as seeks to replace it. It is as if, thematically and rhetorically at least, Europe and the new Mittel-European, yet presumptively universal, psyche turns back the waters of its radically oceanic unconscious, the thaumaturgical unconscious of its religious superego, by keeping itself high and dry, in the rarefied air of a divine law.[10]

Dispensed with, the oceanic feeling will therefore disappear from the second chapter of *Civilization and Its Discontents*. Religion will be transformed from the fluid indistinction of an unbounded ego to Providence in "the figure of an enormously exalted father" (21), from fusion to law, as if consecrating the move from sea to mountain. As I have just suggested, Freud thereby follows Moses onto drier land: religion is no longer to be considered an orgiastic jubilee, a carousing celebration of destruction and deliverance through whose euphony, or within whose silent center, one nevertheless gains access to the universal thalassic concord. Returning to the thesis of *The Future of an Illusion,* Freud worries less about the "deepest [oceanic] sources of the religious feeling" than about the opposition between pleasure and reality principles (21). Religion is henceforth a palliative, compared with a series of other remedies for the toils and travails of existence. It helps cope with reality.

Given Freud's rejection of the oceanic, it is tempting to examine the thematics, metaphorics, and logic of fluidity that nevertheless function in the development of his ideas about religion as a palliative. Were we to do so, however, we would be left with a very confused situation indeed. Now, that might simply be because such a thematics does not remain operative from one chapter to the next; or because a figurative coherence or consistency between the fluid and solid is not required as the mark of logical rigor. However, given the peculiar semantic register and rhetorical operation of the oceanic feeling, given its strange employment of a figurative mode—the immensity, force, and fluidity of an ocean, the whole rhetorical network that that word unleashes—in order to express a precise, literal, and identifiable feeling of absorption into unboundedness, the use and the abandoning of reference to that feeling, especially considered in the context of Freud's never having felt it, can be neither a simple nor an arbitrary matter.

Rolland has a sensation "as of something limitless" and calls it oceanic, and as a result calls himself religious (11). Freud presumably understands the feeling but cannot discover it in himself, adding that "it is not easy to deal scientifically with feelings" (12), and later reinforcing the same: "It is very difficult for me to work with these almost intangible quantities" (19). He understands it to the extent of comparing it with a "limitless narcissism," although he does not say whether that is also a sensation, or whether he has felt it or not. Freud's argument thus seems to be not with the *oceanicity* of the oceanic but with its religiosity. In dispensing with the oceanic feeling in the context of religion, therefore, he cannot for all that have rejected the ocean, inasmuch as he would still want to talk about the potential limitlessness of narcissism, and, as we shall see, other such forces. Yet it is precisely the oceanic as signifier that disappears from his argument, being replaced by other versions of implacable billowing or fluidity. I suggest not only that Freud, consciously or unconsciously, rejects the oceanic feeling both because he hasn't felt it and because it is supposed to be religious, but also that he finds a way, consciously or unconsciously, to avoid a signifier that confounds the distinction between literal and figurative, a most tangible signifier of *intangibilization*. The ocean is both precise, as literal as blood and soil, and nonscientific, intangible; it is both pure difference, the binary opposite of dry land, of the constructible, of the inhabitable, and what destroys that difference, the great torrential leveler.

Therefore, I am arguing, a thematics of fluidity necessarily continues to operate in Freud's argument to the extent that distinctions are being made; for it is, in its opposition to dry land, a prime rhetorical operator of distinction itself. Yet whenever the distinction made is that between fluid and solid, then the ocean of indistinction is never far away, for it is, as the deluge that still haunts us (not to mention as harbinger of the fire next time), the psychopathological signifier of that very indistinction. As soon as and as long as distinctions are being drawn, the line is being drawn in the ocean, between the confusion of the ocean and the distinctness of dry land. And as soon as that line is drawn, it is confounded. That seems to be the case when one tries to distinguish, in the later chapters of *Civilization and Its Discontents*, between fluid encroachment and territorial resistance.

Still in chapter 1, Freud suggests that the oceanic "'oneness with the universe' . . . sounds like a first attempt at a religious consolation . . . another way of disclaiming the danger which the ego recognizes as threatening it from the external world" (19). The fluid oneness covers over the distinction defined by the external world, giving the ego the impression that it can expand unfettered, whereas in fact it must recognize its limits. This means that rather than there being two more or less solid, even though disproportionate entities, namely, ego and external world, the ego expands like an ocean over the external world, allowing itself to discount that world. In chapter 2, Freud recasts the same problematic in terms of the pleasure principle, which, of course, repeats this fluid "structure" of the ego in presuming it can operate unbounded. But the pleasure principle also operates differentially, such that its preferred form is a release and a relief: "What we call happiness in the strictest sense comes from the (preferably sudden) satisfaction of needs which have been dammed up to a high degree [hoch aufgestauter Bedürfnisse], and it is from its nature only possible as an episodic phenomenon. When any situation that is desired by the pleasure principle is prolonged, it only produces a feeling of mild contentment" (23). In this rendering, the pleasure principle functions like a potamic rather than an oceanic feeling, but its force remains decidedly fluxive, even diluvian; it is capable of bursting like the feeling that causes the children of Israel to break into song when the waves of the Red Sea crash over the Egyptians.

In the end, however, this ocean of pleasure will come under the control of a reality principle that functions in the form of the law, as a form of the law, drawing the line, allowing the psychic (and physiological) organism to survive, to stay reasonably dry. Instead of unbounded pleasure, one will settle for avoidance of unpleasure. As a result, pleasure seems to switch sides, figurative sides at least, abandoning its fluid form to become a territorial principle, going head-to-head with reality. We are told that the program of the pleasure principle is at "loggerheads with the whole world" (23), that we are "threatened with suffering" (24), that "misery has to be kept at a distance" (25), suffering "fend[ed] off" (26). From here on, the psyche functions according to terrestrial, and indeed territorial, principles, coping with forms of unhappiness that are in fact "much less difficult to experience" than are our possibilities of happiness, defending itself against "suffering from three directions: *from our own body,* which is doomed to decay and dissolution . . . *from the external world,* which may rage against us with overwhelming and merciless forces of destruction; and finally *from our relations to other men*" (24; italics mine).

Freud has, as it were, again followed Moses, from Red Sea to Mount Sinai and now to Canaan: the distinction between ocean and dry land has been superseded by attempts at the partition and defense of parcels of that land, by interminable territorial disputes. Again the sea has parted, distinguishing and defining the land, defining it as principle of distinction, in opposition to the indiscriminate sea; but again the sea has returned, for lines drawn in the sand of the land need to be constantly redrawn. They are exposed to the billows of political change and military force, are difficult to defend, changeable, undecidable, always threatened with disappearance or reimposition, subject to waves of conquest or flight, the stampede of armies or the panic of refugees. They are lines drawn in the ocean.

Freud makes three distinctions within the psychopathological territories he defines, three dry realities that the organism is exposed to and defends itself against, drawing the line and the wagons around itself: body, world, others. They obey perhaps a questionable taxonomic logic given our previous analyses of the human in its relations to exteriority, given a technologized or prosthetic body that always already articulates with the world and with others. But it is clear that those three forms of reality obey above all a rhetorical logic, that of psychic territorialization. As such, they also imply a politics—indeed, a politics of community—which has come into play well before it is explicitly recognized by Freud later in the same discussion. Faced with "the suffering which may come from human relationships" and "against the dreaded external world," one is inclined to withdraw by one means or another, retrenching, as it were, into one's citadel. But Freud recommends a "better path: that of becoming a member of the human community and . . . going over to the attack against nature and subjecting her to the human will. Then one is working with all for the good of all" (24–25). Better to work together to build a dam on the Rhine than remilitarize the Rhineland. The politics he recommends amount to a relinquishing of reflex territorial claims, of a certain form of psychic identity politics, in favor of a reimmersion within more fluid community relations, but this is still in order to better go on the attack against whatever threatens from a further remove of exteriority, here called "nature." It is still a question of territorial superiority, of defense and offense.

When it comes to more general "methods of averting suffering that seek to influence our own organism," Freud's catalog of remedies is, by his own admission, "most interesting" (25). There we have the series developed in an earlier context, namely, gardening, painting, and cocaine. Or rather, *deflections* such as gardening à la Candide or, what amounts to the same thing, science; *substitutions* such as art; and *intoxications* such as drugs: hence, via my résumé, gardening, painting, or cocaine. And then, of course, there is psychosis. By this point a certain taxonomic rigor has been sacrificed, and Freud concludes modestly that "I do not think I have made a complete enumeration of the methods by which men strive to gain happiness and keep suffering away and I know, too, that the material might have been differently arranged" (28). Ripples of indistinction, cracks within the dry order of things, perhaps even a few drops of oceanic thaumaturgy, are revealed. And indeed, a certain fluidity, forms of wavelike sensation, always existed within the very citadels of resistance just promoted: appreciation of art is a "mild narcosis" (28), intellectual effort is a sublimation, intoxication is a "drowner of cares" (25). In each case what is offered, and what the organism returns to as the path of least resistance, is a type of euphoria produced by more pleasure and less reality, a form of reliance on more oceanic feelings. Forsaking its limitless narcissism in order to cope with reality, the ego will therefore nevertheless resort to simulacra of types of unboundedness, seeking some form of reimmersion in the sea of indistinction from which it has emerged. All that, as Freud apologetically insists throughout the rest of his essay, is "common knowledge" (33), "self-evident" (64).

I LEAVE FREUD snorting coke in front of a canvas in the garden, with the psychic organism easing itself back to the seashore, preferring perhaps a good swim to a good fight after all. But even where gardening, art, and intoxication are concerned, the law isn't far away: we know how God's refusal of Cain the gardener's offering, in favor of that of Abel the rancher, led to the first murder, a breaking of the law before the law; we also know the proscriptive word of the law in respect of the graven image, as well as the long history of repression of intemperance. Beyond that we encounter the myth of certain narcophile outlaws, the Hashshashin celebrated by Rimbaud in his poem "Matinée d'ivresse," presuming we can agree that he is indeed alluding to them. We know at least that in his poem he juxtaposes a "faith in poison" with the exhortation "Voici le temps des Assassins." The myth, with its progressive amalgam of cultural, religious, and political practices, is instructive. The Webster's dictionary entry for "assassin" refers to "an order of Muslim fanatics, active in Persia and Syria from about 1090 to 1272, whose chief object was to assassinate Crusaders." That "chief object," no doubt, clearly distinguishes them from the Crusaders themselves, who are presumed not to have had any such schemes of assassination in mind. It shows what little distance we have traveled from the eleventh century to current references to al-Qaeda, Hezbollah, or Hamas, or to the Iraqi resistance to foreign occupation, as the rhetorical and political lines continue to be drawn in the watery sands of Europe's central edge, or peripheral center.

"Matinée d'ivresse" is not, in fact, the Rimbaud poem that I want to concentrate on here, but rather an earlier, more famous example. For it is by explicitly following a type of psychochemical countercurrent, advocating a voyage to the "true life" of an oceanic elsewhere, embarking on the ecstatic drift of a salutary intoxication, that his drunken boat charts its watery meander in the poem of the same name. The countercurrent followed by "Le bateau ivre" is inscribed explicitly as a renunciation of Europe, at least in the sense of a journeying beyond it. The drunken boat makes a willful *regression* (in Freud's terms) and couches it in the terms of a *progression*, seeming to embrace an unbounded narcissistic indulgence without justification, regret, or guilt. The terms of this trip are canonical: "lighter than a cork I danced on the waves . . . blue wine stains and vomit washed over me . . . henceforth I swam in the Poem of the Sea . . . I sometimes saw what man thought he saw," and the first two-thirds of the poem inventories those sights in hallucinogenic detail. But then, supposedly, reality returns and along with it a nostalgia for "l'Europe aux anciens parapets" (131), and the drunken boat is content instead to be as frail as a May butterfly, a tiny vessel set loose by a sad crouching child upon a cold black puddle in a European twilight (131). It would seem that the Mosaic and Freudian schemata are repeated, that the phantasmatic setting forth and cutting loose on the ocean leads to disillusionment and flight back to the safe harbor of the familiar. The oceanic expanse is renounced in favor of a derisory liquid enclosure, an insignificant puddle, safely contained within a terrestrial Europe. The narrator, who by the end of the poem is prosopopoeically and undecidably either boat or poet, or perhaps both, desires now only what he calls a "European water": "Si je désire une eau d'Europe, c'est la flache / Noire et froide où vers le crépuscule embaumé / Un enfant accroupi plein de tristesses, lâche / Un bateau frêle comme un papillon de mai" (in a literal translation, "If I wish for a European water, it is the puddle / black and cold where, toward the embalmed twilight / a crouching child full of sadness lets go / a boat fragile like a May butterfly").

However, the force of Rimbaud's exemplary poetic experience in general has led to a serious hesitation, on the part of his readers, between what is finally embrace and what is finally renunciation, concerning what follows what, whether he ends on the ocean or on terra firma. This is as true with respect to his work as it is in respect of his life, and indeed in terms of the relation between work and life, and it has led analysis of Rimbaud's work to be more singularly about the ideological predisposition of the reader than would be the case with many other writers. What is undeniable is that Rimbaud stopped writing poetry at the age of twenty, but that abandonment does not tell us whether he wanted thereby to say, "I have written everything I possibly could, taking poetry as far as it can possibly go," or "My experiment is a failure, I give up." Either interpretation is possible, and the questions about his disposition raised at any point during his brief writing career, and especially at its end, remain unanswered all the way to the close of his thirty-seven-year life.

"The Drunken Boat," with its seeming renunciation of the ocean, is the poem Rimbaud has in his pocket when he sets out once more, and more definitively, from his provincial backwater home for Paris. It is the poem with which he sets out toward a life of poetry and of *dérèglement* or debauchery. He takes it to give to Verlaine, in order to seduce him. It can hardly be, at least not simply so, the world-weary recanting of *voyance* or of the poet as visionary that many have read it to be. In the same vein, it will have taken decades of scholarship and the discovery of incontrovertible historical evidence to force critics to accept that the *Illuminations* were written after *Une saison en enfer,* again disqualifying a reading of the latter poem as the remorseful prelude to Rimbaud's abandoning literature altogether. Furthermore, at the time of "The Drunken Boat," Rimbaud has only just begun the travels that will take him all over Europe—Belgium, London, Germany, Italy, Austria—then to Holland and, oh, by the way, to Java and back; then Germany and Scandinavia; then, progressively via

Switzerland, Italy, Egypt, and Cyprus, to Ethiopia. It is only because he is rapidly losing his legs and succumbing to gangrene that he will return to France to die, not, however, in Roche in the bosom of the family, but back in Marseille once more, setting out yet again.

The celebratory tone of most of "The Drunken Boat" comes therefore at the other end of Europe's story from Moses's and Miriam's song. It exalts the sea for its own sake, the voyage instead of the destination, indirection rather than orientation, a type of polymorphous profanity instead of a resolute monotheism. And it comes at the other end of Europe's history in more than one sense, in August 1871, in the wake of the Franco-Prussian War and the Commune, at the moment when a Europe defined more than ever by its overseas possessions begins to implode, dissolve, and reassemble around the lines drawn in the murderous quicksands of the twentieth century. Perhaps it tells the story of the paradox at the heart of Europe, that which exists between the sort of drunkenness for conquest that is expressed through the mayhem of its colonial expansion, and its retrenchment within the parochial confines of its separate borders, jealously protecting the puddle in its own backyard (such that the same mayhem came to be played out on the local level). It is not a paradox that is specific to Europe, for it is the rhetorical impasse I referred to at the beginning, that of the discourse of the proper, hesitating between literal retreat and rhetorical expansion.

There is a difficult interpretive moment in "The Drunken Boat." After the boat-poet-narrator begins to miss Europe with its ancient parapets, and just before he describes the cold European pond with which he will content himself, he invokes an apocalyptic end to his oceanic experience, it seems, with an exhortation to a type of immolation: "O que ma quille éclate! O que j'aille à la mer!" (O let my keel burst, let me go to [the] sea). The second formulation, as ambiguous in French as in English, has been interpreted as "let me sink," and that concords with both the expressions of regret that have preceded it and the compromise of the last two stanzas (where the ocean is reduced to a cold black puddle). Wallace Fowlie takes the liberty of translating *que j'aille à la mer* as "let me go *into* the sea."[13] But what is written in black and white, in the first, literal instance, is that the narrator wants to go to sea. In spite of that, Suzanne Bernard, *agrégée de l'université, docteur ès lettres*, paragon of excellence of French literary scholarship and editor of the Garnier edition of my graduate school days, will have none of it.[14] As she affirms in her copious and assiduous annotations, "Chadwick's interpretation [Chadwick would have to be a paragon of excellence of Anglo-American literary scholarship], according to which the Boat wants to return to the sea, beginning its navigations all over again, seems to me completely impossible, since the Boat wants its keel to burst: *aller à la mer* means to annihilate oneself in the waves" (428). According to the poem's narratological syntax, her insistence, like Fowlie's interlingual decision, is not without justification. But the confidence with which she draws the interpretive lines in the sand is truly impressive, and at the same time frightening. She presumes her task to be to adjudicate on such matters, and she will therefore do so without flinching. Besides, she has a great deal of knowledge at her disposal. She is able to inform us of the "remarkable fact" that Rimbaud had never seen the sea (422), surely remarkable for a poet as scornful of realist composition as Rimbaud.[15] She observes sympathetically—as one who would know from experience of such things—that "perhaps it isn't easy to give oneself over to complete debauchery [*s'encrapuler*] every day, to seek out [as Rimbaud described the poet's task in his famous *Lettre du voyant*] 'all the forms of love, suffering and madness,' and one is allowed . . . sometimes to wish for the modest but tranquil fate of those who have limited their horizons to an everyday pond" (423). Armed with such knowledge, Bernard will allow the poet's supposed renunciation of the end of "The Drunken Boat" to return to infect analeptically the entire poem: for her the whole poem becomes a lament even when it appears to celebrate and revel. Hence the line "I sometimes saw what man thought he saw" becomes, for her, less a celebration of the experience of *voyance* than an ironical or "half-skeptical" allusion to it (424). Presumably it is blue stains and vomit that take the pleasure out of dancing on the waves and swimming in the Poem of the Sea, leading to the fractionally philosophical school of half-skepticism. But the teleological force of the boat's or poet's regretful end, retroactively imposed on the whole poem, which leads her to read *voyance* as half-skepticism when she sees fit, also prevents her from recognizing any such irony or critical distance in the later line about going to the sea. "I sometimes saw what man thought he saw" is ironic and half-skeptical, but "Let me go to the sea" does not suggest nostalgia for what has been retreated from. The reference to *voyance* is less than literal, she decides, whereas a desire for annihilation in the waves is purely literal.

Now, I don't want to suggest that a lamentation cannot cohabit with a celebration, nor would I want to discourage Suzanne Bernard from her interpretive efforts, for this is one of the rare moments throughout her voluminous annotations where she actually seems to be reading in something like a proactive sense, rather than attributing sources as she is usually content to do. What I want to emphasize is the extent to which the interpretive dilemma of a line such as "O que j'aille à la mer!" describes the space that opens between literal and figurative language. It seems banal enough to say that poetry develops its rhetorical force precisely within that space, and one would presume criticism or analysis of poetry—to the extent that it is concerned with the semantics of the poem—to concentrate on what occurs within that space, on the relations of figurative force.

Poetry is presumed to make an explicit virtue out of what a diatribe of, or on, the proper would seek to occlude. The diatribes or discourses of blood and soil purport to retain a literal, elemental connection to real blood and soil even as they multiply the metonymic references to family, nation, country, and so on, disavowing their figurative impulse. Poetry should be an antidote to that, which is not to say that we could not find numerous examples of the poetry of blood and soil. How the rhetorical excess of, for example, enflamed and inflammatory political discourse is to be distinguished from the rhetorical excess of poetry is a complicated question. But we find here striking evidence of how a stupefyingly gigantic industry of traditional poetic criticism or interpretation itself works to reduce the figurative effect of poetry, operating in parallel with more reductive discourses of literality, returning the sense of the poem to a native soil of its own. That is achieved by closing the semantic space so that a commentator will systematically decide questions of reference in terms of allusion, as a matter of accurate attribution (or restitution) of sources. It is only when a Suzanne Bernard cannot find an allusion to, or borrowing from, some other source—Chateaubriand, Hugo, *Magasin pittoresque*, Rimbaud himself—that she will venture an interpretation such as we have just seen.

A poetry of rhetorical excess on the level of Rimbaud's raises that practice of explicative insistence to a frenzied pitch and demonstrates clearly how the literality of attribution of sources functions in concert with much more adventurous strokes of interpretive genius. In both cases, whether the poem is brought back to its genetic source or sent out toward an ultimate hermeneutic destination, a similar reductivism is at work. This can be seen in exemplary action in interpretations of Rimbaud's "Voyelles" (Vowels). That poem's first line—"A noir, E blanc, I rouge, U vert, O bleu"—inscribes an incompatible apposition of two literal series, that of vowels and that of colors. One can reconcile those series as the fact of a nominalizing and literalizing fiat, say, "Okay, A is black, E is white, and so on, Rimbaud wants it that way"; or one can wrestle with the figurative space that is simultaneously opened and try to explain why, according to what metaphoric or other logic, A would be represented as black, E as white. The rest of the sonnet raises the stakes for both of those choices, expanding on the initial qualifications ascribed to each vowel, so that A becomes the "hairy black corset of shining flies that buzz around cruel stenches," and so on. From 1904 onward, many presumed that Rimbaud had created his poem on the basis of a colored childhood alphabet primer. But the presumption of that literal point of departure did not deter later commentators from searching for a rigorous and systematic interpretation; knowing where the poem began did not answer the question of where its meaning ended. A claim to the definitive interpretation of "Voyelles" was made by a provincial high school teacher, Robert Faurisson, in 1961, who opined that the sonnet's ultimate sense was erotic: the vowels develop a pictographic rendering of the female body, the sonnet describes the sexual act, its title reads "Vois-Elles" (See-She[s]). Such a sexualization of the text provoked fulminations from traditional Rimbaud scholars, among them the redoubtable Sorbonne professor René Étiemble, who saw fit to bring Faurisson into line and bring Rimbaud back down to a different type of earth, that of "the literary modes of his time and the dominant images of his work."[16] But Faurisson's interpretation simply insists on a different form of literality than that of Bernard or Étiemble; it similarly wants to contain the semantic ocean within circumscribed borders, however exotic or erotic they be; it wants to draw the lines and stem the tide. On one side and the other, such commentators presume that poetic sense has an identifiable origin and source. As a result, they are able to anchor it here in a children's book, there in an act of coitus. Supposedly excessive rhetorical departures, like Faurisson's interpretation, are possible precisely because they are employed in the service of an ultimate return to a nonpoetic literal soil.

As it happened, after solving the problem of "Voyelles," Faurisson went on to build a reputation as one of France's most notorious gas chamber revisionists, bringing his interpretive prowess to bear on proving that the Nazi Holocaust did not take place. That repeats on the one hand his propensity for the provocative, the contrarious, and the fantastic, whether he is reading Rimbaud or the historical record regarding the production and delivery of Zyklon B; but on the other hand, it may also confirm—to the extent that we can equate Holocaust revisionism with pro-Nazi ideology—a type of hermeneutic will to purity, an interpretative partiality or dogmatism that is underwritten by an ideology of the literal, by the presumption that wherever it is planted, meaning will nevertheless be rooted in the pure autochthonous soil, that whatever the climes to which the boat sets sail, it will nevertheless always come to be anchored at home.[17]

Suzanne Bernard's failings are not those of Faurisson. Yet she displays an extraordinary facility in her adjudications employed in the service of truth, in the presumption that even where she, or one of the other scholar-hounds she relies on, has not managed to unearth the veritable attribution or source of Rimbaud's words, such a source remains nevertheless to be found; that in the final analysis the proper sense of the poet's linguistic drunkenness will be found sober and at home in its literal and proper place (although what "literal" means, when a poetic word has been traced back to another poem or work of fiction or nonfiction, is itself an interpretive dilemma of no small dimension).

After noting so astutely that Rimbaud had never seen the sea, Bernard concludes that he had recourse to "memories of childhood navigations on the Meuse, and his readings," in order to compose his poem (422). Madame Noulet, who, Bernard tells us, has made a list of such "numerous possible sources," nevertheless warns that "it would be too easy to multiply the references [rapprochements]." Bernard seems to agree that caution is in order. Rimbaud, she avers, "chose his materials where he found them" (422). Based on that sound science and impeccable logic, she sets about adjudicating. In note 2 she disagrees with a certain M. Mespoulet when he attributes something to Chateaubriand, opting not to identify it as a literary borrowing, declaring that "in fact, this detail seems to me to represent a rather banal exoticism" (423). Two notes further on, however, she affirms with conviction that a reference to children is "significant" because it is "evidently of an autobiographical character" (423), although she declines to specify what the autobiographical experience referred to might have been (apart from the experience of being a child). Following that she reverts briefly to a greater level of imprecision—"probable allusion" (note 6), "perhaps an allusion" (note 8)—before again drawing lines in the sand in note 11, where there "seems to be a double memory of Hugo" (424), and in note 15, where, as I noted, the expression "what man thought he saw" seems "especially to allude" to Rimbaud's theory of "*voyance*" (424). A reference to Leviathan becomes the occasion for her to evoke the literary allusions made explicit by Colonel Godchot and H. Béraud, adding one of her own before suggesting that Rimbaud could, all the same, also have been thinking of less precise sea yarns (425–26). However, about the word *entonnoir* she is categorical: "It comes from Poe, translated by Baudelaire" (427). This crater is a crater and nothing more, but it is Poe's and Baudelaire's crater nevertheless. "Future vigor," on the other hand, she thinks she wants to insist, must be given a "wider philosophical and perhaps social sense" (427). And so it goes, right to the end. In her final note, she hesitates, regarding the final line, between a reference to a precise experience in the life of the young poet, and merely the "fatigue, somnolence and desire for annihilation that so often took hold of Rimbaud" (429).

I do not doubt that what a poet writes is in some, perhaps great, measure determined by what he or she lives and reads. That is a commonplace. Nor do I want to suggest that interpretation does not have to rely on the intertextual network of references a poem makes. My quarrel is, first and as already developed, with the presumption that the task of the scholarly reader should reduce to attributing a precise and identifiable literary or biographical significance to each term employed by an illuminated poet reveling in the carnival of an oceanic expressive binge; and second, with the staggering imprecision of such an allusive treasure hunt or witch hunt, which seems to give the critic license to successively occupy different and seemingly random points along the gamut of referential possibility, here borrowing from a literary source, there from a childhood experience, here perhaps or maybe, there definitely, here philosophical intent, there just a word.

That reading is definitively adrift on an ocean is something I want to affirm rather than deny. Reading begins only once one consents to cross the ocean of the expanse of tropic possibility, within which the literal has to be understood as one *figurative* position among others; the ocean of the contextual inexhaustiveness that results; and the ocean of an interminable labor of interpretation that is required. Reading begins only once one has left the home soil of the original text, and it drifts thereafter, buoyed by what is never anything more than the lure of a return to that soil, to identifiable, definitive, literal meaning. There is no line in the sand for it, but rather an ocean of possibility. Similarly, a Europe that did not fall back on the model defined by the crossing of the Red Sea—an ocean for a wall on either side of it and the threat of annihilation of anyone with the temerity to follow it without permission into its future flowing with milk and honey—would have to begin precisely by renouncing the strict European context, by recognizing, and immersing itself in, the ocean at the limits of Europe, beyond its colonial reach, the ocean at the limits of the limit by means of whose imposition Europe defines and redefines itself. That was the ocean whose figure I outlined in reading Exodus, as the Europe and reading of Europe (and of political and nationalist aspirations in general) that begins where a line is drawn in the sea to inaugurate a religious and geopolitical entity, a line that seeks to define and discriminate, as if drawn in the sand, but is obliged to recognize that the presumptively singular line drawn is also redrawn, drawing back to itself, to confound itself, the ocean itself. In the ocean that is reading there is always more reading, and more to be read: it takes place in and as such an abyss, can never reduce to any identitarian singularity, finally resolves nothing.

It is therefore as if, as suggested from the beginning, this will have amounted to nothing, nothing that is not the banality of a self-evidence. I could no doubt have put it more simply; I didn't need to give myself over to the rhetorical excess of the preceding pages. But within the space of that rhetoric or that discourse, as I also stated at the beginning, history and politics fall and occur. Not just because political discourse of the type leading to or ensuing from momentous historical events often takes on the rhetorical dimensions of a song like the one Miriam danced to; nor because history and politics fall and occur in the same way as words in a song or poem. Rather, because there is something of a common space and an ocean of indiscrimination between the pure literality of history and politics and the discursive or figurative structures that they are supposed to produce. Now, on the one hand, this is to accept the commonplace that political discourse folds back into political action; there is a certain cr tensivity of word and deed. But, on the other hand, there is mo· than that. While I was writing what precedes, there was blood ·

remained "there," as if literally. It flowed, it was poured into the soil, the soil itself was fought over. That takes place all the time; it is another commonplace. But I would venture that none of it took place without being inscribed in a discursive gesture, that even for the flowing, pouring, and especially the fighting to take place, the blood and soil had to be *rhetoricized*. That is to say, moreover, that such discourse or rhetoric was never just an accompaniment to a literal act that could have taken place without it, but functioned rather as the figuration that precisely gave to the act its supposed literal sense. The most elemental and violent acts are, it seems, the most in need of the rhetorical expansion that they so often, grandiloquently or silently, give rise to; a rhetorical expansion that, conversely, they perform. Cut-and-dried stabbing and shooting, sniping or bombarding, are awash in that ocean; however silently and cruelly they are performed, however secret their crimes and traceless their victims, they derive their force from a type of rhetorical potential, from being able to speak outside the pure literality of the act itself. This is not just to say that the mute political act has no sense, that to have a political sense, it has to advertise itself as such, send a message. It also means we can presume and hope that there will be no unuttered crimes and no permanently silenced victims. In singing the defeat of the Egyptians, Miriam's oceanic song and dance necessarily brings horses and riders back from destruction and oblivion; it washes up the buried corpses that it celebrates, and renders itself susceptible to a turning of the tide. The ocean washes both ways.

One would have to say in the end that history and politics, of the type involving blood shed over parcels of soil, are undecidably the literal reduction or the figurative extension of the inflammatory discourses that accompany them. They fall and occur within a similar ocean, and we need to set out across that ocean to read them, to adjudicate among them, resorting neither to presumption nor to imprecision, following rigorous protocols that respect the lines wherever they are drawn yet allow for the invention of a journey within them and within their self-divisions, an aquatic or "desertic" sojourn by means of which there would arise the possibility of seeing anew "what man thought he saw." Rimbaud's narrator exposes himself to the ocean's extremes and comes to see things differently, as if correcting the record. Far from being a half-skeptical allusion to the theory of *voyance,* seeing sometimes what man thought he saw can be understood to describe history's possibility of being rewritten, the possibility that the undiscriminating ocean will, in its extreme overwash and over-load, become the context, however difficult and interminable, for the very inventory and dedication to archival precision that is history itself; the possibility that, within rather than in spite of, or against the ocean itself, lines will come to be drawn.

Regrettably, we are far from that possibility. As I write, we see anew what we thought we had seen on another side of the relation between history and politics and discourse. We see it again, and it looks all too familiar. We have seen lines drawn, just when we thought we had seen it all, more than we needed to, long ago and yesterday, in Europe, in the Middle East, and in Africa, lines drawn clear through villages, through houses, through kinships, through bodies, making irrevocably solid distinctions that nevertheless serve to reduce villages and houses, kinships and bodies, to seas of dust and bloodied sand. History and politics thus also fall within the space of discourse to the extent that they fall as appalling and unimaginable, unspeakable things. In every sense, everyday. Such unspeakable things fall on both sides of the rhetorical equation, being both banal and everyday commonplaces, and excessive, intolerable, outrageous, even inconceivable extravagances. They fall so deviantly, so monstrously, yet with such commonplace frequency, blood flows so freely, sufficient that the "multitudinous seas incarnadine" as Shakespeare has Macbeth awfully presage, making the green ocean red.[18] Everyday death and suffering are a commonplace, yet there is nothing banal about them. At a certain point nothing more should be said or written about that for fear of reducing it to the banal on the one hand or over-rhetoricizing it on the other. One should draw the line there. But in doing so, one needs to remember, positioned as we inevitably are never very far from it, before us and behind us, never immune from the effects and sensations of it, pacific and not so, exposed to one wave or another of it every time we plot the lines and outlines of our discourse, which means that we can never just speak and write without also living and dying, saving and annihilating, one needs to remember that there is ocean, the ocean that we will likely hear or even smell before we see it, harking back to our quadruped animal origins, and the ocean that, like an immense natural earthmover, effortlessly erases the line of that origin and sweeps us from the beginning into technology, the ocean keeps coming and keeps coming upon us, even as it stands back, it keeps coming upon us here and everywhere, now and always.

And after the telephone call, I will turn my back on you to sleep, as usual, and you will curl up against me, giving me your hand, you will envelop me.

—JACQUES DERRIDA, *The Post Card*

5. Friendship in Torsion   Schmitt, Derrida

CARL SCHMITT'S LINE OF 1927, HOWEVER SPECIFIC TO POST-1648 Europe, is drawn as if straight from the mythology of the Red Sea, defining "the specific political distinction" as an "antithesis" of friend and enemy:

The distinction of friend and enemy denotes the utmost degree of intensity of a union or separation, of an association or dissociation. . . . The political enemy need not be morally evil or aesthetically ugly; he need not appear as an economic competitor. . . . But he is, nevertheless, the other, the stranger; and it is sufficient for his nature that he is, in a specially intense way, existentially something different and alien, so that in the extreme case conflicts with him are possible.[1]

Yet that antithesis relies on a further specific distinction between *hostis* and *inimicus,* between *polemios* and *ekhthros.* Schmitt's politics relate not to a private adversary but to a collective public enemy; the enemy he is talking about must be someone with whom one is so much at odds that one is capable of taking up arms against him, and not within the context of some private dispute. What makes a public enemy is precisely her specially intense otherness, her existential difference; she must be someone far enough removed to make it unlikely or impossible that one could have relations with her that would lead to a private friendship or personal enmity. For Schmitt, Christ's admonition in the Sermon on the Mount to love one's enemies applies only to the private adversary and "certainly does not mean that one should love and support the enemies of one's own people."[2] Never in a thousand years would it occur to one to forsake the cause of one's own people, even presuming those people included private adversaries, even presuming the enemies of one's people included personal friends. For that to occur, one's private adversaries at home or personal friends abroad would have to become numerous enough to constitute a new people with whom one might conceivably identify. Schmitt's political line thus explicitly redraws that of Exodus,

133

with Christians replacing the Jews and Turks replacing the Egyptians: "Never in the thousand year struggle between Christians and Moslems did it occur to a Christian to surrender rather than to defend Europe out of love toward the Saracens or Turks."[3]

In order to reinforce the distinction between public and private enemy, as precondition for the distinction between enemy and friend that defines the political, in order, by means of a strangely circular logic, to make the decision concerning the friend-enemy distinction an affair of "the state as an organized political entity,"[4] Schmitt further defines the enemy as someone one is capable of killing in a war. This raises the question of how to define a killing that gives rise to a war, such as, in the case closest to Schmitt, the assassination of Archduke Ferdinand, whether we should understand it as an act of private animosity or a strike against a public enemy. There is, however, no doubt in Schmitt's mind that war is what allows the enemy and, by extension, the political to coalesce:

> To the enemy concept belongs the ever present possibility of combat. . . . The friend, enemy and combat concepts receive their real meaning precisely because they refer to the real possibility of physical killing. . . . [War] is the most extreme consequence of enmity. It does not have to be common, normal, something ideal, or desirable. But it must nevertheless remain a real possibility for as long as the concept of the enemy remains valid.[5]

One should not underestimate the conceptual innovation introduced by Schmitt, the importance of a reasoning that extends backward from war to enemy to friend-enemy to public-private and thence to the political. In spite of his recourse, in examples at least, to familiar notions of ethnicity and religion as markers of difference and hence producers of enmity, his concept of the political does not derive, strictly speaking, from the organic immanence of a collective entity. It is less the constitution of a polis that represents the evolution from a state of nature than a retroactive fact of armed combat. Politics is not something that comes about once the friendship that is a natural function of human pity is no longer able to regulate communal relations, once an agricultural existence comes to be urbanized, as in Rousseau; nor is politics offered as the solution to the natural enmity of a war of all against all, as in Hobbes. Instead it is as if politics begins once a state decides on an enemy and goes to war against it. War is what makes the concept of the enemy valid and so permits the distinction between friend and enemy that defines the political. The enemy, and hence politics, are facts of war; but so too is friendship. According to the same logic whereby the enemy, emblematized by war, is the positive term for a definition of the political, it will have to be the virtuality of war that also defines friendship. There are friends only because there are enemies, and enemies only inasmuch as there are wars. Friendship is therefore something of a technomilitary by-product.

It goes further than that: Schmitt's distinction between friend and enemy does not just rely on the possibility of armed combat; from what we have already seen, warfare must function explicitly as a *confront*ation. A frontier must be drawn between combatants; the enemies must carry out their mortal dispute along a front. Hence his hesitations concerning civil war, the partisan, and the guerrilla. A distinct line between frontally opposed combatants is what serves to figure and to define the opposition between friend and enemy. An enemy, no more than a friend, cannot in this sense appear at the back, come from behind, be dorsal, for that would mean that the homogeneity of a space and people that Schmitt's reasoning ultimately falls back on had been disturbed. The spatial integrity of a frontier and the contiguity of territories divided by that frontier underwrite his concept of the political, which is also, therefore, a concept of frontality. Whatever disturbs that frontality also problematizes the spatial configuration, interrupting the contiguity, introducing a distance and an irregularity that cause the front to lose its definition. War will henceforth have to deal with that distance and irregularity, to become a form of teleconfrontation, which is indeed what comes to pass in the period of history that Schmitt is observing.

That is made clear in Derrida's analysis of Schmitt in *Politics of Friendship*. From the moment of its title, the book is addressed to Schmitt, and it contests explicitly his definition of the political in terms of the enemy, analyzing in detail certain points just repeated here.[6] Indeed, it is on the basis of Schmitt's *polemios/ekhthros* distinction that Derrida develops his "*genealogical* deconstruction of the political" and argues for another politics and another democracy (104). The genealogical deconstruction of the political is "a deconstruction, at once genealogical and a-genealogical, *of the* genealogical . . . [of] the approbation given to filiation, at birth and at the origin, to generation, to the familiarity of the family, to the proximity of the neighbour" (105). It aims at Schmitt's presumption of a "telluric autochthony," his reliance, in defining the enemy, on blood and soil, on ethnicity and religion. Derrida finds that to be particularly evident in Schmitt's later text *Theorie des Partisanen*.[7] But he also emphasizes the references Schmitt makes there to the increasing motorization of combat, acknowledging how the expansion of space, speed, and the motorization that characterize modern warfare complicate the boundaries separating friend from enemy that seemed so much clearer in 1927. Schmitt thereby recognizes the influence of what Derrida calls "tele-technical automation" and the destabilizing effect it has on telluric autochthony. For it means finally that, coming before or from behind the attachment of a people to a space is an originary deracination that can be called technological. Telluric autochthony is indeed "already a reactive response to a delocalization and to a form of tele-technology" (142); one digs in and holds to one's home-land precisely because one is already, from the beginning, losing one's grip on it. The very space of it, however small, makes one's experience of it tele-relational, requiring the technological artifice of telecommunica-tional apparatuses in order to connect to it.

Thus the front lines on the basis of which the enemy and friend come to be defined are broken up by the dorsal effect of lines of technologiz-ation traversing the community in general. The enemy may not be, for Schmitt, the neighbor who let his old pickup rust and rot on the edge of your property, or the driver who stole your parking place; it may be that the only true political enemy is one who is especially intensely and exis-tentially alien; a line of people not our own arrayed in violent confron-tation against us. But to go to meet an enemy conceived of in that way, we must leave home, traverse the space that constitutes our homeland, and enter into complicated configurations of remoteness and the tech-nological negotiations of that remoteness, beginning with the letters and postcards home that constitute a whole literature of warfare. And further-more, as we have consistently seen throughout these analyses, from the moment we have a home, just by emerging from the soil, we have made some sort of break with our natural attachment to that soil; we have left it and crossed a boundary into exile.

Thus the unmanned warfare of drones and smart bombs no doubt takes to its logical extreme the motorization that Schmitt already observed in the first half of the twentieth century, problematizing irrevocably the relations among territory, enemy, and indeed politics; but, as Derrida makes clear, an originary and generalized teletechnology operates as it were behind and within autochthony itself, giving rise to it as a reactive response. It is at work at home itself, in the mythic homogeneity of the self-constitution of a people, well before that people finds another people over the way to be its enemy, and well before the military hardware is rolled out and the forces deployed. Because of that, the front is never constituted in any purity; its regularity and integrity are disturbed by other lines of force. And because of that, a certain indistinction comes to invade the opposition between friend and enemy, the indistinction of a teletechnologization. If, in Schmitt's terms, the front defines the warfare that defines the enemy that defines the friend (all of which define politics), then a front destabilized by technological fault lines emanating all the way from home will transmit those fault lines and that technology through the definitions of enemy and friend (not to mention politics). According to that logic, somewhere between 1927 and 1963, friendship will have come not only to depend on technomilitarization but to be defined as teletechnological.

WHAT SENSE could one give to that? What would be the sense of a technological or technologized friendship, a friendship that operates in that manner, by definition, against nature? We can imagine friendships that might be deemed unworthy of the name because something in them betrays the very positivity we ascribe to amity: the friendship of rogues, an unholy alliance, or friendships of convenience. We could also imagine a friendship that demeans for one reason or another, or a friendship that is excessive according to this or that norm or expectation, and so is considered reprehensible. We could even imagine what some might consider an unhealthy relation between human and animal (he spends all his time with his dog), or human and machine (she spends all her time with her car), but it would still be a matter of the various moral rights of inspection by which what is supposed proper to friendship is controlled and determined. Such relations would be held to demean or pervert friendship without, for all that, calling into question what constitutes it.

What if, instead, we were to imagine a friendship that was unnatural in its very conception, a concept of friendship that did not suppose it to issue from a beating heart, or some seat of emotion, obeying instead some mechanical automation? In short, a friendship artificially conceived or produced, what we might call a technological or prosthetic friendship? In spite of where a certain reading of Schmitt's logic takes us, we still presume that no such thing exists. And in spite of Derrida's analysis of Schmitt, its possibility is not entertained by the various philosophical discourses on friendship that are the objects of study in *Politics of Friendship*. Friendship, it seems, is systematically an affair of the natural and of the living. An unnatural friendship might be conceived of as an immoral friendship, an uneconomical or wasteful one, but one that in no way impugned the vital originary force of its pathos, its pneumaticity. However, it is also evident, from Aristotle on, that the life that animates friendship does not have to operate on both sides. As Derrida reads Aristotle, "being loved . . . always remains possible on the side of the inanimate" (12); one can love the dead or, by extension, an object. Indeed, it seems precisely an unnatural friendship, at least some form of a *postnatural* friendship, that Derrida is promoting once Schmitt's distinction between *polemios* and *ekhthros* leads him to evoke "a deconstruction *of the* genealogical schema . . . to think and live a politics, a friendship, a justice which *begin* by breaking with their naturalness or their homogeneity, with their alleged place of origin" (105). As we saw earlier, the deconstruction and originary rupture he has in mind in that context have to do with the thinking and implementation of another politics or democracy, and not with my idea of deconstituting the concept of friendship that is limited to the living. But clearly, a friendship that is also a politics has in some way been *impersonalized,* if not *depersonalized.* It has gone public or become something of a business relationship in a way that exceeds, or acts in competition with, what we naively understand friendship to be, even if it hasn't gone all the way to a relationship of allies as a prelude to combat. For if we follow Schmitt at all, the very question of friendship is posed as a problematics of public versus private space. On one side, the enemy is, for Schmitt, always and necessarily a public enemy. But on the other side, friendship is a more complicated matter. Whereas amorous and familial relations are presumed to be private, and economic or political relations public, friendship should be able to function across the border separating the former from the latter. Friendship would be always already "corrupted" by politics, by a politics that is presumed to function outside it, and it therefore raises the question of its own supposed originary naturality. If friendship partakes of politics, would not the naturality that founds friendship also be seen to enter into a relation with some form of unnaturality?

Let me add another layer of questions. What would such an unnatural friendship look like? What does any friendship look like? What is its phenomenological representativity, or appresentativity? How do we know, visibly, for example, that such a thing exists, and what would the sense of it be, outside its performance? How could it operate outside a frequentation (seeing two people, say, corresponding or keeping company), or outside an exchange (of embraces, of gestures, of tokens, and so on)? Not that a secret friendship isn't possible, but we would have to presume its very secrecy to be a function of its performativity. I mean by that that the very effects of its secrecy would have to be negotiated in function of the fact that most friends show signs of affection; one could keep a friendship private only by scrupulously avoiding the public; one could keep it secret only by scrupulously declining to show the signs of it, by *performing the nonperformance of the signs of friendship,* which is not the same as *not performing the signs of friendship* in the way that nonfriends do. Furthermore, how would a phenomenology of friendship be distinguished from, or opposed to, that of something called love or passion? Is there a figure for friendship analogous to, but distinguishable from, what exists in a relation of passion; analogous to, but distinguishable from, the act of love, lovemaking, the carnal embrace? Or is it rather that friendship acts like a "preliminary" subset of the carnal, with looks, smiles, touching, embraces, and so on, but stopping before it gets to certain types of kiss and all the rest? If the carnal includes all the signs of friendship (as well as much more), then does friendship—at least to look at, the way we see it—have any specificity other than that of a domesticated or controlled carnality? For if, to follow Schmitt, the confrontation that constitutes enmity requires a specific regime of visibility—attitudes and acts of aggression, having the enemy in one's sights, the whole oculo-ballistic paradigm—then a friendship modeled otherwise would have to be approached from and with a different regard, according to different forms of knowledge. How that might be so is a question that will be left somewhat in suspense but in circulation, as if caught in the fact and figure of its "pose," while we return in more detail to *Politics of Friendship.*

Politics of Friendship inscribes an originary heterogeneity in friendship as a means of arguing for a different genealogizing of it, and so of politics; its argument is that friendship needs to be otherwise politicized, and politics needs to be otherwise structured, in terms of amity. But Derrida's book also raises questions concerning the rigorous purity of the distinction between friendship and love or friendship and the madness of passion. While raising those questions, Derrida to a great extent respects the tradition of the distinction; to do otherwise, he writes, would involve an impossible analytical project ("it would take another book" [221]). But his whole analysis comes and goes between the two, via an extraordinarily complex configuration, as I hope to show. One is left, in a sense, twisting and turning between love and friendship, as between *philia* and *eros,* and it is as if, in the final analysis, it all adds up to nothing so much as the turning itself, the *torsion* of a *tropic* catastrophe through which one continues to hear the disembodied voices of Diogenes Laertius, Aristotle, Cicero, Montaigne, Nietzsche, Blanchot, and others, repeating something while no longer knowing where they first heard it. But it might, at the same time, add up to a different *configur*ation among them, a set of different poses for friendship that amount to different positions for politics.

In order to quickly approach the vantage point I want to work from, I will contend that friendship presumes the figure of an *inter-view,* a reciprocal perception, a face-to-face symmetry. That is what Schmitt's definition of the enemy conversely presupposes. In referring to the "figure" presumed by friendship, I am both evoking and avoiding the ethical relation, with its complicated relations both to visuality and reciprocity, which I analyzed in detail in chapter 2. Rather than return to the existential functioning of the ethical relation that concerns Levinas, I wish here to suppose that if a classical friendship looks like something, it looks like an interview. That would be its paradigmatic figure, which would not exclude its overlapping with what, in certain cases, the confrontation that is enmity also looks like, or with what eroticism looks like; but in general terms, the paradigm erotic figure would be a form of embrace, and the hostile figure a violent contact or the back-to-back that initiates a duel. Within those same figural terms, a repoliticized friendship would look like a dissymmetrical something; it would involve a turn out of symmetricality or a torsion of it; it would therefore tend toward the back to front, to the dorsal rather than the frontal. I contend that only from the perspective of such a dorsality could a friendship and a politics, and in the end a sexuality, of and for the technological age begin to develop. Only by turning out of what appears as a natural face-to-face amicable relation, which means acknowledging the detour through a type of tropological machinery—nothing more to begin with than the tropo-technology of the turning itself—can there be another politics of friendship, a politics other than what Schmitt prescribes. Such a politics, which we should not too hurriedly call a posthumanist politics, would seem, after all, to be the very wager of *Politics of Friendship*.

Thus a certain figurality—a word I will distinguish from "positionality"—of love and friendship, sex and politics, will form the basis of this analysis. Roland Barthes described his fragments of a lover's discourse as choreographic figures, "to be understood, not in [their] rhetorical sense, but rather in [their] gymnastic or choreographic acceptation.... the body's gesture caught in action."[8] I would argue that, short of a thesis, there is a type of choreography to be drawn out of the relations between politics and friendship as Derrida discusses them, a series of turns and tropologies that articulate a complicated figural or figurative set of gestures. It is as if, in looking at friendship as it articulates with politics, we see certain corporeal gestures or movements; as if there were complicated turns of amicable discourse deriving as much from friendship's relation to the political as from its relation to the carnal, turns that imply and implicate, therefore, both a rhetoric and an erotics. And a technology, for (as I have argued from the beginning) the turn is to be conceived of as the originary corporeal tropology by which the body extends out of itself, into the space of a dorsal otherness where its technological other has always been waiting to surprise it. What follows will play across the distinction between love and friendship in pointing toward a figure, or set of figures, common to both and yet remaining consonant with the lines of argument that are developed and the distinctions that are drawn in *Politics of Friendship*; a figure or set of figures that gesture toward friendship's dorsal otherness. While being sympathetic to Derrida's arguments and distinctions, the discussion will perform something of a torsion of them, a turning, *détournement* or diverting, yet still within the context of a re-con-figuration, a particular rearrangement and perspectival shift.

The choreographic tropology of friendship emerges from two directions in Derrida. First there is the explicit strategy of *Politics of Friendship*, a book that grew out of a seminar that, from week to week, repeatedly staged that epigraph of doubtful origin, "O my friends, there is no friend." That, in Derrida's words, was in order to have the "scenography" of its interpretation turn as if "around itself" (viii, *Politiques,* 12). Much later we are reminded that zigzagging is the very mode of a history of friendship, which consists in "a series of ruptures which intersect their own trajectories before turning back along a different one" (221). Second, turning, and versions of dorsality *(tourner le dos, dans le dos, derrière le dos)* represent a complex thematic figurality in Derrida's work, especially the work with an autobiographical strain of one sort or another, beginning perhaps with *Glas* and becoming explicit again in *The Post Card,* where we are told that "everything is connoted in *do,* there are only the backs *[dos]* that count," and "there will only be back *[du dos],*" and whose penultimate paragraph declares: "I will ask myself what *to turn around* has signified from my birth or thereabouts."[9] It would be hard to overestimate the importance of this figural nexus, which generates the signatory effects of many of Derrida's texts and functions as a structuring force for the rhetorical gestures discussed hereafter. As we shall see, Derrida turns as if dancing in and out of the texts he is analyzing, here and elsewhere, finally giving more back than anything else. In Jean-Luc Nancy's words, "He puts himself forward, in order to turn around and be nothing but his back. . . . Not only to be seen only from behind, but in order to *be* simply the back, in the absolute sense of being."[10] There would necessarily be something of that back in his relation to friendship, in his politics of friendship.

Turning is thus explicit from the beginning of *Politics of Friendship;* one of its major chapters is entitled "Recoils,"[11] and by the end, with Blanchot's formulation of a friendship of abandon(ment) through death (301–2) seeming to reprise the model inaugurated by Aristotle (9–12), the choreographic sense has been developed far enough to suggest that friendship involves turning one's back. The ultimate friend, in this sense, is the one we permit to leave us. Hence, if there is to be a figure for distinguishing friend from enemy beyond both interview and confrontation, it will be the gesture of turning one's back, a politics of friendship as *dorsality.* It would be a choreographic instance that looks neither like a breaking off of negotiations—walking away from talking, from the table, the end of diplomacy that for Schmitt does not exist as long as it retains as outside possibility its continuation by means of war—nor like turning the other cheek, which can occur only after friendship has foundered on an

initial act of violence. And if I am still insisting on a visual version or phenomenality of that gesture, it would be because it takes place only once
friendship has broken out of the circuit of the sentimental, out of the self-
enclosure of its organic privacy or secrecy, become political and—this is
my insistence—become technological. Such a turning of the back would
be the figure for a particular fiduciary relation in the world, the opening to
what cannot be foreseen or controlled, what functions without us, and the
trust that that implies, its presumption of nonenmity, something functioning beyond an economics of appropriation, within the *aneconomics*
and *ana*logic of the "perhaps" that is the opening to a hospitality of radical
otherness promoted by Derrida throughout his discussion.

To configure the question of friendship as a *hypothesis* about turning one's back, about "facing" back to front, where "hypothesis" is itself
understood in the similarly choreographic sense of a turning toward a
positionality, we will need to work through the complicated rhetorico-
philosophico-political formulations, and compounding abyssal enfoldings
and reversals, of *Politics of Friendship.* As Derrida makes explicit in the
first of the many parenthetical insertions within his text that will ultimately become the focus of my reading, in "striving to speak . . . in the
logic of [Aristotle] . . . doing everything that seems possible to respect
the conceptual veins of his argumentation," one finds oneself changing
the tone and embarking on "some slow, discreet or secret drift" that is
undecidably "conceptual, logical or *properly philosophical*" rather than
"psychological, *rhetorical or poetic*" (13; italics mine).

A first set of rhetorico-conceptual junctures in *Politics of Friendship*
may be identified simply as turns, beginning with the pivotal role given
to the epigraph "O my friends, there is no friend," and with the form of
the epigraph itself. As I have just suggested, the reader is led through the
versions the motto borrows in context after context and from the pen
of writer after writer. As Derrida emphasizes, this maxim, by means of
which friendship is analyzed, is a trope (a rhetorical "detour") that is
itself a turning. "O my friends" constitutes an example of the figure called
"apostrophe," that singular form of address that involves, as explained in
the preface to *The Post Card,* "a live interpellation (the man of discourse or
writing interrupts the continuous development of the sequence, abruptly
turns toward someone, that is, something, addresses himself to you)";[12]
or, as repeated in *Politics of Friendship,* "this impulse by means of which I

turn towards the singularity of the other, towards you, the irreplaceable one" (5; italics mine).

However, "O my friends, there is no friend" turns, in turn, within itself. It has the form of a chiasmus, whose two parts intersect by means of a reverse impulse. The end of the saying comes around and back to meet its middle, creating an imperfect symmetry, such that it could be rewritten "O my friends, friend there is none." But this chiasmatic structure, that of a folding back, gets compounded once Derrida draws attention to the alternative version of the expression, where the initial omega of the presumed Greek original is accented to shift from the simple vocative interjection of an address made to "my friends," to a dative. "O my friends" thus becomes something like "he for whom there are (many) friends," and the full sentence shifts to mean "he who has (many) friends can have no true friend." Derrida nicknames the latter version the *repli* (209), translated as "recoil," which is one of its senses, but the English word loses the nuance that matters to me here, that of a folding back or turning in upon itself. "Recoil" does, however, suggest the somewhat vertiginous series of twists or zigzags along which the motto is deployed throughout two-hundred-odd pages of analysis.

To summarize what I have just tried to describe: a trope (rhetorical turn) that is an apostrophe (turn to a single addressee) borrows the form of a chiasmus (a syntagm that turns back on itself) whose exact version (Latin *vertere*, "to turn") is uncertain, potentially diverting or turning its sense, or at least creating a further turn or chiasmus (Derrida's word, 213) between its two forms. But what is all the more telling about the attention given to the alternate rendition and reading of the "O my friends" maxim is the reflective and almost cautious manner in which Derrida introduces it, the explicit reference he makes to the rhetorical ploy or gesture that he is thereby advancing. I am referring simply, for the moment, to the *fact* of that reflection and caution—I will shortly examine their *substance*—and to the gestures of rhetorical, exegetical, and scriptural intervention that they represent as yet another turn in the abyssal layerings that striate the book. The reader cannot help but notice that, above and beyond his "discovering" another version of the maxim, or his reading of that version, Derrida pays particular metadiscursive attention to the means by which his reading is being deployed. More about that shortly.

A second set of gestures in, or movements of, Derrida's text may be characterized as reversals. However difficult it may always have been to conceive of a pure linear movement, we nevertheless understand a turn to be by definition disjunctive, a shift away from the straightforward, and the reflecting chiasmus of "O my friends / there is no friend" reinforces that. Derrida begins chapter one of *Politics of Friendship* by emphasizing the contretemps of the "two disjoined members of [that] same unique sentence" (1). Such a contretemps works against any simple reciprocality that the figure of the chiasmus might seem to imply. In spite of producing a type of symmetry, which would necessarily be imperfect except in the case of a palindrome, and in any case given the two opposing directional movements, the chiasmus involves a disjunctive force that allows, potentially at least, for substitution and reversal. The folded-back second half of the syntagm sets itself up in competition with the first half, overlaying what precedes and effectively having the last word. Indeed, substitute and reverse are precisely what the maxim does, once the "no friend" of the second half replaces and contradicts the "my friends" of the first.

Again, upon examination, more such reversals are to come. Aristotle, we read, breaks with the reciprocity of friendship, its two-way traffic ("the reciprocalist or *mutualist* schema of requited friendship" [10]), to argue for a preference of loving over being loved (or liked). Since it is possible to be loved passively, without knowing it, and since in general terms it is better to be the active party, he gives preference to the one doing the loving, and this makes for what Derrida calls "the necessary unilaterality of a dissymmetrical *philein*" (23–24). Now, while that perhaps says more about Aristotle's conceptions of activity and passivity than about friendship ("Being-loved certainly speaks to something of *philia*, but. . . . It says nothing of friendship itself" [8]), it nevertheless describes a friendship, "friendship itself," true friendship, that would have to contend with two equally perplexing alternatives: the seeming impossibility of two active parties who lack an object for that activity, two parties loving each other without being loved one by the other; or a friendship that remains one-sided or lopsided, where only the active party is defined as a friend. Indeed, still following Aristotle, the really true friendship would be one that was lopsided to the extent of preferring love for the dead or departed. The activity of friendship that makes true friendship, however much it depends on the breath of a living, active soul, depends at the outside (an outside that becomes its innermost possibility) on death and mourning: "Friendship for the deceased thus carries this *philia* to the limit of its possibility. But at the same time, it uncovers the ultimate motive of this possibility. . . . I could not love friendship without engaging myself, *without feeling myself in advance* engaged to love the other beyond death. Therefore, beyond life" (12). It therefore looks as though the Aristotelian logic has reversed the supposed reciprocity of friendship to make it unilateral or unidirectional, and substituted a dead object for its living one.

Nietzsche, in typical fashion, gives his own series of twists to the question. The first is that of volume 1 of *Human, All Too Human*, where, as a riposte to the dying sage's "Friends, there are no friends!" the living fool retorts, "Foes, there are no foes!" For Derrida, the reversal constituted by this inversion or conversion, a simple substitution of the foe for the friend, "would perhaps leave things unaltered" (175). A second version, that of the "good friendship" described in the *Assorted Opinions and Maxims,* involves instead a more complicated "rupture in reciprocity or equality, as well as the interruption of all fusion or confusion between you and me" (62). But when, in a third example, Nietzsche writes in honor of friendship in *The Gay Science*, it is by means of a fable of a Macedonian king and an Athenian philosopher and is articulated through the logic of the gift, with all the disproportion or impossibility of any equilibrium of giving and receiving that that implies. Derrida refers to such a rupture as "a new twist, at once both gentle and violent," one that "calls friendship back to non-reciprocity, to dissymmetry or to disproportion" (63), and whose stakes are high, for it leads him directly into the heart of the aporetic "madness" of the chance of friendship, as of decision, justice, and democracy.[13]

Once again, beyond the reversals uncovered in the maxim, or in Aristotle or Nietzsche, Derrida enacts something of a reversal of his own with respect to the disjunctions or dissymmetries at work in the elaborations of friendship he is analyzing. This takes place precisely with respect to the distinction between friendship and love, along the fault line separating *philia* from *eros* (to the extent that one can presume that line to be the distinction between friendship and love, to the extent that any love can be conceived of as nonerotic), and amounts to a trembling of those differences. As we have just seen, he underlines what, in certain cases at least, appears undeniably as the disjunctivity and dissymmetricality of friendship. But in what seems to be a contrary move, in the context of his analysis of the other possible version of Aristotle's or Diogenes' maxim, Derrida calls on that very disproportionality to define love in contradistinction to friendship:

The request or offer, the promise or the prayer of an "I love you," must remain unilateral and dissymmetrical. Whether or not the other answers, in one way or another, no mutuality, no harmony, no agreement can or must reduce the infinite disproportion. . . . Here, perhaps, only here, could a principle of difference be found—indeed an incompatibility between love and friendship . . . supposing such a difference could ever manifest itself in its rigorous purity. . . . Simply put, friendship would suppose . . . the *phenomenon* of an appeased symmetry, equality, reciprocity between two infinite disproportions as well as between two absolute singularities; love, on the other hand, would raise or rend the veil of this phenomenon . . . to uncover the disproportion and dissymmetry as such. . . . When one names the friend or enemy, a reciprocity is supposed, even if it does not efface the infinite distance and dissymmetry. As soon as one speaks of love, the situation is no longer the same. (220–21, translation modified; cf. *Politiques*, 248–49)

The logic here is complicated and sets up a reverberating reversal between two sides of an opposition that functions as if in permanent imbalance, like some spinning machine that causes the whole apparatus to wobble. Love is unilateral, whereas friendship is less radically dissymmetrical. Friendship presents the reciprocity of two infinite disproportions that have made peace *(une réciprocité apaisée)*, whereas for its part, love rends the very veil of dissymmetry. But this difference, or indeed incompatibility, between love and friendship, is itself "appeased" inasmuch as the rigorous purity of the difference between the two cannot be presumed. It is as if between love and friendship there were either a relation of love (disproportion or incompatibility) or friendship (appeased reciprocity), and so on into the abyss, for each of the terms subdivides within itself ad infinitum.

But Derrida's reversal here is radical in another way. If love *is* to be distinguished from friendship, he maintains, it will be by means of the absence of reciprocity. As a result, "I love you" is spoken into a type of void, performed as a promise or prayer, to which one cannot expect an answer. We might therefore imagine it turned around to the extent of being uttered from behind, spoken into the back of the other, so that even if a response were to be proffered, even a symmetrical "I love you (too)," it would also be uttered into a type of emptiness in front of one. Derrida seems to suggest that only by means of the disproportionality of love can friendship be taken out of Schmitt's schema of amity and enmity and liberated from that version of the political; only by such a means can one gesture toward a different politics, one of promise. But if my analysis of Derrida's logic is correct, this will mean preserving and at the same time breaking down the distinction between friendship and love, dragging friendship kicking and screaming across an abyssal incompatibility that is perhaps not rigorously pure, and into the dissymmetricality of love. I doubt one could successfully choreograph such a rhetorical pirouette without having it teeter like an imbalanced spinning top and fall. But any attempt to do so, and any movement toward a new politics informed by either love or friendship or both, would necessarily involve, like a fleeting glimpse or a languid caress, a relation of front to back. There at least one could begin to see friendship and wait for love in terms of a dissymmetry that did not, for all that, collapse into an impossible contortion.

A TWIST or turn, even a torsion, without, for all that, being an impossible contortion. That would be the risk and wager of a politics of friendship that is called on to reckon with the dorsal. So it is also with the practice of deconstruction. We will have spent our professional lives trying to account for the difficult protocols of intervention within textual form and substance undertaken by such a reading practice, trying to determine what particular twists Derrida gives to the texts he is examining, how and to what extent he either identifies or "causes" the effects of stress on the basis of which the text says, is heard, let, or made to say more than it wants to. Since the exorbitance of the methodological question raised with respect to the analysis of Rousseau in *Of Grammatology*, we will have had those questions before us and been fascinated by the ways in which Derrida makes friends with, or makes love to, the textual objects he analyzes. This chapter has, up to this point, operated on the basis of certain presumptive answers to those questions, purporting to distinguish between turns or reversals that can be identified as the rhetorical gestures of here an Aristotle, there a Nietzsche, there a Derrida.

However, there appears to be a surplus of methodologically reflective moments in *Politics of Friendship,* and a multiplication of forms borrowed by such moments in the text. Most obvious, even if only typographically—no small thing, however—are the multiple parentheses, emblematic of a variety of interruptions, glosses, and diversions, interventions that can only be described, in the context of this discussion and of Derrida's book, as "apostrophic." I am referring here only to those parentheses that are set apart in the text as separate paragraphs, where the normal flow of the text is interrupted by a smaller or larger section that is placed within parentheses. There are also any number of parentheses doing what one might suppose to be normal duty within the text, adding short clarifications with minimal disruption to the reader. At one point, following a slew of those putative minor or everyday parenthetical insertions, Derrida writes, "And let's not talk about the parentheses, their violence as much as their untranslatability" (221; translation modified). Given that reference to violence and untranslatability, and since, in the final analysis, the everyday parentheses differ only in size, not in kind, from the larger inserted paragraphs or sets of paragraphs, we would have to remark the structural violence of any parenthetical insertion as a preface to what I am about to develop.

The larger, "apostrophic" parentheses begin in the foreword with a polylogue of four discursive units (x) and continue throughout the text, ranging in length from a single line (70) to twelve pages (in the French) (*Politiques,* 178–88) or more (I will come back to that "or more" in a moment). I counted twenty-six of them. Two of them use brackets rather than parentheses, and one of them says as much, although according to one reading of its syntax, those brackets can be imputed to Montaigne, which is something that gets lost in translation.[14] Their content varies enormously, and it is difficult to determine the precise logic that justifies them. Sometimes they constitute digressions that are perhaps too long for a footnote, but that has never been an objection for Derrida in the past. Sometimes they are reminders of previous points in the discussion, sometimes openings to other questions. Some of them, uncannily, deal with the question of the female friend or the sister whose exclusion or marginalization from philosophical discussions of friendship is a matter to which the book explicitly wants to draw readers' attention.

Still others, and these are the ones that interest me most, fall into the category of "questions of method" à la *Of Grammatology*. In this vein there is the reference to a "respect" for Aristotle that nevertheless involves "some slow, discreet or secret drift" that I quoted earlier (13). Derrida's next chapter admits to a similarly complicated logic of fidelity to Nietzsche: "Of course, we must quickly inform the reader that we will not follow Nietzsche here. Not in any simple manner. We will not follow him in order to follow him come what may" (33). At a particularly apostrophic moment in chapter 3, Derrida declares: "That is all I wanted to tell you, my friend the reader" (70). And much later, he inserts a perhaps unnecessary reminder that "we have not privileged the great discourses on friendship so as to submit to their authority . . . but, on the contrary, as it were, to question the process and the logic of a canonization. . . . *paying attention to what they say and what they do. This is what we wish to do and say*" (229; italics mine). Such metadiscursive glosses, however, do not always appear within parentheses, that is to say, as interventions circumscribed by a pair of conventional, round diacritical marks. Indeed, not only is there extensive explanation of the methodological protocols in play throughout the analysis of the *repli* version of "O my friends," but one needs to ask whether, following Derrida, one could ever hope to rigorously distinguish between the constative and performative elements of any commentary—indeed, any text—distinguishing what it says in general, and what it says about what it is doing in particular, from what it does. As we just read, Derrida does or says both (what he says and what he does) in the same breath.

Or in a slightly different breath. The matter of the two versions of the "O my friends" maxim turns precisely on the question of breathing, of aspiration, and of the diacritical textual intervention—a subscript iota—that would mark the same in the Greek: "It all comes down to less than a letter, to the difference of breathing" (209). According to how a single omega gets written, with or without the subscript iota denoting an aspirate, a whole philosophical tradition can be reassessed, including, one has to presume, that tradition's distinction between constativity and performativity. On the basis of what Derrida earlier calls "a philological sidetracking" (177)—in French *un mauvais aiguillage philologique* (*Politiques,* 201), bad directions, bad shunting, bad philological flight control, an inattentive switch from one track or corridor to another—there is potential accident and catastrophe. But we have to understand that almost imperceptible difference as also a formidable chance, the chance of a whole other text, a whole other reading, and a whole other tradition for the questions, for friendship and politics. By the time *Politics of Friendship* gets to it, therefore, it is difficult to tell who is taking credit for it, and that is perhaps no longer the question:

The time has perhaps come to decide the issue *[trancher]*. . . . A tiny philological *coup de théâtre* cannot prevail in the venerable tradition which, from Montaigne to Nietzsche and beyond, from Kant to Blanchot and beyond, will have bestowed so many guarantees on the bias of a copyist or a rushed reader by, without knowing it, staking a bet on a tempting, so very tempting, reading, but an erroneous one, and probably a mistaken one. Luckily for us, no orthographic restoration or archival orthodoxy will ever damage this other, henceforth sedimented archive, this treasure trove of enticed and enticing texts which will always give us more food for thought than the guard-rails to whose policing one would wish to submit them. No philological fundamentalism will ever efface the incredible fortune of a brilliant invention. For there is here, without doubt, a staggering artifact, the casualness of an exegetical move as hazardous as it is generous—indeed, abyssal—in its very generativity. Of how many great texts would we have been deprived had someone (but who, in fact?) not one day taken, and perhaps, like a great card player, deliberately feigned to take, one omega for another? Not even one accent for another, barely one letter for another, only a soft spirit *[esprit, breath, aspirate]* for a hard one—and the omission of the subscript iota. (207–8; *Politiques*, 234)

To give this passage its due, one would need, passionately, in and beyond friendship, to study it, as if face-to-back, from the perspective of those famous pages on Rousseau from *Of Grammatology*,[15] to see how far deconstructive reading practice had or had not evolved over the preceding thirty years of its history, and to assess the current *rapport de forces* between "philological fundamentalism" and "invention." Suffice to emphasize here that the glosses that punctuate or *apostrophize* the analysis of the *version de repli*—"where are we heading?" (214), "does one have the right to read like this?" (216), "it is [the temptation] of the book you are reading" (218), "our objective was not to start down this path" (220)—have to be considered to be as much a part of the analysis as the rest. Perhaps they are the very constative part of it, to the extent that they deal with the question of analysis *as analysis,* and perhaps an analysis that does not deal with its own status, that simply presumes to be able to (con)state, in fact reduces to a pure performative. In any case, those glosses, along with the abyssal twists, torsions, and openings, that go all the way from an almost inaudible *ɩ* to lengthy parenthetical excursus, inhabit finally the same structural space of possibility, the same rhetorico-political space as the "risk," chance, or wager of the "perhaps" and more properly philosophical questions—event, *aimance*—around which Derrida's text turns. All such questions derive from minute but uncontrollable textual ruptures, intersecting apostrophically with the secrets or silences of philological chance or accident, with the brilliant inventions of an insignificant stroke of the pen, the slight torsion or curvature of a line that produces or introduces the beginning of a parenthesis of untold promise.

The "perhaps," for example, emerges from Nietzsche's *Human, All Too Human* and is first developed in Derrida's second chapter, whose title ("Loving in Friendship: Perhaps—the Noun and the Adverb" [26]) suggests that it again opens a fault line between love and friendship. It is presented from the beginning as something to which we must be particularly, and particularly sensorially, attentive: "Let us prick up our ears *[Tendons l'oreille]* . . . towards this *perhaps,* even if it prevents us from hearing the rest" (28; *Politiques,* 45). The "perhaps" is then described as an "unheard-of *[inouïe],* totally new experience" (29; *Politiques,* 46), where the adjective *inouïe* refers, in its literal sense, even more directly than does the English "unheard-of," to the impossibility of being perceived by the organ of hearing. Finally its operation is said to depend on its "hold[ing] its breath" to "allow what is to come to appear or come" (29), making the "perhaps" perhaps comparable to a quasi-inaudible aspirate. At the least we could say that it relates to what is on the edge or outside of earshot and of vision ("prick up our ears . . . allow what is to come to appear"). Now, if we were to try to figure or configure that according to our choreographic principle, we would have to imagine its occurring by means of a friendship or love relation that was other than the simple face-to-face, yet not so fractured as not to constitute a relation. It would be a function of friendship or love that operated in or across a type of sensorial *peripherality,* something that could occur only once ears and eyes were required to deal with what was taking place outside their normal frontal hemispheric field, once they had to deal with what comes from behind, required to see, listen to, indeed feel—like uneven breathing on the nape of the neck—what is dorsal.

That would amount to quite a turnabout. Not only does the "perhaps" interrupt and disjoin "a certain necessity of order," but "this suspension, the imminence of an interruption, can be called *the other, the revolution, or chaos; it is, in any case, the risk of an instability*" (29; italics mine). The "perhaps," to say the least, turns things around and perhaps changes everything. It is said here to occur to Nietzsche "in the upheaval of a reversing catastrophe" (30), and is later referred to as a "catastrophic inversion" and "reversing *apostrophe*" (50). The word translated as "reversing" in both cases just mentioned is *renversante* (*Politiques*, 48, 69), suggesting in the first place a radical overturning but including overtones of disorientation, change in direction, backward movement (for example, in the expression *tête renversée*, head bent back as in ecstasy, or *écriture renversée*, writing that slopes backward). Derrida also says explicitly that he is talking about "something other than a reversal *[renversement]*" (31; *Politiques*, 49).

Perhaps, then, a catastrophe that is also a chance, an apostrophe that overturns without, for all that, simply reversing. Both "catastrophe" and "apostrophe" should be heard in more than one sense: a climax or cataclysm, but also a change in poetic rhythm or stress; an interruption in favor of a single addressee, but also an ellipsis. Some minimal thing that changes everything in the context of a philosophical discussion of love and friendship marked by persistent parenthetical attention to its methodological principles—that would seem to be what we are looking for as we read *Politics of Friendship*. And some specifically Nietzschean *controversion* of the political whose parenthesis begins here and will remain open until our final chapter. In the meantime, short of drawing a conclusion on all that, we should try to draw something in conclusion here.

As I previously made clear, apostrophe as discursive interruption and readdress is a conceit of "Envois" in *The Post Card*, playing as that text does across the face-off between a singular private loved one *(toi)* and just any reader *(vous)*. But apostrophe as the form of punctuation that represents a textual omission also functions in "Envois," by means of the blank spaces in the text whereby, one might suppose, the most intimate pieces of the correspondence, the most apostrophic apostrophes, remain undisclosed, excised, censored. As a result of that, perhaps, there is a parenthesis in "Envois," about which I have written at length elsewhere, that opens but never closes.[16] But the possibility of the text's being irremediably or irredeemably opened already exists as soon as there is apostrophe, or any *punctuation* whatsoever. Indeed, any mark whatsoever, any barely inaudible breathing effect whatsoever. The principles of iterability, detachability, and substitution that determine that fact are explicitly repeated, in formulations echoing closely those of "Signature Event Context," within the analysis of the *version de repli* discussed earlier: "Every mark has a force of detachment which not only can free it from such and such a determined context, but ensures even its principle of intelligibility and its mark structure—that is, its *iterability* (repetition *and* alteration)" (216). And as is made clear a few pages further along (219), iterability also means undecidability, the motor and fulcrum of Derrida's ethics and politics.[17] So this is no ordinary or no simple nexus. Everything hinges on it, even its center of gravity. As I have maintained from the beginning, every turn, every displacement, implies that, even walking. So however flippant what follows may appear to be, it remains a serious question of the choreographic reconfiguration of friendship as the latter relates to politics.

ONE GOOD REASON I kept on reading Jacques Derrida's writing after 1980 was in the hope of finding an end to the parenthesis he opened in *The Post Card*. And I would like to think that the reason he kept on writing was because he was still looking for just the right place to bring it to a close. So I was heartened to see the multiplication of parentheses in *Politics of Friendship*, and I searched carefully for an amicable end to the violence of that moment from *The Post Card*. I searched for a westward-facing arc (")") to match the easterly one ("(") of the text from fifteen-odd years before, for the closure of two parenthetical faces, face-to-face and smiling like an e-mail abbreviation, to resolve the unilateral challenge or ultimatum of that opened parenthesis. Instead, sadly, I was confronted with a serious case of recidivism. On page 58 of *Politiques de l'amitié*, Derrida opens a parenthesis and writes, "Let's leave this question suspended" (*Politics*, 38). He never closes it. The English translation follows the French to the letter, or at least to the absence of a ")". Suddenly the "(" of 1980 is inexorably drawn in to the context of the "(" of 1994. Two massive bodies of text slide into some sort of compromising position. There they are, henceforth, for me at least, side by side, or rather front to back, "(. . . (", a couple of nestling parentheses.

I'm tempted to say that they come to exist in *aimance. Aimance,* which is somewhat unfortunately translated as *lovence,* is a term Derrida borrows from Abdelkebir Khatibi to deconstruct the opposition between love and friendship, between passive and active, to mean something like "lovingness" (7). Unable to "take place figurelessly" (69), it is said to "cut across . . . figures" (70), to be "love in friendship, *aimance* beyond love and friendship following their determined figures, beyond all this book's trajectories of reading, beyond all ages, cultures and traditions of loving" (69). The gesture of two unclosed parentheses is thus made, in the first place, toward a figure of that sort of lovingness. But it is also, obviously, a figure that cuts across figures, a figure of catastrophic inversion, or at least of the disruption of the symmetry and closure of a love or friendship that is presumed to function only by means of the face-to-face. For that figure to be fully drawn, for an aimance beyond love and friendship to be clearly delineated, we would have to develop fully the erotic phenomenology or semiology that I have been hinting at. And we would have to trace not just the aimantic pose between friendship and love, but also, presuming it is not already implied, that between *philia* and *eros.* For, in contrast to the face-to-face, the back-to-front relation, or embrace, is more difficult to conceive of outside an erotics; the rhetoric of its figural pose cannot but refer—both because of the version of intimacy it represents, and because of its trangressive turn—to a carnal embrace. Once friendship turns out of a relation to enmity and into a type of aimance, it also opens to the erotic drift of a dorsal repositioning, turning toward a different intimacy.

I would argue that Derrida allows for that in the very metadiscursive parenthesis without parentheses within his analysis of the *version de repli,* which I referred to earlier concerning the violence and untranslatability of parentheses (221). The parentheses he is alluding to might as well be the two I have just brought into proximity across the texts of *The Post Card* and *Politics of Friendship;* their proximity might be said to draw a figure of them, of their very violence and untranslatability. But also of the simple fact of their juxtaposition, their apposition. Two open parentheses, front to back, form the figure and something of the dance of text and commentary, the means by which a text opens itself to another text, decoration, paratext, quotation, metatext, commentary, exegesis, any insertion at all. In this way it is the very model of the rhetorical relation in general, inasmuch as we conceive of that relation, in its classical sense, as establishing and refining relations between discourse and quotation. The two textual forms or levels, say quotation from the canon and commentary on it, are brought not into opposition but into apposition; one slides in adjacent to the other, molding itself to its fit, in the manner of two open parentheses. Yet the two texts retain their differences: there is some effect of rupture and hence violence, and some effect of interruption, hence untranslatability, a failure to simply carry over. But by the same token there is an effect of what we could call textual friendship, *aimance,* or even love. The paragraph in which Derrida refers to the violence and untranslatability of parentheses is the same one where he had been emphasizing the unilaterality and dissymmetry of the "I love you" that was said to perhaps be the only difference between love and friendship. The nestling parentheses appear precisely as the chance or scandal of a mutual unilaterality, a doubled dissymmetry that interrupts reciprocity by means of a turning, some *détournement* of a presumed face-to-face of the same.

Textual friendship—love or *aimance*—and hence politics are not something foreign to this discussion, beginning with Schmitt, for whom "the fact that the substance of the political is contained in the context of a concrete antagonism is . . . expressed in everyday language. . . . All political concepts, images and terms have a polemical meaning. They are focused on a specific conflict and are bound to a concrete situation."[18] Now, this means on the one hand that words are party to the polemology that defines the political; they are as capable of dividing friend from enemy as is the taking up of arms. Schmitt mentions words such as "state, republic, society, class, as well as sovereignty, constitutional state, absolutism, dictatorship, economic planning," which affect, combat, refute, or negate one group of people or another.[19] But this politicization of language is impossible to contain: any piece of everyday language is capable of dividing friend from enemy, not least in the textual situation within which it occurs, beginning with the way it divides itself as it is written, and the way it distinguishes itself from its immediate, and not so immediate, context. Any piece of text so divides, all the way, I would argue, down to punctuation or parentheses, even before it comes to divide groups of people out in the world. Language in general thus becomes polemological, and the polemical value of Schmitt's attempt to determine a rigorous conception of the *polemios* will not be lost on Derrida, who analyzes the question in some detail (114–19). Words or other elements of language are in this sense bodies that are at least potentially armed against each other, capable of conflict, and they remain so as long as they depend on a conceptual opposition that is ultimately rooted in the soil of a bounded territory. But should their relation be understood to be generated through various rhetorical turns, always already detouring thanks to a techno-tropology, they will also reveal themselves to be capable of friendship, love, and *aimance*.

Much later, when discussing Montaigne's version of friendship, Derrida has recourse to a textual model, or rather his own precise model of textual relations as grafts, to refer to the logic, rhetoric, and politics of fraternity, and problems of distinction and opposition—hence some version of Schmitt's polemological relation—among blocks of culture (e.g., Christian versus Greek): "We are here in the vicinity of a generative graft in the body of our culture. 'Our' 'culture' is such an old body, but such a young one too. . . . A patriarch, born yesterday, who knows but forgets, too young and too old to remember that his own body was grafted at birth" (185). The grafting or iterability principle appears here as Derrida's version of Schmitt's originary conflict. It is in any case the teletechnology of the origin, the structure, means, or figure by which the body forms a nexus with the rhetorical and the political, a politics of textual friendship, love, and *aimance*. Derrida calls it a graft or prosthesis, which I am rewriting here as an always-already-becoming-dorsal: "There is no body proper without this graft. This body 'begins' with this prosthesis or this supplement of origin. *Among other consequences, endless political consequences should follow from this law*" (185–86; italics mine).

Originary graft or prosthesis means a body that starts from nonintegrity and exile from identity, a body that relates from and in the beginning to unassimilable otherness, a foreign or inanimate body growing into an animate one or vice versa, the body facing what it cannot foresee, having the other come upon it as if from behind, a face with a back melded or artificially attached. Such a body *inhabits* its own dissent or conflict without clear definition of friend or enemy, of life or death; it is within itself friend-enemy and life-death beyond any pure opposition between the two. As a result, war as outside possibility regulating conflictual difference falters in its very possibility: *it possibly cannot break out.* As soon as there is that type of difference, some sort of technological symbiosis of other and same, intestine conjunction, a front-to-back nestling of sameness to produce difference, there is no longer the same enemy. Endless political consequences should follow.

And so this love, friendship, and politics of dorsality is finally also a love, friendship, and politics of prosthesis such as would allow for that scandal or chance of a love, friendship, and politics of the inanimate. A prosthetic or dorsal politics that would perhaps be more productive a concept than a posthumanist politics. From the beginning of Derrida's book, friendship has had to be understood within the structure of *revenance* and *survivance,* of spectrality and inanimation. Derrida refers to a "convertibility of life and death" (3), to the fact that, as we have seen, after Aristotle "one can still love the deceased or the inanimate," and that it is through the possibility of such loving—whose directionality I am letting turn here so as not to limit it—that "the decision in favour of a certain *aimance* comes into being" (10). And again, in the same passage where the incompatibility of love and friendship is described in terms of the dissymmetry I have been insisting on, Derrida writes of the "non-assurance and . . . risk of misunderstanding. . . . in not knowing *who,* in not knowing the substantial identity of *who* is, prior to the declaration of love" (220). Not knowing the substantial identity of *who* means not only doubting about different *who*s but also not knowing the substance that distinguishes the identity of a *who* from that of a *what.* In the end, therefore, we are asked "to think and to live the gentle rigour of friendship, the law of friendship *qua* the experience of a certain ahumanity" (294).

That would be the force of a friendship, love, or politics of dorsality; it would happen something like an "I love you" spoken from behind, behind the human, the caress of an automatic voice speaking the technological in the back of the human. It would involve a catastrophic turning "toward" the ahuman other as a turning of one's back, something like the passive decision that Derrida describes at length (68), which is a patience in no way reducible to what we are used to understanding as passivity. It means an *act* of confidence that lets the other come in the figure of *surprise,* coming like a "perhaps," the chance of being taken by surprise from behind, something that one might contrast with the economics of an appropriative preemption that increasingly seems to be the single permissible version of political discourse and practice. The dorsal does not account for every figure of this surprise, which could as easily fall on one from various frontal or lateral horizons. The back is not its place but simply the structural space of whatever falls outside frontal knowledge and visibility. It is in that sense that I referred earlier to the choreographic *hypothesis* of a dorsal friendship figured by the front-to-back. One of its versions, one of its turns, would also involve the principle of substitutability that comes to function as soon as anything like an "I love you" is proffered, as soon as a singularity of address is determined, as soon as the supposed general discursivity of the text is interrupted, a parenthesis opened, as soon as there is any apostrophic turning whatsoever: "Would the apostrophe ever take place, and the pledge it offers, without the possibility of a substitution?" (5). Turning one's back allows the other to come as other to the other, as other other, as another other.

But in spite of the formulations I have just been attempting, a dorsal or prosthetic love and friendship, erotics and politics should be understood as something different from a raising of the stakes of nonidentity or desubjectivation, different from simply taking things beyond the human, even beyond the animal, to the inanimate. Dorsality no more refers to the symmetrical substitution of the front by the back than does prosthesis refer to the replacement of the human by the inanimate; rather, it refers to the articulation of one and the other. So such a love and friendship, erotics and politics, would, as we saw to begin, break with the naturalness of the supposed homogeneity of those concepts; it would, from the perspective of an always already prosthetic, allow us to begin to think the subject of love and friendship, erotics and politics, in its biotechnological becoming, to think the radically inconceivable otherness of the other as coming upon and coming to bear upon, a being let come upon, and let come to bear upon, the sameness of a presumed reciprocal relation; and it would be whatever is required to let that come, behind one's back, unable to be known, in the vulnerability of an unrestricted hospitality, in a fiduciary relation reaching toward or arching back upon the possibility of a friendship and a politics at once *unheimlich* and *aneconomic*. Such a love and friendship, erotics and politics, would encourage us to think differently detachment, substitution, dissymmetry, disjunction, something to be imagined or envisaged as the interruption of an apostrophic or parenthetic reversing catastrophe, the figure of a double *retrait* in torsion, ((, a coupling, if that is what it is, whose only ending would be another opening, to another.

to see the history of philosophy as a sort of buggery or (it comes
to the same thing) immaculate conception. I saw myself as taking
an author from behind and giving him a child that would be his
own offspring, yet monstrous.

—GILLES DELEUZE, *Negotiations*

6. Revolutions in the Darkroom   Balázs, Benjamin, Sade

WE HAVE COME TO ACCEPT THE LIMITATIONS OF PHOTO-graphic representation. But that wasn't always so. Béla Balázs believed that "close-ups are often dramatic revelations of what is really happening under the surface of appearances. . . . the faces of things. . . . The close-ups of the film are the creative instruments of [a] mighty visual anthropomorphism. . . . In the isolated close-up of the film we can see to the bottom of a soul."[1] For Balázs, a silent film such as Carl Dreyer's *Passion of Joan of Arc* was the prime example of the "new dimension of the soul" that Balázs called "microphysiognomy."[2] Such a microphysiognomy supposedly fades from sound cinema, but I suspect that a comprehensive analysis of the close-up on the human face since the 1930s would show that it still played a similar role. And I suspect that contemporary film has not yet finished wrestling with the paradox that Balázs found himself caught in back then: on the one hand, a cinema that is called on to reveal the soul under the surface, according to the traditional notion of art that unveils hidden truth; and on the other hand, a cinema that functions thanks to immediate revelation, according to the laws of realist representation and photographic instantaneity, such that "the facial expression on a face is complete and comprehensible in itself."[3] Either an image of fullness and light or one brought back from less visible depths.

Balázs's paradox can be seen to haunt Benjamin's famous essay on technological reproducibility if one juxtaposes the latter's reference to the last gasp of the cult value of art in a photographic portrait, in "the fleeting expression of a human face," and film's "insight into the necessities governing our lives by its use of close-ups, by its accentuation of hidden details" by means of which the camera reveals the "optical unconscious."[4] As if the portrait or close-up were able to capture and freeze-frame such a fleeting expression of a face and reveal it to be a nonreproducible soul with fully restored aura, belying the technological mechanism of cinema; and as if the camera were able to record and transmit both the symptom (the face) and its analysis (the optical unconscious). Of course, those observations are not the principal reasons why we remember Benjamin's essay; rather, we remember it for its explication of the social significance of film, and the fact that the function of art after photography is no longer ritualistic but political, that cinema had coincided and collaborated with a fascist "aestheticizing of politics" to which "communism replies by polit-icizing art."[5] Yet perhaps those two cinematic questions—the one that inherits from Balázs concerning what the camera reveals, and the other that describes how cinema becomes a function of politics—are not for-eign to each other, inasmuch as both presume the operation of an appa-ratus. In Benjamin the camera is the nexus through which politics comes to be aestheticized or art politicized, and it is via the cinematic apparatus that communism and fascism opt respectively for politics and aesthetics. Perhaps, therefore, the chiasmus of politics and aesthetics and of fascism and cinema is to be understood as a function of photographic revelation itself, or at least of the apparatus itself, something that takes place in the darkroom or camera obscura, a space of invisibility through which the real comes to representation.

Indeed, as scholars such as Samuel Weber, and later Eduardo Cadava, have underlined, the logic of Benjamin's conclusion derives from the fact that technological reproducibility aestheticizes politics by allowing the mass to express itself—once the cameras roll at rallies, sporting events, and wars—by "look[ing] itself in the face."[6] Philippe Lacoue-Labarthe defined fascism precisely as "the mobilization of the *identificatory* emo-tions of the masses," and for Deleuze and Guattari, "certain assemblages of power require the production of a face. . . . The face is a politics" that requires another politics of dismantling the face.[7] The mass sees thus its own close-up, takes an optical glimpse into its unconscious, but, failing to see the pathologies revealed there, is instead comforted by a narcissistic pleasure. Both the camera that films and the mass that looks itself in the face mistake politics for aesthetics. As a result, the ugly face of fascism is perceived not as that but instead as a flattering portrait whose aura still beckons, where "the cult value of the image finds its last refuge,"[8] reen-dowing the cinematico-political scene with the fervor of a cultic experi-ence. Weber will insist that, far from disappearing, aura gets reinvested in modern technological media and in fact "*thrives in its decline*. . . . Fascism allows the mass to look itself in the face and thereby to find a gaze that ostensibly looks back. Fascism thus reinstates the aura of the world-picture by means of the very media that undermine it."[9]

It is a commonplace to understand that Benjamin attributes to fascism via photography, or more precisely via cinema, the "introduction" of aesthetics into politics; that he discovers the nexus between cinema and the age of the masses on the one hand, and the aestheticization of politics on the other. This is the basis of Jacques Rancière's somewhat summary rebuttal in advancing his own thesis of the distribution of the sensible.[10] But as Cadava reads Benjamin, the latter identifies rather a disjunctive structural fact of photography that applies, as if in retrospect, to all art: "For Benjamin, as soon as the technique of reproduction reaches the stage of photography, a fault line traverses the whole sphere of art: photography transforms the entire notion of art."[11] It is as if, after photography, we have to go back and read the artwork as always already reproducible and therefore always already political. Photography and cinema would be specific modern instances of that structure, with specific effects relating to the age of the mass, such effects being concentrated in the self-recognition of the face of the mass that is enabled by films of "great ceremonial processions, giant rallies . . . mass sporting events, and . . . war."[12]

Weber's insistence on the self-reflexivity of the mass via film, which Benjamin mentions in a footnote to the epilogue of his "Work of Art" essay, is owed to a comparison with "On Some Motifs in Baudelaire." There Benjamin relates the aura to "the expectation that [the gaze] will be returned by that on which it is bestowed. . . . To experience the aura of an object we look at means to invest it with the ability to look back at us." Painting provides such a possibility, whereas "the camera records our likeness without returning our gaze."[13] As Cadava emphasizes, photography therefore involves a particular form of dehumanization, or what he calls "petrification," deriving from "a kind of rhythm or oscillation between a gaze that can return the gaze of another, and one that cannot, between a thing that is becoming a person and a person that is becoming a thing."[14] The objects we look at in a painting, on the other hand, are humanized, returning our gaze in the manner of "the relationship between humans and inanimate or natural objects."[15] It is as if we were looking into the face of another. An *auraless* photograph cannot do that unless or until it becomes a photograph of the mass seeing itself looking back at itself.

From that point of view, the aura would itself be a strange version of the darkroom of inversion that I discuss here, allowing nature or the inanimate to be reanimated and to return to the observer as though a human interrelation were involved, making what is close appear distant.[16] Paradoxically, the aura that fades from art with the arrival of the photograph would have something of the photographic about it, namely, the ability to invert a reality that, as a result of such an inversion, the photograph comes to reproduce. What disappears from the photograph is thus a type of photographic apparatus, and the aura, which we might ordinarily understand as a supplementary dimension of signification hovering about or above the work of art, its supplemental dimension of enlightenment, appears in fact as an apparatus of transformation, and of automation, that operates, as it were, behind it. I say that especially in view of Benjamin's comparison, in the same section of the Baudelaire essay, between the loss of aura in the case of "techniques inspired by the camera and subsequent analogous types of apparatus" and the Proustian and Bergsonian *mémoire volontaire*. The camera, unlike a madeleine, "make[s] it possible at any time to retain an event . . . through the apparatus," but the image produced is "vapid."[17] Aura again comes and goes in function of the approaching or receding spaces of memory, of voluntary or involuntary processes, clustering in the latter case, dissipating in the former, operating through a complex relation of light to dark that is played out in the mind, but also in the body. Cadava fills out the complexity of Benjamin's relation to Proust and Bergson and analyzes to what extent memory functions in Proust in a properly photographic space, so much so that "the body is a kind of darkroom" whose movements produce "a technology wherein body and image interpenetrate one another."[18] For that to be so—or at least this is my persistent claim here—the body would have to "contain" its own unattainable or invisible space, a space of automatic reproduction that I call dorsality.

Benjamin ends "On Some Motifs in Baudelaire" by referring to the poet's piece entitled "Perte d'auréole" (Loss of a Halo). Given the French title and the context of Benjamin's discussion, it is hard not to read that it was an aura that Baudelaire describes as being lost, knocked off one's head on a busy street and fallen "into the mire of the macadam." Depending on the version, in Baudelaire's diaries or in the prose poem, the poet either picks it up or laughs at the idea of coming across someone else, "some bad poet," wearing it. Benjamin's point concerns Baudelaire's disillusion with the crowd and "the disintegration of the aura in immediate shock experience *[Chockerlebnis]*."[19] But given what we have so far developed, one would have to imagine the aura as a detachable artifice, or as an organic emanation detached to reveal its artificiality. Either the poet picks it up and puts it back on, but cannot henceforth avoid the possibility that it will again slip off the next time he is jostled in the cheek-by-jowl of the industrial age, that it will finally be abandoned, left behind like some stray hubcap; it is even possible that he will be jostled by some halo snatcher precisely so that he can be divested of it. Or else one of the mass will find it, shine it, look at himself in it, and try it on for size, convinced that it looks back at him and suits him just fine, showing him in his best light. Both eventualities occur in the flash of shock experience, in a photographic moment that is also the moment of history, a moment that, because it is photographic, is also aesthetic.

THE MASS expresses itself fascistically, therefore, thanks to a camera that allows it to see itself in close-up, face-to-face. It is not clear whether the fascism of the mass will necessarily be there on the surface—as at Nuremberg, dancing and chanting in unison in front of the lens of a Leni Riefenstahl—or existing more discreetly as a form of optical unconscious, behind the scenes of less explicit manifestations, waiting to be unleashed; whether the camera shows a simple perceptual excerpt, a surface of the real, or the depth or soul behind or below the surface such as we expect on the basis of traditional artistic norms. One or the other, or both, are presumed to be transmitted in the service of a politics of the mass, causing fascism to reproduce itself. Benjamin's analysis not only preserves something of Balázs's paradox but also seems to require a confusion between two forms of mechanical reproducibility: that of the work of art, able to exist in multiple copies, without the aura of a single original; and that of the photograph itself, as a mechanically induced reproduction of the real. The photograph is reproducible by virtue of both its multiplicity and its mimeticism, and the transformation of the cultic and ritualistic into the political, which comes into focus in the case of cinema, is a function of not one but two forms of reproduction. That is how the mass sees itself in face-to-face close-up and how, as those images are seen by more and more mass audiences outside the original moment, there develops a communion or fusion of reactionary political sentiment.

For Lacoue-Labarthe, it is in mimeticism that the aestheticization of politics begins, and perhaps ends, precisely via the means by which "*techne* is conceived as the accomplishment and revelation of *physis* itself,"[20] the presumption of an organic relation between art and nature. As a result, the polis is produced as a work of art, but one that is nevertheless presumed to have organically reproduced itself out of its natural origin: "Greece is quite simply the very home of *techne* (or—and this makes no difference—of *mimesis*)."[21] The contrived artificiality of the polis—and the Greek polis will serve as the model for Nazism's self-representation and Nazi Germany's identity—comes as a result to be celebrated not as technological fact but as a form of organic immanence.

From this point of view, the reply to any aestheticizing of politics would involve further aestheticizing it in the sense of emphasizing its originary technicity; it would mean uncoupling aesthetics from the "fundamental mimetology" that governs it,[22] disjoining the *techne* from any organic relation to the *physis*. Politics, it would have to be insisted, is art, but art is technological, involving a rupture with respect to its presumed mimeticism.[23] To understand how politics is aestheticized by the cinema, we therefore need to analyze cinematic reproducibility from the perspective of its apparatus and of its technology of mimetic representation, of what happens between one face of the mass and its other, the face in front of the camera and the face in the image; we should examine the ideology of realism that allows one to be seen as a mirror image of the other, follow the face back through the darkroom behind the lens, into the dorsal chiasmus where its image passes through serial inversions before emerging framed for our narcissistic comfort and consumption. For neither aestheticization nor politicization can take place, it seems to me, without such a passage and such an inversion, and the place of their intersection or chiasmus is precisely what escapes our gaze.

The problem that Benjamin reveals in reproducible art, therefore, what he calls the fascist "aestheticizing of politics," is above all its ideology of mimeticism, its realist aesthetics understood as a problem not just for art and aesthetics but for politics itself. A realist politics presumes the operation of social and economic transformations that nevertheless preserve immediacy, directness, and transparency, transformations whose revolutionary inversions manage only to reproduce a type of representational sameness, some version of a political mass perpetuating its own narcissistic indulgence. However much it claims to be pure praxis, to avoid any aesthetico-theoretical deviation, it defines itself as politics precisely on the basis of a realist aesthetics: pragmatism as instantaneity, materiality as immediacy, causality as transparency. In the process, it ignores or represses the negotiation that takes place behind it, and on which it relies, the darkroom's technological overturning that reproduces the real, the inversion whose truth cannot survive the light of day, and thanks to whose hermetic concealing there emerges instead the familiar duplicate sameness.

Throughout the rest of this chapter, I seek to demonstrate how that perhaps takes place once the cinema comes to Sade, as in the case of Pasolini's *Saló, or The 120 Days of Sodom*. That film is one of the examples, along with Cavani's *The Night Porter*,[24] put to Foucault in terms of an eroticization of Nazism in the brief 1975 interview that goes by the title "Sade, Sergeant of Sex." Foucault finds connections between Nazism and sadism, such as those made in the films just mentioned, to be lacking in imagination. Whereas he advocates "invent[ing] with the body . . . a nondisciplinary eroticism," he remarks that such films display a penchant for "an eroticism of the disciplinary type." He therefore concludes: "[Sade] bores us. He's a disciplinarian, a sergeant of sex, an accountant of the ass."[25] Now, although we know that that wasn't all Foucault thought about Sade,[26] it is important to note that he here equates bringing Sade to bear on fascism with a retrograde politics, the aestheticization of an extremely conservative politics, rather than a converse politicization of the sexual. It is as if Sade on film cannot but be recuperated by an aestheticizing force of cinema that is stronger than any revolutionary power inherent in sadism itself, or in the writings of Sade.

When Foucault called Sade a "sergeant of sex," neglecting in the end the specifics of a cinematic Sade, he was making explicit a problematic that can already be identified in Sade's writings, referring not just to the essential traits of the latter's theory of sexuality but also to the strange circuit of forces that his theory brings into play with modern politics and the modern state. Foucault's remarks concerned the very site where power exercises its sovereignty, where power in the form of the modern police or military maintains its "right" through a violence that seizes the body and so produces it as a sexualized entity that can be regimented, controlled, and inspected. By following the logic of this "circuit," one would argue that Sade's theory has a "double" status: it is on the one hand the description and advocacy of a sexuality that comes to be "enforced" by modern disciplinary societies; and on the other, the ideology that formulates a program for an "eroticism proper" to those societies and their politics: "I would be willing to admit that Sade formulated an eroticism proper to a disciplinary society: a regulated, anatomical, hierarchical society whose time is carefully distributed, its spaces partitioned, characterized by obedience and surveillance."[27]

In suggesting earlier that the cinema "perhaps" comes to Sade via a certain sense of the political, I was acknowledging that, according to Foucault, it precisely cannot do so. Cinema cannot come to Sade: "I believe that there is nothing more allergic to the cinema than the work of Sade. Among the numerous reasons, this one first: the meticulousness, the ritual, the rigorous ceremonial form that all the scenes of Sade assume exclude the supplementary play of the camera. The least addition or suppression, the smallest ornament, is intolerable. No open fantasy, but a carefully programmed regulation. As soon as something is missing or superimposed, all is lost. There is no place for an image."[28] In other words, for Foucault the rigorous programmatic character of Sade's scenes excludes the possibility of an "additional" intervention such as the camera. Once the camera is there, we get the image but lose the Sadean scene and vice versa: if there is a "properly" Sadean scene at work, there is no image of it. Sade's scenes cannot be represented. That is what films such as *The Night Porter* and *Saló* supposedly overlook. They eroticize a "program" foreign to representation and from which "eros [is] absent," and so reinforce, by aestheticizing it, a reactionary politics. Such films would be based on a "complete historical error. Nazism was not invented by the great erotic madmen of the twentieth century but by the most sinister, boring, and disgusting petit-bourgeois imaginable. . . . I don't say it to diminish the blame of those responsible for it, but precisely to disabuse those who want to superimpose erotic values upon it."[29]

So whether Pasolini felt constrained to have recourse to Sade in order to represent the extreme demented state of siege of Mussolini's endgame republic, or felt he could not not use Mussolini's last gasp as the context for Sade's *120 Days of Sodom*, I would agree with Foucault that in resorting to the context of fascism, the film somewhat abandoned the context of sadism. However, I would argue that a different perspective on the cinematics of Sade and Nazism is possible, a perspective within which certain additions, suppressions, and ornaments are not only germane to Sade but necessary to his scene of sex. For if one were to attempt to account for an articulation of the sexual and political beyond the presumption that the sexual, like the domestic, is necessarily political because it involves relations of power (how does that apply in the case of solitary sex?), or on this side of the equally problematic presumption that sex in Sade is political because it is transgressive (isn't any sex, after Freud at least, transgressive by definition?), then one might argue for that articulation via the very notion of the enclosure itself (Lacoste, Silling, Saló, as well as, conversely, Miolans, Vincennes, La Bastille, and Charenton),[30] the *château fort* as hermetic space within which the sexual seems to seal itself off yet manages to reemerge as the political. It is there, as Pierre Klossowski writes, that the bedroom becomes the "vast layout of an urban showroom at the heart of the city, one with the city."[31] Similarly Barthes, in his *Sade, Fourier, Loyola,* writes at length of the Sadean *cité* (which he compares to Fourier's utopian phalanstery) as enclosure or *clôture,* for which the model is the hermetically isolated Château de Silling in *The 120 Days of Sodom.* That locus, writes Barthes, functions not only as a secret place, the site for every crime against the world it refuses and against which it buttresses itself, but also as the place of a "social autarchy," a precise and strict form of polis.[32] And Deleuze, allowing for a Sade in cinema more than did Foucault, notes that "in *Salo* . . . there is no outside: Pasolini presents, not even fascism *in vivo,* but fascism at bay, shut away in the little town, reduced to a pure interiority, coinciding with the conditions of closure in which Sade's demonstrations took place."[33] Sade's polis is thus the enclosed château, and the bedroom within that château, and the sex that enters that space is found to bring the political with it. In *Philosophy in the Bedroom* such an entry would be emblematized by the pamphlet "Yet Another Effort, Frenchmen If You Would Become Republicans" *(Français, encore un effort si vous voulez être républicains),* as explicit incursion of politico-sexual philosophy within the libertine scene.

I will therefore argue for changing the perspective from the cinema of Sade, such as Foucault critiques, to what might be called the Sadean theater of cinematic representation. Within that perspective, one might examine a particular figure of the enclosed room or bedroom that derives less from a Sade on camera than a Sade *in camera,* namely, the figural space of the camera obscura. In that obscure room, sex is transformed into pure perversion, yet inasmuch as politics follows sex into the dark, it also undergoes a fundamental—or perhaps originary—contamination, such as will irrevocably belie its realist, *anesthetic* presumptions. As I will read it, something takes place in Sade under the cover of a type of darkness, in the more or less hermetically sealed confines of a seat of power, as a result of which everything gets transformed in the representation of the world. But we do and we don't see it take place. As long as the doors, gates, and windows or "shutters" remain closed, then the world can continue as it had before; indeed, one vision or image that finally emerges shows that whatever took place behind those walls was nothing so much as the faithful representation of the warts and all of that world, a repetition or reproduction rather than a representation of it. Screeds of Sade's writings themselves could be adduced to support such an image, repeating that "all I am saying is that this is how it really is, the state of nature itself." But the defiled and destroyed bodies that emerge periodically, flailing, screaming, or in tatters from behind the closed doors of the château, also prove that that logic is not what it seems, and that the enclosure is neither completely hermetic nor entropic. It appears that something is seriously awry in there, that nothing is as it appears, that what we are indeed witness to derives from the rending of the fabric of representability and representativity that is the physical law of the darkroom and of the camera. For, as we know, in that space, by means of the controlled aperture that is the point of entry into it, whatever reproduction does take place can never reduce, repress, or annul the fact that the light and image of the world have been irrevocably reversed.

The "pure" reversal of photographic representation takes place under cover of darkness: it occurs the moment light enters the camera obscura. Yet the back-to-front and upside-down image of the world so produced remains effectively hidden within that darkness. For what emerges on the other side, what we see as printed photograph in the light of day, amounts to a restitution of the original world. That is the effect of the so-called miracle of photographic representation and the basis for the whole conservative ideology of realism, the presumption of a world seen as if through a window, bathed in its natural light. Light is indeed the language that is spoken, or more precisely written, by *photo-graphy*, but the apparatus that renders it possible is a black box, a darkroom; photography's language of light is first spoken in the dark. Furthermore, the light that becomes photographic in the dark chamber of the camera is but the primary instance of a series of reversals required for the world to become an image. The virgin film itself exists unexposed, remaining in the dark until the light from the world brings it to life; but it is not a simple revelation that is required, by no means the total exposure that we understand revelation to be, but rather a negotiation by the light of the film's sensitivity (a totally exposed film, one that is bathed in light, of course appears black). Light, in fact, remains the enemy that film must protect itself from. And a further set of negotiations of light comes into play as the exposed film is developed (the French verb is *révéler*) as negative before being further developed or revealed as positive photograph.[34]

Hence the reversal, inversion, or perversion that the Sadean scene inscribes remains irreducible, and it indeed acts as the condition of possibility—however occluded, repressed, or inverted in its turn—of any ultimate vision of the world. We have come to understand and to accept that there could be no Enlightenment, no emergence into secular rationality without the converse *production-in-incarceration* of a Sade, no utopian sense of progress without his "vision of a society in the state of permanent immorality . . . a *utopia of evil*."[35] But neither is there realist representation, and mechanical reproduction of the real in the photographic sense, without a sense of reversal, inversion, or perversion; and indeed, there can be no representation at all without the minimal—yet radical—departure that is the passage through an apparatus, the artificialization of the natural.

THE BARRIERS on the road to the Château de Silling are numerous; once they are passed, there is no going back. First we cross outside France, then traverse the Rhine, before abandoning the coach and beginning to travel on foot, into the Black Forest. Thieves and smugglers act as sentries once the gate to the domain is closed; it takes five long hours to scale a peak as high as Mt. Saint-Bernard, whose crest is split by a crevice sixty yards wide and more than a thousand feet deep, making it virtually impossible to get back down. A bridge, by means of which the ravine is crossed, is destroyed as soon as everyone reaches the other side. The château itself is surrounded by a wall thirty feet high and a deep moat. Inside, we are taken along a long gallery, through a dining hall, a large living room or salon, and finally to "the assembly chamber intended for the storytellers' narrations . . . seat of the lubricious enclaves."[36] Multiple compounding retreats, therefore, into a citadel for a four-month reclusion that will set the stage for, and take the form of, a narrative performance, and narrative and performance.

Once the players are inside and the château is hermetically sealed, the curtain opens on a scene of excess and cruelty. But the extravagant theatricality of *The 120 Days of Sodom* functions, among other things, as the pretext for developing further a formalist architecture of the recess, for extrapolating within the château itself the structures of retreat that had to be traversed and endured for one to arrive there. Those spatial structures of recess and retreat mean that Sadean theatrics involve a play of light and dark and thus constitute a type of *cinematics*. The narrations performed evening after evening and month after month by the four *historiennes* are designed to provoke excesses that are performed more or less offstage, in the four niches belonging to the male libertines who constitute the audience. Those niches are like private boxes, dark spaces in contrast to the lighted stage ("she was placed like an actor in a theater, and the audience in their niches were situated as if observing a spectacle in an amphitheater" [237–38]). The structure of a separation between actors and audience, and between the lighted stage and the darkened niches, remains in force in spite of certain contraventions of it.[37] Such contraventions include the commerce between the victim-playthings who are disposed on the space of the stage and the libertines who constitute the audience; and beyond that, what transpires when, invoking their right to interrupt the performance "at any point and as frequently as they please," and to suspend it "as long as the pleasures of him whose needs interrupt it continue" (246), the libertines themselves come to be both actors and directors of much of the business, if not of the narrative performance itself. But the separation is again reinforced by the existence of cabinets behind each of those niches, darkened recesses behind each recess, accessible by means of a small door where a subject is taken when "one preferred not to execute in front of everyone the delight for whose execution one had summoned that subject" (238).

The theatrical or performative architecture is further repeated or compounded by the organization of the living spaces. Strictly speaking, these are external to the "assembly chamber reserved for the narrations" (244; cf. *Oeuvres*, 52), but they remain auxiliary to that theater inasmuch as eating and sleeping, and the whole complicated regimen of discipline and hygiene (and punishment and feculence) associated with those needs, not to mention sexual needs, are considered secondary to the nightly performances. In addition to the kitchen and dining spaces, and bedrooms, there is a whole complex of barred and darkened rooms, chambers, cells, niches, and recesses, culminating finally in a type of black hole of "depravity, cruelty, disgust, infamy, all those passions anticipated or experienced" (239), namely, the vaulted dungeon three hundred steps down into the entrails of the earth, the place reserved for "the most atrocious things that the cruelest art and the most refined barbarity could invent" (240; cf. *Oeuvres*, 48). It is there that the whole performance is designed to reach its climax in the mutilations and killings of the final days, there where we will have crossed into either the aesthetics of pure voyeurist spectacle or the politics of raw power and arbitrary murder, or some perversion of each.

Barthes analyzes the recessive structure of Sade's châteaux, emphasizing how the progressive retreat toward the secluded *enclos* becomes, once one is inside it, literally *abyssal*. But what retreats into that abyss along with the libertines is a question of representation, so that the recess is a secret and silent space in form much more than in actual function:

The Sadian enclosure is relentless; it has a dual function; first, of course, to isolate, to shelter vice from the world's punitive attempts; yet libertine solitude is not merely a precaution of a practical nature; it is a quality of existence. . . . It therefore has a functionally useless but philosophically exemplary form: within the best-tested retreats, there always exists, in Sadian space, a "secret" where the libertine takes some of his victims, far away from all, even complicitous, eyes, where he is irrevocably alone with his object—a highly unusual thing in this communal society; this "secret" is obviously formal, since what happens there, being of the order of torture or crime, has no reason to be hidden. . . . And since in Sade there is never anything real save for the narration, the silence of the "secret" is completely confounded with the blank of the narrative: meaning *[le sens]* stops. This "hole" has as its analogous sign the very site of secrets: they are usually deep cellars, crypts, tunnels, excavations located deep within the châteaux, the gardens, the pits, from which one emerges alone, saying nothing.[38]

The 120 Days of Sodom is no doubt too grand and precisely too abyssal a project to be fully accounted for, for its expenditures to be satisfactorily reconciled here. It purports, after all, to be the exhaustive paradigm of what it classifies. *Philosophy in the Bedroom* shares many of its structures while at the same time presenting, as we shall see, its own unique version of the scene of representation, and accordingly that text will be my focus here. It shares, most pertinently, with *The 120 Days of Sodom* the possibility of an abyssal retreat or move offstage, the possibility that what takes place will not be represented, will in a sense remain unuttered; but that possibility is reduced to a single instance at the end of the fifth dialogue. There, in the denouement to the orgy that follows the reading of "Yet Another Effort, Frenchmen If You Would Become Republicans," the libertine master Dolmancé, his mouth already full of this and that, asks permission to retire for a moment with the gardener Augustin "into a nearby room *[dans un cabinet voisin]*," and in reply to Mme de Saint-Ange's remonstrance at his desire for secrecy, adds "in a low and mysterious tone" that "there are certain things which strictly require to be veiled *[demandent absolument des voiles]*." The women insist on not being kept in the dark—"Is there, do you think, any conceivable infamy we are not worthy to hear of and execute?"—so Mme de Saint-Ange's brother, the Chevalier, who somehow knows what Dolmancé intends to do without being told, finally whispers it to them. Eugénie, the young pupil, finds it repugnant, Saint-Ange, blasé as always, says she thought as much, and Dolmancé repeats that "one must be alone and in the deepest shadow *[dans l'ombre]* in order to give oneself over to such turpitudes." So the two men retreat into an extreme or absolute darkness to perform what has and has not been uttered, this *affaire d'honneur* that "should take place between men only."[39] We will have reason to come back to this scene, which obviously takes center stage in the problematics of Sadean representation. Let us note it for now as the single and all the more remarkable instance of the dark chamber that subsumes or supports, acts as the reserve of and for whatever is "seen" in the text; and let us observe also a certain irony in this veil drawn by Sade in 1795 over what takes place between men only, a veil that *The 120 Days* had already well and truly rent without, for all that, resolving its abyssal enfoldings.

Onstage, under the lights, *Philosophy in the Bedroom* prioritizes visibility. When Eugénie is first undressed, it is in front of the mirrors that surround the niche housing Saint-Ange's ottoman of pleasure. Mistress explains to pupil how "they infinitely multiply those same pleasures for the persons seated here. . . . No part of the body can remain hidden: everything must be seen *[il faut que tout soit en vue]*" (203; *Oeuvres*, 387). But the abyssal repetitions and absolute clarity of that realist visibility come at a price: such a pure vision can be reproduced and represented only by means of a darkroom reversal. *Philosophy in the Bedroom* offers at least three versions of that chiasmatic reversal of the world: first, a problematization of distinctions between diegesis and mimesis as between theory and practice; second, a problematization of the very relation of the aesthetic and the political; and third, an undoing of nature by forms of technological artifice.

The first of these problematics is introduced as the text begins, and opens explicitly onto both a pedagogical and a theatrical scene, namely, Eugénie's induction into libertine practice. *Philosophy in the Bedroom* is subtitled *Dialogues Intended for the Education of Young Ladies,*[40] and here, as in other texts of Sade, emphasis is constantly placed on instruction: "It is a matter of an education," declares Saint-Ange (*Philosophy in the Bedroom*, 190); "I came hither to be instructed, and will not go till I am informed *[savante]*," concurs Eugénie (194; *Oeuvres*, 379); "This [is] the lyceum where [the lessons will] be given," confirms Dolmancé (196). There is, of course, no instruction without a disciplinary dimension. Saint-Ange informs Dolmancé that Eugénie "must have a severe scolding if she misbehaves," which he is quick to reinforce: "Punishments . . . corrections . . . I might very well hold this pretty little ass accountable for mistakes *[fautes]* made by the head" (199). But as is demonstrated by these distinctions between misbehavior and scoldings, or faults or sins of the head and slaps on the ass, the quandary of pedagogy is that of representation, of various forms of the show or tell mimetic dilemma, however false a dilemma it be. Eugénie will have to correctly perform the libertine behavior that is demonstrated to her, and also speak so as to demonstrate that she is thinking libertinely correct thoughts, or else she will be scolded and slapped on her pretty little ass, by means of which Dolmancé will begin another cycle of libertine sadomasochistic demonstration, and so on abyssally. Whether she will have learned more by means of the explanations and demonstrations or by the scoldings and slappings, and whether the slappings will have been more demonstrative than explicative, remains difficult to determine.[41]

However, that there is a need for mimetic representation—indeed, realist representation and even a tendency toward photographic representation—is also made explicit from the beginning. A desire for the photographic close-up *avant la lettre,* for the exaggerated dimensionality of the human figure, would seem to motivate the frequent requests for a discursive portrait. "Paint your Dolmancé for me," Saint-Ange asks of her brother, "that I may have him well fixed in my mind before I see him arrive" (*Philosophy in the Bedroom,* 187). And then, when the Chevalier asks her to reciprocate by faithfully describing Eugénie, something she says she can only fail at doing ("As for Eugénie, dear One, I should in vain undertake to figure *[peindre]* her to you; she is quite beyond my descriptive powers [*au-dessus de mes pinceaux,* literally "above what my brushes can execute"]), he insists, "But at least sketch a little if you cannot paint" (192; *Oeuvres,* 377).

The status of the images one represents for oneself is a question from the first page, where Saint-Ange describes the extent of her erotic imagination or the outrageous ideas she has, the products of a "busy brain," as the English translation has it. For she in fact describes those fantasies in terms of a difference between "idea" and "conception," as the inadequation between another's idea—perhaps also her own, for she is referring to the experience of everyone in general (*on*)—and what she conceives: "*On n'a pas d'*idée *de ce que je* conçois" (*Oeuvres,* 371; cf. *Philosophy in the Bedroom,* 186). And indeed, inasmuch as the conceit of all of Sade's texts would be the possibility of *realizing* one's fantasies (at least within the context of literary representation), then they would necessarily be caught in the quandary of any number of representational fallacies. What distinctions are to be made, once it comes to sex and fantasy, between idea and conception; how does one distinguish among the various levels of the representative scene that are played out in the dark recesses of the mind? Can we know whether those dramas take place on its conscious stage or in its unconscious recesses, and can we thereby determine which of those psychic scenes is in fact the theater of narrative and which is the niche where, suspending the performance and reaching for the nearest or most desirable walk-on, *one* resorts to the real sex? Given the fact that, in the Sadean perspective, it is a matter of always going further, of pushing the boundaries of erotic conceiving—which leads one to wonder about the conceit of taxonomic exhaustiveness of *The 120 Days,* its founding limit of six hundred narratives of as many perversions[42]—is there not, beyond the problem of having an idea of what can be conceived, an insoluble abyss where not even conceiving can any longer conceive of what can be conceived? However much the libertine presumes to strive for that unattainable and as yet unknown conception, the ultimate not-yet-dreamed-up-perfectly-perverse-and-cruel coupling, tripling, or quadrupling, is not the limit to such fantasies, or at least a question concerning their exhaustivity, precisely what both excites and frustrates him? Presumably there is a point at which representativity is no longer able to function, a point at which, within the mind itself, a Dolmancean conceiving says to a Saint-Angean conceiving that it has to withdraw into an adjoining chamber of neuronal space, into the strictly veiled space of an *affaire d'honneur* between men, which comes now to be understood as inconceivability itself, the secret place of representational failure that only the honor of men avows and whose secret men of honor would preserve. Yet perhaps, as I shall argue, such a pure aesthetic emptiness is at the same time a very political space.

The form of representational quandary that is explicitly played out in the pedagogical scene of *Philosophy in the Bedroom* is less the distinction between idea and conception than that between practice and theory. Saint-Ange explains to her brother: "I wish to join a little practice to theory, as I like the demonstrations to keep abreast of the dissertations" (*Philosophy in the Bedroom,* 191), and Dolmancé reinforces the presumed hierarchy of that relation: "Demonstrations will be necessary only after the theoretical dissertations" (196). Similarly, Saint-Ange briefly describes the advantages of anal sex to Eugénie while leaving a fuller analysis to Dolmancé, who will convince her by "uniting practice with theory" (202). But the success of the whole venture is threatened at both ends: by the risk they are warned of by Saint-Ange, of spending so much time on theoretical "preliminaries" that the practical "instruction shall remain incomplete" (200), in other words, too much talk and not enough action; or by the risk Dolmancé warns of, asking them to hurry up with their "demonstrations" for fear that his formidable member will ejaculate and no longer be able to "aid your lessons" (202), in other words, too much action leading to inaction. Too much action means too much realism, reality itself, if you will, the reality of ejaculation as physiological impulse beyond both theory and practice. Such a peristaltic automatism will destroy the tension and unmask the false hierarchy between theory and practice on which the pedagogical representational experience is based. The threat or risk of it brings about a strange inversion, or at least a perversion of the instructional relation: the authority of master over pupils and the emphasis on practice over theory are both called into question as Saint-Ange disciplines the erotic master Dolmancé and calls back to order the practice that threatens to exceed itself, calling it back to its theoretical origins: "No good will come of this excitement *[Je m'oppose à cette effervescence]*. Be reasonable, Dolmancé: once that semen flows, the activity of your animal spirits will be diminished and the warmth of your dissertations will be lessened correspondingly" (201; *Oeuvres,* 385). The "effervescence" that is the very aim of the libertine erotic exercise, in which Dolmancé is a seasoned instructor and of which he is repeatedly the model, threatens to overreach itself in its very practicality, requiring the authoritarian intervention of a lesser adept against her teacher, an intervention in favor of theoretical discourse (dissertations) and against practice (excitement). Indeed, by the end of the orgy that precedes the reading of "Yet Another Effort, Frenchmen," we are perhaps supposed to understand that theory less precedes practice than transcends it, for there Saint-Ange avers: "A little theory must succeed practice: it is the means to make a perfect disciple *[écolière]*" (295; *Oeuvres,* 477).

This brief and insufficient analysis—we have mostly remained within the opening scenes of the text—shows at least how *Philosophy in the Bedroom* inaugurates a double structure of the diegetic and the mimetic that is repeated abyssally. To recapitulate: Saint-Ange's superego has no idea of what she conceives and will seek to realize. Dolmancé and Eugénie are either painted or sketched before they appear in the flesh. They all agree to theorize before putting those theories into practice, until the practice threatens to negate itself. And, of course, the grand structure of the narrative involves a progressive dissertation on the range of sexual perversions whose putting into practice serves to enact two major lessons. The first lesson involves Eugénie's participation in the repudiation, defiling, and murder of her own mother, the painfully practical lesson against Mme de Mistival's libertinely incorrect prudishness ("I am finally going to teach you" *[je vais à la fin t'instruire]*, Saint-Ange tells her [*Oeuvres*, 540; cf. *Philosophy in the Bedroom*, 357]). She will be sent back corrected—her body literally rearranged, sewn up *[cousu]* like a well-wrought and ordered discourse—to the libertine husband who regularly disciplined her in less extreme ways anyway.[43] Following that, the second lesson will be achieved by having an emancipated Eugénie sent out into the world, her whole experience inside the château serving as the theory that has now equipped her for the practice of a libertine life.

It is in such ways that, on one level, the Sadean world of representation contains, sustains, and reproduces itself, producing an inverted or perverted mirroring, but, as it were, finally changing nothing. Theory precedes or transcends practice, pedagogy functions by means of a disciplined transmission of information and demonstration, the unformed or misinformed mind and body are formed or corrected, the whole representative apparatus has its content radically inverted or perverted, but without, for all that, having its logic or operations challenged. Yet, on another level, it manages to peel away the tain of the mirror of the world and expose to implacable and detailed scrutiny the archive of that world's inverted and perverted self, everything that has been imprinted, as if photographically, on its reflecting surface. That goes obviously for what is called morality, but also, as I am arguing after Barthes and others, for the world, or rather the theater, of representation that unfolds within Sade's texts. For however obviously the pedagogical dialogue reveals itself as a theatrical scene, however much Sade's work is understood as the mise-en-scène of moral instruction, it in fact rehearses and repeats any number of representational quandaries that extend well beyond those of theatrical mimesis. Hence once the initial opposition between theory and practice is made explicit at the beginning of *Philosophy in the Bedroom,* the text devolves into an alternation among various discursive formations and subformations whose status as either theory or practice is not easy to determine.[44]

Beyond that, of course, there are the long philosophical dissertations, which are perhaps the purest representation of the pedagogical, or at least the informational, whose unmediated transmission is subverted by the failure of such philosophical interludes to preserve their discursive purity, by their inability to prevent themselves from being drawn into the practical demonstrations and from becoming mere preludes to the orgies themselves (even though that seamless transition from philosophizing to sex act could also be understood as the transcendent ideal Sade was striving for). The reading of the revolutionary pamphlet "Yet Another Effort, Frenchmen" epitomizes such interludes, and by means of its status as autonomous text, it can claim to circumscribe itself in a way that the other discursive digressions fail to. Its status is therefore the distinguishing question of *Philosophy in the Bedroom* and focal point for an examination of the chiasmatic darkroom inversion of the sexual and the political. If we can identify the space in which the pamphlet is read, indeed assign a status to both the space of its reading and the performance that its reading constitutes, we will know, I am arguing, what and where politics is, at least what politics is and where it resides in the age of mechanical reproducibility.

Thus it is that the enclosure of the château, as a type of darkroom, reveals or develops for us an unexpected tableau of unbridled sexual depravity: what we know to go on in certain benighted corners of human activity and in the dark recesses of some, perhaps all, minds. Sade's camera obscura realizes, according to a simplistic realism, what should be only imaginable; it photographs the wild libidinal fantasies that various forms of the reality principle and the superego presume to contain within the imagination, and then lets those images loose, at least within a more visible if less visual medium, namely, as words on a page. However, by means of its realist rigor, the château also becomes a theater in which the stakes of representation as realization are constantly raised; whatever can be conceived of must be urgently performed. That requires the chiasmatic overlap of another form of realism, of a discourse designed to be the pure transmission of a pure pedagogy, unrepresented knowledge or truth, words that would be indistinguishable finally, in terms of their immediacy and transmissibility, from an involuntary physiological spasm or orgasm. It is telling that the verb Sade uses for both male and female orgasm is "discharge" *(décharger),* for at those points of intersection between utterance and bodily function, when one haltingly states and spastically performs orgasm, discourse is reduced to the release or emission of a *secretion.*

Yet the text presumes elsewhere to adhere to a solid distinction between the dry theory of a dissertation and the lubricious practice of sex itself. The simple moral truth that encloses itself within the discursive formation of the dissertation—"Fuck, Eugénie, fuck therefore my dear angel . . . we are born to fuck" (221, 226)—lies supposedly at the other end of the scale from the orgasmic discharge that is that very dissertation put into practice—"Sacred bugger-God! I come [*je décharge*]! . . . Aïe! Aïe! Aïe! . . . fuck! . . . fuck!" (272)—but the representational space that separates them, however much it presumes itself to be absolute, however much it relies on the explicit graphics of a textual configuration, is seriously confounded. As one realism (performance or realization of fantasies) is crossed by the other (the seamless transmission, both practical and theoretical, of libertine knowledge), a type of inversion takes place that, while seeming to mechanically reactivate the representative apparatus, nevertheless calls its operation into question. Klossowski calls such a reversibility "the presence of *nonlanguage* in language . . . a foreclosure of language by language,"[45] in other words, the disclosure of language's darkroom.

In the blink of an eye in which the realist pact is concluded, in the darkroom, under the shroud or gauze behind which everything imaginable supposedly takes place and comes to life, there occurs a crossing and a doubling, such that whatever emerges to satisfy the logic of the system—pure pleasure, pure inverted morality, every fantasy realized—brings with it the tearing of a veil, a type of representational breakdown, everything upside down or back-to-front, the image of the world irrevocably awry. As a result, those within that world are required to inhabit that very breakdown or suspension, and, to the extent that they recognize and acknowledge it (most clearly in *The 120 Days of Sodom*), come to inhabit a place of no return, straddle the very quandary, accept to be the bearers of their own representational contradiction, are stretched on the rack of a chiasmatic switch that will never survive the light of day, but whose tenebrous enactment means the veritable and visual undoing of the world.

THE SECOND darkroom reversal of *Philosophy in the Bedroom* concerns more explicitly the aesthetico-political relation. It comes into focus in the pamphlet that Dolmancé says he picked up on the way to the château, "Yet Another Effort, Frenchmen, If You Would Become Republicans."

There, for the space that represents about a quarter of the entire text, whatever other forms of representation there are, whatever the insistent demands of the theater of practice and of demonstration, coming and discharge themselves are subordinated to the exposition of a radical politics of sexuality. Now, as I have already stated, whereas it is difficult to determine the discursive status of the often lengthy treatises that are embedded in the text via the mouths of one educator or another (pure diegesis or pure mimesis, pure theory or pure practice), the pamphlet does at least preserve the homogeneity of a single textual form. It is a treatise that presents itself as such, a well-demarcated piece of philosophy introduced into the bedroom, ostensibly responding to Eugénie's request for more instruction in the form of something to console herself with following her excesses (295). Hence, in and of itself, like philosophy in and of itself (to the extent that it is able to remain homogeneous), the pamphlet appears to escape the question of its discursive format. However, the articulation of the sexual and the political (or philosophico-political) depends on a problematization of the homogeneity I have just allowed. That is to say, the words of "Yet Another Effort, Frenchmen" as they appear within the homogeneous format of the pamphlet represent one version of that articulation, but they are transformed into another version of it once the pamphlet is inserted into the middle of the text called *Philosophy in the Bedroom*. Philosophy is not the same outside the bedroom as it is inside, nor is a text of philosophy the same when it is distributed on the street and when it is read within the more or less theatrical dispositions of a literary text. Indeed, as we shall see, the supposed homogeneous interiority of the pamphlet is called into question in a number of ways, all of which derive from its being inserted here, from problems of framing and contextualization, and from a certain rupturing of the textual surface that necessarily results.

But let us attempt to confine ourselves for the moment to the content of the pamphlet, to its argument in favor of what I'll call a radical sexuality as a radical politics. It makes that argument in terms that do not go substantially beyond the commonplace presumption that a "transgressive" sexuality is by implication revolutionary. Rather than bringing politics into the bedroom, it takes the bedroom into the street. We need to ask whether, as a result, politics becomes liberated, liberalized, or revolutionized, invested with a libidinal charge, or whether on the other hand a polymorphously perverse sexuality gets disciplined and systematized, policed. Sade, via the pamphlet's anonymous author, via Dolmancé, clearly believes in the former alternative, and "Yet Another Effort, Frenchmen" proceeds on that basis. It reserves much of its force for its anticlericalism, arguing the necessity of an atheism in the service of the revolution, the need for the church to be ridiculed to death following the guillotining of the monarch. It therefore reminds us how another supposedly revolutionary nation, modern America, remains to this day "under God" in more ways than one. The pamphlet also argues against "the atrocity of capital punishment" in terms that are surprisingly modern—"impractical, unjust, inadmissible . . . it has never repressed crime" (310, 311)—terms that again serve as a salutary reminder of where the supposedly first revolutionary and the supposedly primary democratic state still stands in that regard. It argues that the crime of theft has no sense in an unequal society, that murder cannot offend nature, and has in any case always been the very stuff of politics, especially via the continuation of politics as the failed diplomacy that is war. With respect to laws regarding sexual practice, apart from the expected plea in favor of adultery, incest, and sodomy, what there is that could be called properly revolutionary reduces primarily to a vindication of the rights of woman, "able to give themselves over to [carnal pleasure] wholeheartedly, absolutely free of all encumbering hymeneal ties, of all false notions of modesty" (321). Except that such rights have to contend with uninhibited "proprietary rights of enjoyment" *(droit de propriété sur la jouissance)* (320; *Oeuvres*, 503), and all of a sudden sex appears to be transformed into pure power, pure politics, such that the question of whether that politics can be called revolutionary or reactionary becomes hard to resolve.

Although both man and woman have a de jure right to enjoyment, only man, whom nature has given "the strength needed to bend women to our will" (319), is able to exercise that right de facto. But this aporia of the libertine's unbridled pleasure principle is finally less a question of sexual inequality—in a state of revolutionary or insurrectionary republicanism, women can presumably invent the means to bend men to their will or even count on legislation to do so—than it is a question of another distinction, indeed, another formulation of the distinction we have been dealing with all along, that between politics and aesthetics. For the seeming contradiction between freedom and the right to submit another to one's pleasure occurs in the middle of the text of "Yet Another Effort, Frenchmen," as if bisecting it along this fault line, and it is recognized as a contradiction by a footnote that thereby rends the formal surface of the tract in a way that I did not previously acknowledge:

> Let it not be said that I contradict myself here, and that after having established at some point further above, that we have no right to bind a woman to ourselves, I destroy those principles when I declare now that we have the right to constrain her; I repeat, it is a question of enjoyment [jouissance] only, not of property. . . . I have no real right of possession over such-and-such a woman, but I have incontestable rights to the enjoyment of her. (319)

In reality the contradiction is itself bisected: in the text itself, the distinction that gives rise to the footnote is quantitative, concerning time: "It likewise becomes incontestable that we have the right to compel [women's] submission, *not exclusively, for I should then be contradicting myself, but temporarily*" (319; italics mine). As long as submission remains temporary rather than exclusive or permanent, there would be no contradiction with the idea, made explicit in the preceding paragraph, that "never may there be granted to one sex the legitimate right to lay monopolizing hands upon the other. . . . The act of possession can only be exercised upon a chattel or an animal, never upon an individual" (318, 319). Temporary submission preempts monopolization or exclusivity; that is to say, it precludes the permanent subjection that would imply possession. In the footnote itself, however, the question of temporary versus permanent possession gets somewhat displaced: time comes to regulate a qualitative difference between *jouissance* and property. The essence of the aporia may indeed be temporal, but it cannot easily be resolved by this introduction of a new distinction between enjoyment (*jouissance*) and possession. Can we still presume one to be temporary and the other permanent or exclusive? Is enjoyment something less than exclusive, something vicarious? How long is it? How long is a *jouissance*—120 seconds, minutes, hours, days? Doesn't the libertine strive for a type of enjoyment in perpetuity? On the other hand, can property not also be enjoyed? How long does it have to be enjoyed to become a property? How would we understand the enjoyment in usufruct, defined as the right to (enjoy) a piece of property that belongs to another (in French, *avoir la jouissance d'un bien sans en avoir la propriété*)? And is possession not in fact rendered problematic and nonexclusive by the finiteness of beings?

Enjoyment and property are maintained, therefore, in an uneasy opposition that risks becoming a contradiction. Time will tell the difference between them. They appear to cross into each other's space in the impossible simultaneity of text and footnote, in the fissure or abyss that is thereby opened, in the recessive space where an argument retreats into the difficulties of its finer details at the bottom of a page. One domain where we distinguish enjoyment from property is that of aesthetics, although the terms and definition of that enjoyment are the subject of debate. We would impute to Kant the insistence that the pleasure associated with a work of art should outlast or transcend what we understand in terms of *jouissance*, but perhaps the critique of Benjamin amounts similarly to a reproach that the narcissistic enjoyment of the mass fails to rise far above or beyond a sexual or physiological type of pleasure. Once enjoyment cedes to the idea of property as possession, on the other hand, however narcissistically invested that idea continues to be, we are obviously faced with juridico-political questions. In fact, the point at which supposedly private pleasure and individual will become susceptible to juridico-political regulation appears as the all-consuming political debate of the contemporary era, be it a matter of individuals, families, or nations. The aporia of "Yet Another Effort, Frenchmen" is, by means of what it invokes concerning individual autonomy and subjection, quite clearly that of sovereignty.

It might be said, therefore, that politics and aesthetics undergo some sort of reciprocal or mutual inversion on the sidelines or in the wings, relatively unseen, in what I am calling a recessive space in the center of "Yet Another Effort, Frenchmen." More specifically, it is within this same context that the possibility of an eroticization of a reactionary or fascist politics intersects with the possibility of the erotic subversion of that reaction, and by extension of fascism. The absolute right to one's own *jouissance* could on the one hand introduce an indomitable disorder into authoritarian politics, oppose to fascism's regimentalization the very "insurrection" as "the republic's permanent condition" (315) that Blanchot underlines in *The Infinite Conversation*.[46] On the other hand, insurrection necessarily intersects at some point with fascism's capacity to wield its own arbitrary power and to clothe it in the fabric of aesthetic uniformity, to be precisely the enactment of its own absolute right to *jouissance,* to be the dirty secrets of an autarchic or autocratic theater of sexual cruelty.

However, as Thomas Keenan develops in his *Fables of Responsibility,* following Blanchot, it is precisely within such a question that the political properly resides, as a matter not of "interpretation" but of "unreadability." The absolute right to one's own *jouissance* is first and foremost a textual datum, one that comes to reading as the aporetic pronouncement within "Yet Another Effort, Frenchmen" that we have just seen, or as a discursive utterance and narrative enactment within *Philosophy in the Bedroom.* In this way we first "see" it put into practice as what Blanchot calls the madness of writing and of reason, as "the freedom to say everything,"[47] if you wish a state of permanent insurrection of language itself, the right to *jouissance* but not possession of it, with all the attendant risks (and in Sade's pages and pages, we begin to understand how he measures the temporality of this linguistic usufruct). It is this "possible impossibility" of writing, and of reading, that, according to Keenan, "makes politics . . . ineluctable." That is not to reduce the question of politics in Sade to that of the freedom of expression, though a claim is explicitly laid to such a freedom in "Yet Another Effort, Frenchmen"; even less is it to reduce the political to the textual or to encompass it within an artistic or aesthetic field. Rather, it means passing again through the darkroom of representation, what Keenan calls the "withdrawal of security" common to reading and politics, a politics understood as different from "something a subject does when it knows."[48] What I am reading as a chiasmus or even aporia of the political and the aesthetic, an inversion or perversion of one and the other, therefore goes beyond a contradiction or confusion that it is our responsibility to resolve, some static in the way of a clear political message. It is an irreducible unreadability, both the shadowy doubtful place where daylight logic is confounded, and the means by which what the world sees as its own reflection and immutable perpetuation is subjected to an inescapable overturning; *the possibility, therefore, of an inversion or reversal that we might call revolution.* As long as the possibility of a revolutionary or even any transformative politics of power as potentiality or becoming means reconciling some imagined version of the world with the reality of it, as long as it means *realizing* emancipatory desire, then there is no eluding the camera obscura. This darkroom operates as a powerful apparatus, and an ideological apparatus of stasis, as a result of which revolution is consistently preempted by reproduction; but it is thanks to the blind moment of that same apparatus that the world can be turned upside down. The confined opening into such an apparatus, the point of entry where the rays of sex and politics converge, is the moment of crossover into its innermost recesses where nothing can prevent an inversion.

The recessive fissure in the middle of "Yet Another Effort, Frenchmen" is echoed by cracks that appear in its exterior frame. It is supposedly a type of throwaway given to Dolmancé on his way to the château, but immediately after it has been read, Eugénie will opine that she is tempted to believe that Dolmancé in fact wrote it. Dolmancé replies that "my discourses . . . lend to what has just been read to us the appearance of a repetition" (339). We can hear the French word *répétition* in at least three senses. First, as the repetition of the libertine discourse that Dolmancé has already developed prior to the reading of the tract. Second, as a *rehearsal* for the orgiastic representation that is about to be enacted (itself a more or less approximate repetition of previous orgies), which would again crack the distinction between theory (dissertation, discourse, tract) and practice (orgiastic enactment), bringing the pamphlet itself, or at least the *viva voce* reading of it, into the structure of theatrical representation, or else setting it up as the pose on the basis of which the realist sexual theatrics will be produced. For the third sense of repetition is precisely the most literal one, that of repetition as reproducibility.

"Yet Another Effort, Frenchmen" is of the age of the reproducibility of the printed document. As the three libertines and their apprentice are reading and heeding it, the pamphlet is presumably being read all over Paris and inciting the people to implementation of it, just as Sade himself sought to effect with his atheistic speech delivered from the tribune of the Convention in November 1793, three weeks before his rearrest. It is produced as a manifesto destined for immediate consumption and implementation as a set of revolutionary libertine principles, a dissertation that hopes to find an immediate demonstration. In this way its logic appears to be that of a realist politics: it should be understood as the discursive model, the emancipatory call to arms that will find its perfect copy in actual revolutionary action such as will bring a libertine world to fruition. It presumes that sort of photographic fidelity, as does, no doubt, any such call to arms: repeat my words as actions, the tract says, be the very portrait of what I call for, reproduce me as if in close-up, I expect to see what you are reading enacted and so revealed or developed for the historic archive, as my photographic image. Hence the age of such a document is in fact in doubt; it perhaps extends beyond that of the printed document to that of a representational mechanism that risks aestheticizing the political, the age of cinema. When the mass enacts this program, it will hope to see itself coming into focus and into close-up out of the relative imprecision of the prescription for it: it will take the program, put a human face on it, and as a consequence find the image of itself reinforced. When the program of the manifesto is enacted, the significance of the printed document will be as if developed and revealed in its photographic fidelity to itself; historical document will become historical event. For the faithful enactment of a program, theoretical discourse becomes social reality or history, would seem to be the dream of every politics understood as something a subject does when it knows. A successful politics thus involves history painting its self-portrait, taking a photograph of itself, the implementation of a realist reproduction.[49]

Dolmancé's tract comes thus to read like a photographic sequence within the film of *Philosophy in the Bedroom*. It appears between two orgies and, by virtue of its formal configuration within the text, occupies the *recessive* position that I have already alluded to, functioning within the space of a retreat. But that retreat has a precise and formal frame. Before the tract is read, the gardener Augustin is ordered to retire—"Out with you, Augustin: this is not for you" (295)—and following its reading, he is recalled in order to respond to Dolmancé's erection. In fact, we are told, "this fine lad's superb ass" has been preoccupying Dolmancé's mind while he has been talking—"All my ideas seem involuntarily to relate themselves to it. . . . Show my eyes that masterpiece" (346). But how are we to understand that? That Augustin's ass was simply being held in abeyance as the piece of reality that would provide the means by which libertine theory as expounded in the tract would be followed immediately by practice? Or rather that the explicit politics of the pamphlet were all the while being aestheticized offstage by thoughts of Augustin's ass, his real historic piece of flesh functioning as the masterly portrait that gives vigor and energy, and cult value, to the libertine manifesto? Or again, is Augustin's ass the idealist repository of political meaning of the pamphlet, banished precisely so that it might "occupy Dolmancé's head"—"il est inouï comme le superbe cul de ce jeune garçon m'occupe la tête" (*Oeuvres*, 530)—in other words, so that it might function as a concept and as the transcendental signified for the whole revolutionary libertine enterprise, out of sight but not out of mind, the sense of it in fact being articulated coextensively with the utterances that refer to it?

Whatever precise relation of politics and aesthetics is represented by the automatic or involuntary diverting of Dolmancé's attention, it seems that, in retreating, Augustin takes with him offstage and into the shadows the force and significance of the libertine's, or the pamphlet's, words. In spite of its explicit address, by means of the reference to Augustin's ass, the tract's sense gets redirected out of the space of its visualizable representativity, into what is necessarily invisible and inaccessible. That means less that a public politics is reduced to, or corrupted by, private desires—even though that may or may not happen in fact, more or less systematically—than it suggests that what is promoted as, or presumed to be realizable as, a political program, relying as it does on the reproduction of a pure realist surface, nevertheless answers to a space of inversion or perversion, an unseen recessive niche through which every realist representation must transit in order to be reproduced, and where things are not the way they turn out, and why things, especially things political, rarely turn out the way we expect or desire them to. As I have already mentioned, following the orgy that follows Augustin's being summoned back, Dolmancé will again retire with him, back into nonrepresentable space, so that he can indulge the fantasy that he is so reluctant to describe. And as I have already argued, the "turpitude" that "one must be alone and in the deepest shadow" to give oneself over to, the as if unutterable scandal that men of honor must protect yet confront, perhaps consists in nothing more than acknowledging the functioning of that veiled space: Dolmancé wishes to visit the absolutely recessive place where the culminating libertine act, the pure politics or pure aesthetics of it, inverts into and confronts its own inoperativity.

NATURE IS the third arena of chiasmatic reversal. Presumably the same ideology of realism that we have already so consistently observed enables Sade's characters to insist that libertine practice derives from it. In *Philosophy in the Bedroom* nature is the touchstone of human behavior. As

Blanchot points out, by the time of *La Nouvelle Justine,* nature becomes a deceitful bitch to be abhorred.[50] But here at least, nature stands as the antithesis of the law, the ultimate law that renders human laws all but unnecessary. The references to it begin with the Chevalier's apology for homosexuals whose only wrong "is Nature's" (188), they being no more able to choose their preferences than is one to be born with a limp or not ("bancal ou bien fait" [*Oeuvres,* 373; cf. 188]), and end with Dolmancé inviting his syphilitic valet to spurt his venom "into each of the two natural conduits" belonging to Mme de Mistival (362). Shortly before that, Dolmancé has reminded one and all for the last time that "one single motor is operative in this universe, and that motor is Nature" (360). In between, the repetitions are countless, the recourse to nature systematic, and especially so within the excursus "Yet Another Effort, Frenchmen."

Nature, indeed natural resemblance, is thus called on to accredit every libertine credo, all the way from feminine cupidity ("Woman's destiny is to be wanton, like the bitch, the she-wolf" [219]), to sodomy ("Is not this aperture circular, like this instrument?" [264–65]), to coprophagia ("When [Nature] created men, she was pleased to vary their tastes as she made different their countenances" [227]), and of course to murder ("Destruction being one of the chief laws of nature, nothing that destroys can be criminal" [237–38]). Everything reduces to such a mimetic fidelity, and politics (in the form of human law) as much as aesthetics (*Philosophy in the Bedroom* is mostly roses and myrtles, whereas *The 120 Days of Sodom* vaunts nature's ugliness and disorder) consists in returning to the degree zero of the natural state.

Yet the logic of natural resemblance is as generous and as varied as nature itself. Blanchot has well described Sade's "shameless contradictions,"[51] and nowhere is the latter's rhetorical legerdemain more obvious than when it comes to the productions of nature. If we can understand how a circular anus matches a circular penis, we are less clear on why differently shaped faces make for an innocent smile in one case and a literal shit-eating grin in another. Throughout "Yet Another Effort, Frenchmen," the recourse to nature, whose most faithful imitators are animals and primitive peoples, in fact systematically functions via the multitudinous differences of cultural relativism. Because Rome, Athens, Thebes, and Sardanapolis did it as much as Batavia, Mindanao, Louisiana, and Algiers, not to mention mythological deities, so should we also; a universalist nature spontaneously generates myriad different cultural practices. Within this unbroken mimetic circle, whatever is de facto is also invoked de jure: what is, is and so should be. That paradox has an explicit formulation in "Yet Another Effort, Frenchmen," where it is explained that when nature comes to teach its lessons, they will be articulated not just through differences of culture but specifically through the artifice of agriculture: "All intellectual ideas are so greatly subordinate to Nature's physical aspect that the comparisons supplied us by agriculture will never deceive us in morals" (333). Such is the rationale for euthanasia, for "do you not prune the tree when it has overmany branches?" (336). Sade's nature, it would seem, is always already cultural and agricultural. Though it serves as the transcendent order, it can operate as effective morality only via a cultivational or agricultural representation, by means of the transformation and deformation implied by agriculture or horticulture, in the final analysis by means of the technological.

When it comes to the orgiastic scene, of course, the technological transformation of nature is on full display, and the mechanization of corporeal relations at maximum efficiency. The *tableau vivant* retains a link to the pastoral on the one hand and the family portrait on the other, but the acts of nature that are staged and set in motion in Sade amount to nothing so much as a complicated mechanics, the bodies being bent to the service of a well-oiled desiring machine. So the discursive recourse to a nature that reveals itself to be instead culture and agriculture, in short a technology, finds its analogy in the machineries of the erotic scene, natural couplings refined into multiple moving parts. But that analogy in turn comes full circle, for the machine that is most actively at work in Sade's recourse to nature is that of discourse or rhetoric itself; as Barthes has extensively analyzed, in the final analysis "the scene is merely discourse. We better understand now upon what Sade's erotic combinative [combinatoire] rests and toward what it tends: its origin and its sanctions are rhetorical."[52] Barthes notes certain figures operating by means of the scene: metaphor, asyndeton, anacoluthon.[53] Yet the rhetorical gesture that I am examining here is perhaps nothing more than a form of tautological repetition whereby nature extends itself from some presumed degree zero, through shapes of orifice or difference of countenance, all the way to sodomy and coprophilia, while still managing to say, "This is the nature that is." Or in another version, a discursive and performative mirroring allows a master or mistress of discourse to say, with frequent recourse to nature, "Watch these bodies bend this way and that, and even break and bleed, because they can," and the bodies do just that in order to say it is so. It works like clockwork once the pieces are made to fit and the mechanism is set in train, and whenever it falters, the defective part is replaced, and the machine is rewound or refueled to begin all over again. There is indeed one single *motor* operative in this universe, and that motor is Nature.

Tautology thus feeds into the rhetorical darkroom, the space of a realist technology of discourse. In it nature reproduces itself as well as perversion does; indeed, nature can even reproduce itself as perversion and still remain nature, or perversion can reproduce itself as a natural morphological conformity yet still blaspheme and offend. Any twist is possible, for it all takes place in a discursive black hole, in the recessive space that necessarily exists and functions behind the self-evidences we see and hear being repeated. Sade is only possible on such a condition: his untroubled narrative and discursive surface, his confident rational insistence, repeats, not parodies, the intellectual, pedagogical, and epistemological heritage of the Enlightenment. He is its pure product in the sense of its pure reproduction. If he perverts its project entirely, symmetrically, it is because he understands that the camera obscura of realist reproduction functions by inversion, or even "before" that, he knows how every repetition opens the space of a difference that is a transformation, a substitution and a reversal. There is in that sense always cinema in his work, he is always in cinema, the cinema has its own indispensable niche within his writing. Not in the form of a "supplementary play of the camera"—in that sense, Foucault was perhaps right, and no doubt right about Pasolini or Cavani—but as a recessive darkroom that supports every realist enactment played out before our eyes. But neither is it a hidden recess in the normal sense, nor is it even a space for what is imagined but remains repressed, for whatever takes place there or thanks to it will be exhaustively inventoried; and even in that rare case where we aren't privy to it, someone whispers it to someone. If there is in Sade a revelation of what was previously unknown, it is no more than his pointing to the existence of the apparatus itself, the dark place or darkroom itself, the space of inversion behind what we see with perfect reproductive clarity, the very space that enables it to be seen with that perfect reproductive distinctness, and with the keen focus of a violent and purgative illumination.

My argument throughout this chapter has been that in such a space, at its point of entry, the vector of politics also and necessarily crosses that of aesthetics; that it would be naive to imagine that one comes to be perverted by the other according to a program being enacted in front of the camera, something that can somehow be neutralized or reduced to inaction, leaving a pure form of one or the other. What we see as a realist or realistic political agenda, as well as what we see as an unabashed aesthetics, albeit of cruelty or sexuality, depend one and the other on the same space of inversion, and their very reproduction, repetition, and transmission take place only to the extent that they pass through the darkroom that lies behind the clarifying lens. In this we are not as far as we might seem from Rancière, whose distribution of the sensible *(partage du sensible)* identifies first a politics that emerges, and indeed becomes confused with the aesthetic, as soon as a visible space of operation is determined, and then a particular aesthetic regime where thought "has become foreign to itself" (23). The darkroom of inversion is invisible only in the sense that it is what realism represses even as it requires it, in the sense that its apparatus rigorously controls and over*sees* what enters there. But it is by no means in the dark about what it is lodging there. Rather, it is a space of pure visibility, of an as if panoptical presumption about what will go on there, a regime of pure political surveillance. A certain version of politics is no doubt at home in such a space, in a tightly controlled regime whose elements and operations are limited enough to be reducible to the laws of physics; no overt apparatus of control, just an incontrovertible arrangement dictated by the movement of light rays; and a certain aesthetics no doubt enables itself there also, opting for ever so little more light while it claims to be doing no more than letting the world emerge in its pristine clarity.

Yet the same logic—indeed, the same conception of controlled and transformative space—leads from the camera obscura of realist reproduction to the vaulted dungeon of *The 120 Days of Sodom*. The torture chamber would similarly be a place of raw power and pure spectacle. It would seemingly function as a place we have not yet been to, the site of some promised yet deferred revelation—"a little patience, friend reader, and we shall soon hide nothing from your inquisitive gaze [*nous ne te cacherons plus rien]*" (*120 Days*, 485; *Oeuvres*, 270), we are promised on day twenty-one—but in the end, it offers but an extreme version of the logic, structure, and architecture of the libertine enterprise in general, a place where the ultimate fantasies of cruelty are able to be realized, where arcane erotic and psychopathological imaginings are brought from the back of the brain into the most secret recess of the château. *It is the darkest of the darkrooms, but finally just a darkroom.* In it the line between politics and aesthetics remains as difficult to draw as ever, for its economy of voyeurism and ecstatic transport intersects even more stringently with one of absolute manipulation and subjection. Does the power reside in subjection and the ecstasy in the spectacle, or is it the very voyeuristic positioning that renders possible the exercise of power, as Foucault has detailed for us, and the very seduction of power that is the figure for and means to any rapture? It should be possible to understand murder as pure politics and sex as pure aesthetics; we should be able to distinguish will and libido, the sanctum of power and the boudoir of pleasure. But Sade has shown us once and for all that that is not the case, and that the further we delve toward a purity of one, the more we find it traversed by vectors of the other. Thus the ultimate recessive space of the dungeon, once it is put to use, immediately loses its exclusive status. At the end of *The 120 Days,* as the maltreatments are multiplied within the main theatrical space of the château and the murders become systematic, there is less and less distinction among the different forms of recessive space; and by the very end, the upstairs chambers have become cells within a generalized carceral architecture. That means that the logic of the darkroom is finally its own insoluble paradox: it was hiding everything and nothing as long as it functioned to reproduce what was seen outside of it; yet on the other hand, once it is exposed to reveal the inversion that takes place within it, nothing any longer preserves visible space from its effects of inversion, and all possible transformative perversions spread across the surface of the everyday.

Such is the cinema in Sade. By filming it as *Salò,* Pasolini may have given to fascism an aesthetic credibility as Foucault charges. But Pasolini did not impose that aesthetics on fascism from the outside, for, according to what we have seen here, there would be no *an*esthetic politics that a fascism could choose to aestheticize or a communism to politicize. Neither, however, would there be an apolitical aesthetics. Sade's camera obscura offers a type of infinite chiasmatic regress of one and the other and at the same time shows how the realist surface of the world is traversed by creative as much as degenerative inversions of it.

THE INVERSIONS THAT TAKE PLACE via the camera obscura are positioned adjacent to, as if behind, the visible world whose representation they assure. They are not, finally, buried in some concealed vault that searching, discovery, and illumination will bring to the light of day. However much Sade continues to have recourse to underground enclosures that hide a depravity defined by depth, his recesses are in fact spaces of more or less patent operations, to which one retreats in order to return to the theater with further confirmation of what is being narrated. Sadean sexuality is in that sense practiced in a space that I would call "dorsal"; it is the polymorphous paradigm of a sexual relation conceived of from behind, of a sexual that "continuously surprises, takes from behind, works from the back."[54]

That is to say, and not to say, a number of things. It is to say that whatever passes for a frontal sexuality receives its confirmation, is reproduced—for example, as norm or normative—by passing through the space, and we might say the experience, of its own overturning. It sees itself the way it imagines itself to be, receives back its own accredited image, only on that condition. It is replicated as frontal only by risking the dorsal. It continues to be represented as sexuality's open surface, can claim to be its real, dominant, or legitimate field of practice only because there exists behind it, providing its very *endorsement,* the close dark space of inversion.

That is not to say, not in the same way or in the same terms at least, that perversion is the oppositional condition of possibility for normative sexuality. There is no doubt that the perversions Sade describes taking place behind closed doors are resolutely transgressive: his libertinage posits itself in violent opposition and resistance to normative laws, for example, virginity, marriage, and so on. But he is for revolution; his is not the transgression of a taboo that would serve to reinforce it, and he seeks nothing less than the ruination of existing laws of sexual conduct and whatever is controlled by them. No doubt he hopes to institute something like a normative libertinage, but we would have difficulty recognizing any code in it other than, perhaps, the license of the six hundred passions enumerated and classified in *The 120 Days,* the polymorphous perversity that has become his trademark. Reading the dorsal in Sade means reading through his transgressive, oppositional practice to develop a concept of invertibility that is different from, although at times consonant with, what is called perversion. It means reading through both transgression and perversion into what they offer in terms of ascesis, as Foucault might call it, or *apathy*, the emptying of pleasure referred to by Klossowski.[55] This has, of course, on one side the refusal of sympathy that permits a crime; but on the other side it involves the "expropriation of one's own body and of others" that is the beginning of every new sexual experience.[56]

Dorsal inversion would represent the adjacent space of a normative sexuality that it nevertheless overturns. Because of that overturning, because there is turning, there is no simple continuum of practices on the basis of which the so-called normal would find its borders problematized and made more accommodating, so that the so-called perverse could come to be recuperated within it. Rather, what is practiced in the first instance is a turning itself—there are *versions*—beginning with the one that *turns to* what is behind in order to vindicate itself, beginning in a sense, therefore, with that very behind and the turn to it. From a frontal perspective, what takes place behind inverts, in order to restore, what appears before, the visible scene enacted with repetitive certainty and assuring regularity and presuming to preserve a satisfying image of itself. From the dorsal perspective, however, what takes place in general begins with a turn, producing serial disjunctions that are nevertheless related by the fact and effect of that turn. Once there is that turning, that dorsal inversion, then any practice becomes accountable for any other within the serial structure of invertibility. What takes place behind, within the space that makes inversion possible and renders it necessary, is therefore a whole disruptive tropological repertoire, a taxonomy of passionate instances that means variation and exorbitance, but from within which figures such as those of submission and cruelty, constraint and spectacle, can never be excluded. Tenderness is not continuous with cruelty, or voyeurism with sadism, but neither are they mutually exclusive. Each requires the inversion of the dorsal to validate its representation of itself, to affirm its realism, but through inversion each enters the structure or darkroom of transformation, deformation, and perversion.

For similar reasons, a dorsal sexuality cannot be reduced to the anal, any more than it can be reduced to the animal. If it risks the figure of a type of regression, that is because it evokes the fetal pose, a type of amniotic submission beyond desire or even consciousness, an openness to something that might be as much somnolescence as arousal; something not even sexual in the strict sense, a letting come that is ultimately, as we have seen in previous discussions, the opening to ethics. To the extent that it is *a tergo*, to use Freud's term, and therefore *more ferarum* (as though the Latin terms will help us either to rarify or pathologize it), it implies, precisely, a shift in the function ascribed to language, the realignment of phatic utterance that becomes necessary once partners speak not face-to-face but into parallel structures of the void. Already we would presume the sexual performance of speech to operate differently from either the interview or the dialogue, and to "degenerate" all the way to the sublingual groan, cry, sigh, or moan; sounds uttered from an absolute ecstatic solitude that still manage to say, "I am here (with you)." What there is of animality in dorsality recognizes and valorizes those forms of utterance, or even the type of regressive context—infancy, insanity, zoologicality—within which they can be validated, just as it recognizes and valorizes also a gestural and sensorial activism that is no longer governed by the visual—scent, the caress of hair and breath—as well as a passive or regressive sensory deprivation of one vis-à-vis the other, the face buried in the nape or in the pillow.

Anal sex is no more necessarily dorsal than is dorsal sex necessarily anal. Quite clearly, Sade wants nothing more than the "the nature against nature" of sodomy, but he wants it as a form of transgressive normality, and he will get it there by way of various misogynies, homophobias, and misanthropies alike. On the other hand, however, the anal exists within the space of dorsal inversion. In that respect, we would have to go so far as to say there is no sex without anality; to the extent that dorsality refers to the human body, the anus functions as its darkroom in all the senses that have been developed earlier. It is behind the sexual while being adjacent to, or coextensive with, it; it is what or where the sexual turns around in order to remain the sexual. But it is the place of a sexual crossover, where sex crosses over, from regeneration into putrefaction, of course; yet also, therefore, where the sexual turns out of itself, into a type of sexual *indifference*. Hence by implying anality, the dorsal disavows gender, becoming as indifferently male and female as it is indifferently heterosexual or homosexual.

It does so in other terms as well. The dorsal means a turning away from the morphologico-visual regime of sexual identification, a turning toward the body of another as indifferently sexualized. I say a "turning toward" because I am not suggesting that, within that regime, the back coded as female looks the same as the back coded as male. But from behind, the sexual organs themselves, and what might be called the purely sexual morphology of the body, no longer provide the governing basis for sexual attraction or the sexual encounter. Once sex or sexuality is back-to-front, then the sexual relation begins precisely with a type of asexualized clean slate on the basis of which the construction of genders and sexualities will take place. However fleeting that beginning, however quickly touch might impose a morphological sexuality, the dorsal will have first been that neutral space or virgin territory of every sexual possibility. In the encounter conceived of from behind, the sexual morphologies, organs, or protuberances that come to be imprinted upon the back will signify first in a space of impersonality.

Dorsal space may well function as the black box where real or realist human bodies are reproduced in their secure sexual identities, always photographically and photogenically, photogenerically more of the same; that happens when the frontal turns its back on the dorsal and calls it an empty space, a null set. By the same token, however, what also operates through the dorsal is the recognition that any such identity is reproduced in the unseen moment of an inversion, in the same space in which any other number of turnings are generated and out of which sexuality is produced. The dorsal camera obscura is the realist mechanism by which sex—say a physiological morphology or sex organ—represents itself to itself as a form of sexuality; but for being the space of a reconfirmation, it is also that of a remodeling. Dorsal inversion means that sexuality has to be constructed in order to be represented—even reproduction is a construction—but it also implies that any such construction is susceptible to reconstruction and can be neither confirmed nor endorsed without a passage through the darkroom, into the recess of instability.

The invertibility of a dorsal sexuality means a different sense of the reversible, and by extension of the reciprocal. Sade, we know, strove for a systematic symmetry of passions. As Barthes points out, he thereby installed a rigorous "rule of reciprocity." But reciprocity in Sade is to be understood differently from the frontal mirroring of simple couplings, of subject and object in a type of equitable give-and-take of activity and passivity. If Sade's characters take turns at being "whipper and whipped, coprophagist and coprophagee . . . sodomist and sodomized, agent and patient, subject and object," they do so not to level the playing field by means of a simple interchangeability, but rather to destabilize the identitarian basis of such oppositions. Sade's reciprocal couplings produce "classes of actions, not groups of individuals. . . . Sexual practice is never used to identify a subject."[57] Similarly, the subject-in-dorsality forgoes face-to-face reciprocity, as well as eye-level or head-to-head equality, in favor of a reversibility of role, function, and activity. And its reversals or interchanges of activity and passivity call into question how we understand those roles. Whoever "takes" the dorsal position, molds oneself to the back of another, exposes at the same time one's own back. Whoever "gives" dorsally, to the safety of being embraced or the adventure of being exposed, knows that in the reverse mode no comfort will come, not even the gaze of another to keep one, ideally, positioned and defined. Unless, precisely, coupling be itself "inverted" by the arrival of a third, another other, which is the outside possibility that haunts dorsal space.

The dorsal is therefore also multiple. But the multiplicity of dorsal relations should not be understood simply, in the sexual context, to imply the orgy; it is more transgeneric than that. For where we have been leading, or turning, via Sade's darkroom is finally into the very sense of the apparatus itself, into what, in being dorsal, necessarily leads from gender to kind, and then beyond, to a certain conception of what exceeds the human in the form of the technological. In Sade, there are of course numerous inanimate sexual apparatuses, from dildos to complicated pleasure or torture machines. Besides, as we have already discussed, the sexual scene itself functions as a machine, turning increasingly mechanistic as it becomes multiple, a finite *combinatoire* with no inactive parts.[58] But the conceptual space of the camera obscura that I have been developing here refers only in passing to that sort of prosthetic mechanical compounding or supplementation. Dorsal space, where a machine for realist reproducibility doubles with mechanisms of invertibility, returns us to the technology in the back that is my consistent theme. In the dorsal space behind the back extends a darkroom that is a type of converse to the house that, in Levinas, defined the subject as interiority and by extension enabled the face-to-face relation. But a dorsality beyond the face is also beyond the back in the sense of an exteriorization. By means of it the human rejoins not the element but an irrecuperable technological otherness that nevertheless forms part of it.

Dorsality means opening to the apparatus behind the back, the technological in the back. Dorsal sexuality suggests something beyond Sade's counternature; its polymorphousness is not that of *perversibility* but that of a type of pure *invertibility,* an originary invertibility as if prior to representation but functioning adjacent to it. Dorsal sexuality turns beyond nature (or before nature), to the nonnatural rather than to the unnatural, suggesting a rupture with respect to the body-to-body animate sexual scene, incurring exposure to the inanimate or technological. That does not necessarily mean that one couples with a machine, that the only touch is henceforth coarse fiber or cold steel. But it does mean that we have henceforth to share our most intimate space—and the dorsal is a different sense of what constitutes the body's most intimate space—with foreignness of gender and kind, but also of matter, thinking being in relation to what we cannot yet imagine that we can invite or accommodate. What comes to one from behind cannot be seen and thus can no longer be known or presumed to be even human to the same extent or in the same way as what we thought we counted on as the basis for our relations. Which way one takes the other, who takes whom or what—for that there is neither sketch, nor painting, nor even photograph, we are beyond the image of it, there is only the darkness of the darkroom concealing and producing the constant reversals of an absolute reversibility and the softness or surprise of a sensation like breathing that falls upon the nape, as easily raising hackles as feeling like home.

BACK TO BENJAMIN in the end. He has his own version of dorsal space: it is the future behind the angel of history, whom we encounter in "On the Concept of History," face "turned toward the past."[59] Such a prophet, as he is also called, is able, by turning his back on his own time, to make it "far more distinctly present to [his] visionary gaze."[60] In contrast to the historicist who interprets past events in their supposed continuity, the historical materialist sees the object of history "blasted out of the continuum of historical succession," and as a result seizes the past as a dialectical "image flashing up in the now of its recognizability."[61] Benjamin's emphasis on visuality and on the image could not be more explicit, especially in "Convolute N" of *The Arcades Project:* "Image is dialectics at a standstill. For while the relation of the present to the past is purely temporal, the relation of what-has-been to the now is dialectical: not temporal in nature but figural *[bildlich]*."[62] Referring to the formulations of "On

Some Motifs in Baudelaire," he calls the dialectical image "the involuntary memory of redeemed humanity,"[63] but this now seems not to mean that the angel survives, as it were, on a steady diet of madeleines, or that the shock of recognition of the past derives from its auratic return gaze. Instead everything points to the angel's existing in photographic space, to his being precisely a camera, the apparatus wherein "what has been comes together in a flash with the now."[64] But the "constellation" so formed is no simple reproduction: the past flashes back through the angelic darkroom to emerge into the present as a different configuration, in a dialectical process that involves constant transformation. For that reason, the constellation is a "constellation of dangers," and any rescue of the past for the revolutionary chance of the present runs the risk of catastrophe as much as of triumph.[65] That is because the darkroom behind the angel, the space that escapes his gaze, has been explicitly identified as the future. Which is what it always was, in a sense, no doubt; the photograph produced in the camera obscura always took place as the birth or invention of a future. However much we envisage it simply as the preservation of the past, it is the instantaneous production into a future moment of what was not before. The angel operates as the technological moment, interrupting the organic historical continuum to reconstellate it, to launch it into a different orbit, albeit simply by re-cognizing it. The angel's technology is, for that reason, no longer simply the technology of reproducibility; indeed, the angel is no longer just an analog camera. But that is not because he is sent by some new digital god, or good, for nothing assures us, in spite of its possibility and promise, that some new technology will shift us from our realist entrenchment. It is rather because the angel progresses steadfastly backward, consenting against all rational perspective and perspicacity to leave technology to the future or to leave the future to technology. Still, neither does that mean that he cannot or will not have anything to do with it, for he is employed precisely in producing it, he is where it takes place, he is an angel prosthetically divided between prophet and phantom, focus and reflex, scrutiny and exposure. The angel turns his back toward the future in the sense of knowing that however much he gazes and whatever he captures from his active field of vision, what comes to him to change the present and produce the future, will flash up *from out of* that field, beyond visibility, in the irretrievable past in front and the imperceptible future behind.

That's the effect of living backwards . . . it always makes one a little giddy at first.

—LEWIS CARROLL, *Through the Looking-Glass*

7. The Controversy of Dissidence Nietzsche

ZARATHUSTRA, NO DOUBT OTHERWISE UNLIKE DOLMANCÉ, has his own moment of discursive demurral. As evening falls in section 2 of "The Other Dance Song," near the end of the third part of Nietzsche's text, Zarathustra is conversing with, or rather provoking, Life, expressing his love-hate relationship to her, threatening to have her dance to the tune of his whip. Life answers by appealing for calm, insisting that they are too alike not to love each other, but reproaching Zarathustra for a type of infidelity, for wanting to retreat to the darkness of his cave:

"There is an old heavy, heavy growling bell: it growls at night all the way up to your cave—

—when you hear this bell toll the hour at midnight, then you think between one and twelve about—

—you think, oh Zarathustra, I know it, about how you will soon leave me!"

"Yes," I answered, hesitating. "But you also know—" And I said something in her ear, right in it between her tangled yellow, foolish shaggy locks.

"You *know* that, oh Zarathustra? No one knows that."—

And we looked at each other and gazed at the green meadow, over which the cool evening had just spread, and we wept together.—But at that moment I loved life more than I ever loved all my wisdom.[1]

Nietzsche's scene has none of the contextual apparatus of Sade's. We would be hard pressed to imagine what form of knowledge, unknown by all and whispered in secret, here manages so to surprise and move life itself. This secret knowledge does not represent itself as one of those things that must be kept veiled, as some infamy that certain of us are not worthy to hear of. On the other hand, however, it does function as a type of raised stakes within the set of rhetorico-discursive strategies that constitute, in the first place, the range of Zarathustra's utterances, everything he *speaks* and that is narrated about him, and more generally, the philosophy of Nietzsche. What could Zarathustra be whispering to life that we cannot know? What do he and life alone know that nobody else does? Or more precisely, what is the discursive—indeed, epistemological and ontological—status of such a secret? How does Nietzsche continue to philosophize through the muteness of an inhuman knowledge; how does his character come to an ultimate reconciliation with life beyond wisdom by bending his mouth to her ear, by so turning from speech into a form of silent intimacy? What we do know is that such an utterance is far from simple, that it involves a complex tropology. For if, as we are told, the dancer Zarathustra "has ears in his toes" (181), then we cannot presume to easily locate his mouth, and we must imagine him bending into some fantastic contortion as he whispers into life's ear, presuming we have already determined the location of her auditory organ. So what teratological scene of transplantation, prosthesis, and mutation is taking place here in order that a knowledge outside human experience be communicated?

Nietzsche's scene is not, then, that of the darkroom. Zarathustra's cave contrasts in various ways with Sade's recessive enclosures, and as we shall see, it is via the shadow, a very different play of light and shade, that a certain phenomenon of otherness is developed. However, one does not require the light of noon to discern in Nietzsche a machinery of reversals. As we saw in chapter 5, Derrida identifies in a "perhaps" uttered in the context of a "reversing catastrophe" the risk and chance of an interruption that "can be called the other, revolution, or chaos."[2] Nietzsche's reversals turn explicitly on rhetorical hinges, and their sway is usually considerably more broad than the chance displacement of a perhaps. Moreover, they are consistently played out for their very rhetorical effect, and in full view of those effects.

Yet what those reversals enact is nonetheless a type of revolutionary moment that is as forceful as the inverting physics of the photographic apparatus, the moment of contravention and dissidence that, as I have argued elsewhere, "can only develop out of the instant of the law, and necessarily develops out of the instant of the law by dividing it against itself in the moment of its constitution."[3] Nietzsche's dissident rhetoric does function as if through that photographic moment, flashing up in absolute contradiction and contravention. And what intersects with that rhetoric in the same moment, and emerges transformed by it, is something we will not hesitate to recognize as the political. But what is transformed in Nietzsche's oppositional moment, according to my reading, derives its particular pertinence from producing a politics adequate to our age, with the question of technology as firmly behind as in front of it: a type of dissident politics I call *controversion*.[4]

THE TASK of developing a systematic rhetoric of Nietzschean utterance, to account, for example, for what is silently communicated in Zarathustra's flirtatious exchange with life, represents a tall, if not impossible, order. From aphorism to poem, from parable to dance, from Wanderer to Zarathustra, from genealogy to interpretation, he permanently resists the attribution of anything like "face value" to his discursive adventuring. As Derrida has it, his "genealogy inscribes itself in the back of reason."[5] In Nietzsche everything is uttered tropologically or, we might say, by turning, often, of course, out of turn. Yet interpret we must, and persistently, if we are to continue to rescue his work from being relegated to literature, on the one hand, and protofascism, on the other. It might therefore be strategically advisable to approach the question from the perspective of something that Nietzsche, along with Zarathustra, does say loud and clear, with patent constative neutrality, and precisely to affirm life and deliver thinking from reaction, namely, that "God is dead." For, I contend, it is on the basis of that statement, or rather the rhetorico-discursive status of such a statement, that Nietzsche opens the path to the political, and precisely to a politics that gives a new sense to resistance and opposition.

We know that Nietzsche died on August 25, 1900, and that he was effectively lost to the world from about January 3, 1889. We also know that Nietzsche is not, and never was, Zarathustra, however much the end of the first edition of *The Gay Science* (1882, book 4, aphorism 342) overlaps with the opening of *Thus Spoke Zarathustra* (1883), and even though book 5 of *The Gay Science,* published in 1887, opens by again announcing news of "the greatest recent event—that 'God is dead'" (aphorism 343).[6] The announcement by the aphorist in *The Gay Science* looks back to the astonishment of Zarathustra, who, early in that text, speaks "thus to his heart: 'Could it be possible! This old saint in his woods has not yet heard the news that *God is dead!*'" (*Zarathustra*, 5). We should note already that he speaks it, as if mutedly, perhaps silently, to his own heart. He is speaking what he presumes everyone to know, repeating old news, a commonplace that everyone except the old saint knows, not some recent revelation. Yet we have to suspect that some part of Zarathustra, perhaps indeed his heart, is not so sure that everyone except the saint knows that God is dead, that in fact enough people have not yet heard the news that it needs to be said out loud even when one is speaking to one's heart. It may well be that no one except Zarathustra (and perhaps life) really knows that God is dead, that it is something requiring rather to be shouted from the mountaintops than whispered to one's heart. However, when Zarathustra begins to deliver his message to the public in the following chapter, it is not the news of the death of God that he brings but his teaching of the overman. God's death, therefore, whether whispered by Zarathustra to his own heart or announced by the aphorist, is a fait accompli become a *fait divers,* some miscellaneous thing that was reported recently or long ago and requires no further discussion. It appears to barely require uttering.

That was in August 1881. We can imagine how old the news is some century and a quarter later. Perhaps we have no further need to speak of it at all, not even silently. Or, on the other hand, to be quite sure, it should be written one more time, without rhetorical flourish, without reporting or indirection of any sort, or even quotation marks, patently, in its own virgin space or camera lucida, without even any expectation of transformative effect.

God is dead.

The fact that, via either the inner speech of Zarathustra or his aphorisms, Nietzsche first presents the death of God as a report—something even the hermit-saint should have heard, something quotable—gives the information the status of a supposition, something that remains to be argued; presuming it to be common knowledge would be a form of wishful thinking. For his part, Zarathustra has to repeat the information—as a more constative matter of fact, it is true—in elaborating the teaching of the overman ("but God died" [6]). And indeed, it is a question that remains all the way to the end of the book (255). Similarly, the aphorist goes on to concede that most will receive or will have received the news with an incredulity akin to the ignorance of the old saint, that "for many people's power of comprehension, the event is itself far too great, distant, and out of the way even for its tidings to be thought of as having arrived yet" (*Gay Science,* 199). Furthermore, we know how much effort of Nietzsche's previous and subsequent writing was invested in combating the force of Christianity in particular, and religious belief in general. If the assertion of *Human, All Too Human* that "our own age . . . no longer believes in God" were a simple fact, it is doubtful that Nietzsche would still need to be legislating a "war to the death against . . . Christianity" in *The Anti-Christ,* or "reject[ing] God [in order to] begin to redeem the world" in *The Twilight of the Idols.*[7] The horizon that finally seemed clear again in *The Gay Science,* allowing "our ships [to] set out again, set out to face any danger," into the sea that lies open again—"*our* sea . . . maybe there has never been such an 'open sea'" (*Gay Science,* 199)—remains fraught with the storms and shoals that Nietzsche will have spent a life of writing attempting to overcome.

My interest here is to attempt to account for the performative effect of the statement that God is dead as both fictional utterance (Zarathustra) and philosophical argument (Nietzsche), in order to develop a sense of dissent beyond ressentiment that nevertheless functions as a type of affirmative politics. A politics that begins not in some impossible-to-determine consensus, contract, or compact but rather in dissent, detraction, and disintegration, without, for all that, being simply reactive. That sense of politics will be argued, in line with my project throughout this book, within the structure of the dorsal, as a type of turning away, objection, or contradiction, which, instead of offering a cold shoulder, reveals the other side, another position, a nonconciliatory controversary dissidence.

Nietzsche seems an obvious guide here. No philosopher in the tradition presents himself as more contrarian, indeed polemical; no one abandons himself more to the perils of what would normally pass for contradiction and illogicality, intemperance and *intempestivity* or untimeliness; no one uses declamation so consistently as a strategy against platitude, value as a weapon against morality, irony and sarcasm in the service of rhetorical demystification, interpretation, and affirmation. For the same reasons, no one pirouettes or dances more provocatively, and indeed no dervish ever drove himself to such irrevocable vertiginousness, to the point of collapse. No one *tropologizes* more exhaustingly; no one *controverts* more unfailingly. He would therefore be the model for a controversial, or rather *controversary,* dissidence.

By calling Nietzsche the guide or model, I want to restate the obvious, namely, that his rhetoric cannot simply be analyzed; it requires the activism of an interpretation.[8] First of all, his rhetorical tergiversation is too complex to be susceptible to a systematic analysis or typology; but more than that, there is no returning, after him, to straight or plain speaking, however much he himself seems to indulge in it, no reducing discourse to *constatation,* which also means, no doubt, that there is no longer any pure mountain air such as he finds indispensable for thinking. One starts from Nietzsche by departing from him, and indeed, Nietzsche starts by departing from himself: "This thinker needs no one to refute him: he does that for himself" (*Human,* 371). The start, as we have consistently seen, is a tropological divergence from itself; it is only such a concept of departure that can provide the basis for a return to, or recurrence of, Nietzsche's thinking, and only such an activist injunction vis-à-vis the reading of that thinking that, from the beginning, makes Nietzsche political, makes the philosopher a legislator.

The single example already provided can serve as paradigm here, the news or event of August 1881 that God is dead. (It came along with the end of the first clashes between English and Boers in South Africa, the signing of the Treaty of Pretoria that would lead to the real Boer War of 1899–1902, like a Treaty of Versailles in preparation for a real Second World War. At the same time as Anglicans sat down with Huguenots and Dutch Reformed Protestants, in order to better subjugate the Zulu and other native peoples, Stanley was shaking hands with the Congolese monarch on

behalf of Leopold II, inaugurating what would become the most murderous colonial experience of the nineteenth and twentieth centuries; while
in Cairo, the Turkish, those good Islamic Europeans, were facing nationalist resistance from the Egyptians that would ultimately force them to
retreat from the south just as they had previously retreated from Kosovo
and Bosnia in the north. One gets a sense of the scene, its epidemic discourses of religion and identitarianism.) Although we may yet live to see
the day when proclaiming the death of God in the marketplace is no longer
considered to be an (ill-considered) political act, there is, from the perspective of 2006 within which I am writing, no more generalized and strident
form of provocation (for it implies all varieties of ethnic insensitivity), no
more raw version of the political. As a result, Nietzsche's immoderation
seems ever more salutary, his declaration ever more necessary. When the
religious is no longer a question of politics, or when politics is no longer
overshadowed by religion, the world scene will certainly have been transformed, and thinking will have moved to another stage. Activism, in the
meantime, remains mired within the religious perspective.

The death of God that is whispered or cited by Zarathustra or by the
aphorist also stages the abyssal or chiasmatic relation between political
discourse and what calls itself pure politics, the politics of deed rather
than word. The supposedly watertight distinction between the words of
a fictional persona who wanders down from his cave on the mountain,
and those of a historical philosopher who strolls along the lakeside at Sils-
Maria, around the bay of Rapallo, or up the mountain face to Èze, seems
to founder on the basis of such a statement. Nietzsche will be held responsible for it whether he writes it or Zarathustra cites it. Similarly, the distinction collapses between the words of either and what are commonly
presumed to be political acts. I shall shortly elaborate on how saying or
writing "God is dead" is a political act beyond its being an example of free
expression. But such distinctions are nevertheless systematically pressed
into the service of a concept of the real (real philosophers, real-world consequences) that relies on an organicism of the natural as opposed to the
contrivances of artificial confections such as language or fiction. Against
that, the controversary dissidence of the utterance "God is dead" will be
developed here as a form of politics that functions beyond such organicist
reductions of the natural and of the human. "God is dead" is beyond the

human or animate in the first place because the statement evokes a God beyond the human. However much God is that from which all life flows, he or it is also that from which mortality, as the "quick" of the human, has been extracted. "God is dead" means that a certain conception of the nonanimate is dead. But that very tautology points to the other reason why the statement reaches beyond the human, namely, that it necessarily operates with the force of a maxim or even an axiom. It is beyond rhetoric in that sense; it has passed into automatism.

A politics beyond the human would contradict, on the one hand, the presumption of a politics formed by a community of subjects, and promote, on the other hand, a technology of the political subject. That technology emerges, paradoxical as it might seem, once the human turns its back, and reveals what is in a sense its most human, the vulnerability of the dorsal. Behind us all operate manipulations that go from vertebral spasms to explicit political straitjacketing. But what is also revealed dorsally—and this Nietzsche shows us more clearly than any other—is the space of a shadow and of a prosthetic automaticity. I am referring here to something quite different from the future emergence of the overman as sleek posthuman machine, or the necessity of a politics to manage some imagined cyborg insurgency. Nor is it simply a matter of calling to account the increasing role of machine and information technology in the operations of contemporary governments. Of course, the dorsal political shadow does refer to the increasingly complex set of prosthetic relations that I just evoked, which begin once the human articulates with the world by standing up to straighten the spine, putting on clothes, building a house, negotiating the extrafamilial. Within those relations, what we call the political marks a particularly contrived moment, in which the subject concedes its physical (in contrast to its psychic) management to an unattainable, invisible, and as if mechanistic set of functions that will take it progressively and indefinitely into an articulation with the foreign, all the way from automatic payroll deductions of taxes to death on a distant battlefield. But my emphasis here, thanks to the example of Nietzsche, is rather on the possibilities of analysis of, and resistance to, that structure of the political instance, different versions of turns against it by means of the rhetorico-performative *controversions* that dance through the impasses of identitarian agency, of what "a subject does when it knows."[9]

God is dead. To say so, perhaps even in a whisper, does not currently escape political consequences. Among those who agree little, if at all, over the concepts and definitions of sovereignty and war, terrorism and torture, rendition and detention, there seems to be more universal agreement than ever that such a statement represents a serious provocation. But what is the discursive status of such a statement, and why does the aporetic force of something seemingly lacking in constative content attribute to it such impossibly high performative stakes?

If God is dead, that means she was previously alive. But one understands someone who proclaims the death of God to be at the same time refuting God's existence. To declare that God is dead is to declare that God was never alive, that God is not now and never was a member of the party of existents; or else it is to murder her. And for that reason, the declaration inscribes itself as an act of resistance or contradiction against those who believe God to be alive, and is received by them as a provocation. If God is that which cannot die, then the declaration of God's death, the simple utterance of it, amounts to a deicide. Still, how is it that a statement that, at least on one reading, is semantically nonsensical can become such a crime? Speech that becomes not just the threat of an act but the act itself? A supremely provocative political act, on the basis of which bombs will explode?

The simple answer to that question would seem to be that for those against whom the declaration is directed, the statement carries a heavily overdetermined semantic force. Refuting the belief of a religious person becomes tantamount to an attack against his person. To those for whom God is alive, his death is unwelcome news, like that of the murder of a family member. Saying God, "your" God, is dead to someone whom that God inhabits is not just an insult but also an injury, a type of blow to the heart or soul. It is received in the same manner as statements such as "Your country stinks," "Your mother is a whore," "Your race is degenerate," or, indeed, "Your religion is apostate." And perhaps the reason for that is the consistency with which such statements and attitudes have been historically amalgamated, so that one never impugns the religion of another without also impugning his race, his country, or his mother; or that impugning someone's mother automatically means impugning his religion (because of the play of the maternal or matriarchal within that religion), and so on.

Hence a number of things become clear, however obvious they should always have been. In the first place, God's existence is not some pure metaphysical fact that functions outside material conditions of existence and outside a whole ideological complex of the national, the familial, the racial, which prevents believers who are informed of God's death from simply shrugging their shoulders in disagreement or disbelief. The death of God is profoundly deracinating not just because God functions as the transcendent home and anchor—the ultimate rhetorical abstraction from blood and soil that nevertheless sanctifies both—but more precisely because his disappearance exposes us to the fact of the technological. That might mean on the one hand exposure to functions of technoscience, in particular, as Avital Ronell has extensively discussed, in the form of testing: "Now we godless ones test, we rigorously experiment. We are the Christian conscience translated and sublimated into a scientific conscience. . . . The experimental disposition, and the provisional logic of testing that evolves from it, occurs, in its technological sense, as an event, after the death of God."[10] Or on the other hand, it might mean, as Lacoue-Labarthe formulates it, that the world becomes *refabulized:* "The world has become a fable (again). Creation is canceled. This is as much as to say that God is dead, and not only the metaphysical God. . . . The discourse of truth is now revealed as fictional. This discourse was itself a fable: the world becomes a fable again because it already was one."[11] The first version institutes a technology of experimentation, and a new type of faith in the science of tests and proofs; in the second version, a proliferation of narratives sets in train an inexhaustible fictive machinery that, by masquerading as fact or by being always farther fetched, will ceaselessly provoke the lower and upper limits of our credence.

In the second place, therefore, because of, or in spite of, both science and fable, God's existence or nonexistence, belief and nonbelief in God, mobilize the economy of credence and credit that functions in excess of what is called the purely material, the performative economy or *aneconomy* that Derrida refers to as "promise" or "faith." Within that economy, the death of God cannot be decided and therefore cannot be simply stated or refuted. For God really to die, all belief, faith, promise, and commitment would have to be neutralized. Not only would such an event or declaration of that event have to be emptied of performative as well as constative content—saying "I believe God is dead" would thus be a contradiction in terms—but promising anything at all would become logically and discursively impossible. In our thinking, the concept of belief depends on the *possibility* of the existence of God, which means not that in order for anyone to believe anything at all there has to be a God, but that, all the same, belief, faith, and promise mobilize something beyond fact and evidence.[12]

Finally, declaring the death of God cannot function as a straightforward and liberating refutation but is rather a highly complex rhetorical maneuver that engages various signifying functions (and provokes on each level): by reducing God to the mortal or material (God can be here today and gone tomorrow), by introducing argument within the structure of belief (the death of God is logically preferred over religious faith), and by foreclosing plenitude of any sort (where you thought there was God, there is nothing). In the final analysis, as Deleuze puts it, "the phrase 'God is dead' is not a speculative proposition but a dramatic proposition, *the* dramatic proposition *par excellence*."[13]

Nietzschean discourse stages all that and operates as if it were in full knowledge of the whole strategy as well as its consequences; and not just by virtue of how God's death is declared but also through the ways in which it declares in general: *in and into the shadow*. If the death of God cannot finally function as the refutation, contradiction, or silencing of religious belief, for the reasons just suggested, it may nevertheless shadow that belief, both by constantly dogging it, keeping it under a persistent form of threat, and conversely by turning its back to it or on it, resisting and refusing it, dissenting from it and turning away from it. As does Nietzsche's discourse in general, operating in the space of a rhetorical shadow, where every utterance takes a different form of a generalized controversary dissidence, turning away to turn into the political.

THE SHADOW is a familiar Nietzschean figure. In his work it runs the gamut of the value-laden metaphors that are normally associated with the absence of light. When the bald fact that "God is dead" is uttered for the first time in aphorism 108 of *The Gay Science,* we are warned that his shadow will continue to be shown in caves for millennia to come and, as is suggested in the following aphorism, will continue to "darken us" (*Gay Science,* 110). The sinister residue or spectral effects of his existence will remain a threat, and "we must still defeat his shadow as well" (109). In aphorism 343, the greatest recent event itself "casts its shadow over Europe" with a foreboding, and a sense of liberation, similar to the specter of communism announced nearly forty years earlier. To those caught unaware, it is as if the sun had been eclipsed, but for philosophers and free spirits, it will be experienced like "a new dawn" (199). One man's shadow is another's daybreak, and the shadow itself is shown to function as either a rearguard or vanguard specter, both frontal and dorsal, as it were, according to the position of the sun. No doubt that rhetorical variability of the shadow, the fact of its erratic nonstasis, in fact its becoming, is what will allow it to develop into a persona.

In the third aphorism from *The Gay Science* that deals with the question of God's death, aphorism 125, the "tremendous event" that will become the greatest event makes a prosopopoeic leap by being said to be "still on its way, wandering" (120), and we know from *Human, All Too Human* that where there is wandering, the shadow is never far behind. The Wanderer is, in the first instance, he who simply walks, goes somewhere, but who, more specifically, refuses to reduce that experience to a teleology: "He who has attained to only some degree of freedom of mind cannot feel other than a wanderer on the earth—though not as a traveller *to* a final destination: for this destination does not exist. . . . Within him too there must be something wandering that takes pleasure in change and transience" (*Human,* 203). At the end of the first volume, he appears to receive gifts from "all those free spirits who are at home in mountain, wood and solitude and who, like him, are . . . wanderers and philosophers. . . . *of the morning*" (203–4), before reappearing to converse with his shadow in part 2 of volume 2. On that occasion, it is in fact the shadow that first speaks and surprises the Wanderer, and it surprises him precisely by interrupting his silence, giving two distinct impressions: on the one hand that it has already been speaking, perhaps even uttering the entire "Assorted Opinions and Maxims" of the first part of the volume;[14] on the other hand that it is used to being spoken to or whispered to, or confided in, that the discursive relation between shadow and wanderer is a privileged one for the development of Nietzsche's ideas, and that that relation is an interlocution, something of a intimate conversation involving two parts of a single self, or else a human and a more or less disembodied shadow:

THE SHADOW: As it is so long since I heard your voice, I would like to give you an opportunity of speaking.

THE WANDERER: Someone said something:—where? and who? It almost seems as though it were I myself speaking, though in an even weaker voice than mine.

THE SHADOW (after a pause): Are you not glad to have an opportunity of speaking?

THE WANDERER: By God, and all the things I do not believe in, it is my shadow speaking; I hear it but do not believe it.

THE SHADOW: Let us accept it and think no more about it: in an hour it will be all over. (*Human*, 301)

This surprise interpellation of the Wanderer by his shadow is explicitly dorsal: the voice of the shadow comes from outside the Wanderer's field of vision ("where? and who?"), and at the same time from within his corporal space ("as though it were I myself speaking"). The Wanderer, he who meanders or turns as he walks, the one who turns by virtue of the errancy of his very wandering, turns again to attend to his shadow. He turns first one way ("where?"), then the other ("and who?"), seeking an identity for the speaker whose identity must precisely remain in question. That is because, to begin with, it is a shadow who speaks, and a shadow would have, by virtue of a general doppelgänger or uncanny effect, to call into question the identity of whatever it shadows, and conversely its own status. But also because, within the strict narrative logic of the conversation, the Shadow does not identify itself, does not reassure the Wanderer by answering his questions. Instead the Shadow pauses, and allows silence, or the shadow of speech, to respond. The shadow remains outside the identitarian perspective of the Wanderer's questions and continues with its own question, posed from dorsal space. It is the Wanderer himself who will have to decide that it is his shadow speaking.

When he makes that decision, it is by means of what is, for us, a most pertinent rhetorical performance: "By God, and all the things I do not believe in, it is my shadow speaking; I hear it but do not believe it." The surprise of the shadow elicits an oath—"By God"—the automatic performance of a belief that we normally take to be semantically empty, an almost phatic utterance that only a literalist would take to signify faith or religious practice (indeed, religious literalists refrain from using such profane oaths precisely because they believe too much in God to take his name in vain). The Wanderer, however, intent on interpreting as he speaks, on resisting the supposedly valueless innocence of an interjection, allows God to assume semantic content in the oath so that he might all the better record his disbelief. The name of God, uttered "innocently," is immediately associated with "all the things I do not believe in." No sooner is He allowed by the expletive to live than He is declared dead. But this God is precisely sacrificed on the altar of belief, in favor of a system of credence that itself continues to exist, which indeed remains necessary if the shadow is to exist and speak. "I do not believe in God," the Wanderer seems to be saying, "but I do believe in my shadow and its ability to speak." Yet a speaking shadow cannot function without the system of credence that God introduces, which his death should but cannot eliminate, and therefore it cannot simply be read as a constative utterance ("it is my shadow speaking") that operates in isolation from its syntactic context ("By God, etc."). The shadow's existence and speech remain infected by the performative structure of that context. Indeed, that existence and discursive capacity are immediately called into question, returned to the question of credence: "I hear it but do not believe it," as if to say, "I can't believe my ears, I want to believe it but I can't, I have instead to believe it isn't possible."[15] In short, what takes place by means of this performance of credence is a series of controversions, each enacting a type of dissidence, but without for all that presuming the last word, the zero degree of constative truth. What might, on one level, appear or seek to give itself the force of a refutation of fact instead operates as a rhetorical shift that challenges and provokes without disengaging. This is so less because of strategic choice than because of structural necessity, that of the credence or credit within which every utterance (to the extent of its performativity) is performed, and thanks to which the discourses and actions of opinion and evaluation that we call political—conviction, posture, testimony, contract, dissent, conflict—are able to take place. Every utterance is shadowed by that structure as what animates or activates it and by virtue of which every rhetorical turn involves passage into the dorsal shadow. The ideologues who dream of a purely constative politics, something like a science of political fact and truth, forget (as does Nietzsche, perhaps, in certain aristocratic moments) that without such an umbral structure there would be no politics, and certainly not any transformative politics, just the tautological stasis of what is.

The shadow comes, therefore, from behind or from some oblique angle; it speaks to the Wanderer not in the face-to-face of a dialogue but as a form of inexpectancy or caution. The shadow speaks from the shadow, like a condemned daytime ghost haunted by the impending night ("in an hour it will be over"). And in the final analysis it involves a form of intimacy that requires or expects secrecy—"promise you will tell no one how we talked together," it will insist (302)—a secrecy that is precisely the fact of its speaking, the discursive effect of its being part of a more generalized shadowness, a *dorsal umbrality* that structures not only its own speech but also that of the Wanderer. It is as if the conversation with the shadow were functioning in the rhetorical twilight of shadows that shift within the prospect or threat of a discursive night.

For, still within the narrative logic of their conversation, the dorsal surprise remains a question to the end, or at least to the end of this part of their dialogue, but in such a way as to trouble and interrogate the 350 aphorisms that follow. This introductory conversation ends with the Wanderer calling the Shadow to order and foreclosing its questions ("More shadow than light! Is it possible?"),[16] with a response that refers to "my first question": "Be serious, dear fool! My very first question demands seriousness" (302). That "very first" question has to be read in two directions at once, as much back to the Wanderer's "where?" of the first lines, which is obviously interrogative, as forward to aphorism 1, "Of the Tree of Knowledge," for as is the case with all of Nietzsche's aphorisms, the space between interrogative and sententious, between the hypothesis and the tenet, between provocation and affirmation, describes their whole rhetorical gamble. And furthermore, given the structure of *The Wanderer and His Shadow,* whose title covers the entire volume of 350 aphorisms sandwiched between a conversation at beginning and end, we would have to ask where the shadow disappears to during the major part of the text. Indeed, the question remains not only "to where" it disappears, but also "into whom?" Does it fall back into the shadow, melt into the night, deferring to the Wanderer, who alone will utter the aphorisms? Or is it rather the Shadow itself that becomes the aphorist, pronouncing its rapid-fire wisdom in telegraphic form in a race against time, though it is difficult to imagine it getting to the end in the hour before "it will all be over"? The text does, however, explicitly allow for the second alternative when the Wanderer says, "And so enough preamble! There are a couple of hundred questions pressing upon my soul, and the time *you have in which to answer them* is perhaps only brief. Let us hasten . . ." (302; italics mine), suggesting that the Wanderer silently poses his questions to which the Shadow offers its aphoristic responses. On the other hand, the narrative break between preamble and aphorisms inserts a new structural shadow into the exchange, and we must finally understand any number of abyssal possibilities to be in effect throughout the aphorisms themselves: that they constitute (1) the Wanderer's questions, (2) the Shadow's answers (to the Wanderer's silent or whispered questions), (3) the Wanderer's answers (to the Shadow's silent or whispered questions), and (4) a new form of impersonal conversation, or question and response, wherein neither Wanderer nor Shadow can any longer be identified, where voices have become the shadows of personalized utterances, or where discourse turns into a type of generalized *errancy,* a tropicality that is no longer reducible to either dialogue or dialectic but functions instead as the dorsal difference machine of a controversary dissidence.

Could we not say that the particular rhetorical ruse of the aphorism works to open the space of a shadow within the philosophical discourse that it represents, mimes, or ironizes? Nietzsche, commenting on the reception of *Zarathustra,* seems to suggest as much in the preface to *The Genealogy of Morals:* "An aphorism, properly stamped and moulded, has not been 'deciphered' just because it has been read out; on the contrary, this is just the beginning of its proper *interpretation.* . . . In the third essay of this book I have given an example of what I mean by 'interpretation' in such a case:—this treatise is a commentary on the aphorism that precedes it."[17] We should therefore read the aphorism as a boldly outlined, provocative figure standing tall and casting a long shadow of commentary or interpretation behind it. And although that sort of density should finally be allowed, and indeed encouraged with respect to any text, what is particular to Nietzsche's sense of interpretation as transvaluation, and what reinforces the dorsal sense of it, is that the shadow of commentary is precisely designed to surprise, overtake, and reconfigure the figure that casts it. Nietzschean discourse in general thus comes to be spoken from the shadow—"up to now people have perceived in my opinions more shadow than me" (*Human*, 302)—from what I am calling dorsal space. It derives from such initial "dorsal" questions as "where?" and "who?" the questions of a wanderer who waits for the un(fore)seen surprise of some free-spirited event or arrival, who turns to respond to the "good and bright things . . . thrown down to him from their tops and leafy hiding-places" (203); and more precisely, from the questions of perspective ("[from] where?") and of identity ("who?") on the basis of which he strives for the philosophical newness of the genealogical and the affirmative.[18]

The second conversation between Shadow and Wanderer, which occurs at the end of the volume, concentrates on the hierarchy of the relation between the two. The Shadow complains of slander, of being taken for a slave or a dog, for what slavishly dogs the human: "We are to be found very, very often following behind man, yet we are not his slaves. . . . Perhaps today too I have already been following you too long. . . . It occurred to me that I have often lain at your feet like a dog" (394). The Shadow therefore asserts a type of independence, which derives precisely from its "ability" to disappear, which in turn implies a capacity to require independence on the part of man; in short to assist or generate his transformation. That news produces more than a little regret and anxiety on the part of the Wanderer, and the following intercessions constitute his final four contributions to the exchange and the end of the text: "Oh, is it already time for us to part? . . . Is there nothing you want? . . . What shall I do? . . . Where are you? Where are you?" (*Human*, 394–95). In a sense, therefore, the epilogue conversation mirrors—or shadows—that of the prologue. The Shadow returns to the silence whence it emerged, and the Wanderer is left posing the "where?" question, disturbed out of his visual and identificatory assurance, left posing and dealing with the question of the dorsal.

On the other hand, the question has become a larger one. In falling further back into the behind, into a dorsal autonomy, that of darkness, the Shadow has lost its definition and finally its existential status. The Wanderer must again wander alone, in the darkness, without even the comfort and encouragement of his shadow. The dorsal space of the Shadow has expanded to become an englobing night that the Wanderer must find a way to navigate, as it were affirmatively, learning not to rely on a photological thinking. If the Shadow teaches the Wanderer a lesson, it will be less that of its own duplicity—for all its doggedness or slavishness, it is frank about its doubling effect and speaks frankly to alert the Wanderer to that very fact—than that of the duplicity of light itself, which, as Blanchot explains so eloquently, is the medium that passes for immediacy itself:

Light illuminates—this means that light hides itself; this is its malicious trait. Light illuminates: what is illuminated by light presents itself in an immediate presence that discloses itself without disclosing what makes it manifest. . . . Light's deception, then, would be in the fact that it slips away in a radiating absence, infinitely more obscure than any obscurity, since the absence proper to light is the very act of its light, its clarity, and since the work of light is accomplished only when light makes us forget that something like light is at work. . . . The light of day is a false day.[19]

The work of the Shadow therefore involves being the shadow of a light that presents itself as homogeneously pure emanation, and in disappearing from behind the Wanderer, it not only affirms a certain blindness in his wandering but also affirms a darkness or absence of light that is less the threat of an infernal void, or what Blanchot calls "the Stygian night,"[20] than the differential play of a generalized *umbrality* on the basis of which dawn, noon, and dusk, and indeed midnight, will all come to play a role in the *discoveries* of Nietzsche's thinking.

NIETZSCHE SPEAKS in *Ecce Homo* of Zarathustra's having overtaken him: "It was on those two walks that the whole of the first book of Zarathustra occurred to me, and above all Zarathustra himself, as a type: it would be more accurate to say he overtook me *[er überfiel mich]*."[21] It is as if Zarathustra stalks his author and falls upon him from out of the structure of the shadow. When the Shadow itself returns, coming to overtake Zarathustra in part 4 of the book, it will similarly appear as a dorsal surprise, a "new voice behind him" (*Zarathustra*, 220). Zarathustra, unlike the Wanderer of *Human, All Too Human,* is not ready to be importuned, and the Shadow in turn can less afford the leisurely or coaxing approach of the earlier text, instead "crying, 'Stop! Zarathustra! Stop already! It's me . . . your shadow!'" But Zarathustra soon repents of the folly of attempting to outrun his shadow, and once he has stopped and "turned around abruptly" (221), he and the shadow do in fact return to the conversational tone of "The Wanderer and His Shadow." However, by its own and by Zarathustra's accounts, this is now a worn-out shell of a shadow, whose extreme ateleological experience ("'Nothing is true, all is permitted': thus I persuaded myself") has left it weary, restless, and somewhat broken (221–22). It therefore accepts Zarathustra's offer of hospitality among the higher men in his cave. There the shadow is rejuvenated enough to reminisce and sing its Orientalizing song about the daughters of the desert, a desert from which it seems to have since retreated back to Europe (247–52). Its song at least restores some "convalescent" gaiety to the company of higher men, even if that is but a prelude to their kneeling and praying to the ass. The shadow's final appearance involves its being berated by Zarathustra for participating in such a farce and thereby betraying its free-spirit principles (255).

No doubt *Thus Spoke Zarathustra* is too different from "The Wanderer and His Shadow" for us to presume a simple intertextual or transtextual development of our analysis of *Human, All Too Human*.[22] However, the shadow of *Zarathustra* is strangely as well as instructively complex. When it first appears "behind him, crying," it self-identifies as the shadow of Zarathustra ("It's me, oh Zarathustra, me, your shadow" [220]), and when Zarathustra admits that he cannot outrun it ("It seems to me, when all's said and done, that he has longer legs than I" [221]), we can also hear him conceding that the shadow didn't just choose this moment to appear behind him, but was always, diurnally, there. Indeed, the shadow will shortly say, "Even when I concealed myself from you, I was still your best shadow" (221). From that point of view, even when it accepts Zarathustra's invitation to retreat to his cave ("Then go up to my cave. . . . Now I have to run away from you quickly again" [222]), it leaves him without leaving. For "shadowness" remains explicitly with Zarathustra after that, in two forms: first as an encroaching or generalizing cloud that he cannot seem to shake off, such that "already it's as though I'm covered in shadow" (Schon liegt es wie ein Schatten auf mir),[23] which is immediately given as the reason for his having to dismiss his own shadow and "run alone, so that things clear up around me again" (223); and second, as something identified by its absence once noon comes and the "sun stood directly over [his] head" (223), depriving him of the shade he seems to be seeking when he lies down beside a tree to sleep, only to be wakened by a "sunbeam [that] fell down from the sky onto his face" (225). In this context, even sleep itself, which "dances" on him "like a delicate wind" (223), seems to be experienced as the palliative shadow of his waking existence.

Hence Zarathustra has no more a shadow, but there is all the more umbrality. His shadow, on the other hand, no longer *his* shadow, goes off to lead its autonomous existence as one of the higher men. But we will already have recognized its autonomy once it responds to Zarathustra's attempts to shake it off ("What are you doing here? And why do you call yourself my shadow? I don't like you") by calling itself "a wanderer, who has already walked much at your heels; always on my way, but without goal, without home too" (221). This is therefore the shadow's second, more abyssal self-identification: as the shadow of a wanderer (Zarathustra), one who has become a wanderer by virtue of following a wanderer. And in case we didn't already know from *Human, All Too Human* that the Wanderer has a shadow, once this one leaves Zarathustra and enters the company of the higher men, it morphs from being simply "the shadow" (225) to "the wanderer who called himself the shadow of Zarathustra" (247), and persistently thereafter to "the wanderer and shadow [*der Wanderer und Schatten*]" (248, 252, 254, 255; *Werke* 6.1, 376, 382, 384, 387). Thus the shadow, which is the shadow of a wanderer, wanders off to become a wanderer with its own shadow; or else a wanderer, which is or at least calls itself the shadow of a wanderer, wanders off to lose itself within the divided shadow of its former self. For in the surreptitious and unexplained becoming, like any mythological metamorphosis, whereby Zarathustra's shadow becomes both wanderer and shadow, we cannot presume that the shadow has simply seen another wanderer and attached itself to him. It is not simply that the wanderer (the shadow) that was behind a wanderer (Zarathustra) is now shadowed by another unidentified wanderer, or any other sequence involving those possibilities. It is rather that the shadow itself, which we understood from *Human, All Too Human* to be the dorsal question of perspective (where?) and identity (who?), is in fact the opening to a contagion or abyss from which or within which no fixed perspective or identity is any longer possible.

This shadow, unlike the earlier one, appears to survive nightfall. It folds into the night, into what we should understand as nondistinction, or self-contradiction, without for all that failing to exist. When Zarathustra returns to his cave in the "late afternoon," he finds the whole group "he had passed by during the day" sitting there together (225). At this point, the shadow is still just a shadow. By the time it takes its turn at providing entertainment, there has been an evening meal *(Abendmahl)* ("supper," 230; *Werke* 6.1, 349); and the "dessert psalm" (248) the shadow introduces is literally a night song *(Nachtisch-Lied)* or night psalm *(Nachtisch-Psalm)* *(Werke* 6.1, 376). It is at that point that the shadow divides into wanderer and shadow. Thus, even though we are thereafter told that "already evening is coming" (252), night has well and truly fallen by the beginning of "The Sleepwalker Song" *(Nachtwandler-Lied),* for we read how *"one after another had stepped outdoors into the open and into the cool pensive night. . . . There at last they all stood silently together, nothing but old people, but with comforted, brave hearts and inwardly amazed that they felt so good on earth; but the secrecy* [Heimlichkeit] *of the night came closer and closer to their hearts"* (258; italics mine, translation modified; *Werke* 6.1, 391). Soon thereafter we are told, "it was not long before midnight."

In what form the shadow is able to live on in the night is something we can only guess at. Nothing suggests it is henceforth absent from the company of higher men. Is it thanks to "the big round moon" (258), or some other flicker of light from a technological source such as a fire or candle? The immediate context of Dionysian celebration, from ass festival with its "aromatic smoke and incense, as of burning pinecones" (253), to the greater celebration outside, is enough to suggest that the night contains some light. Or, pursuing that sense, does the shadow live on precisely as the light that shadows, and so differentiates darkness, as what tells the lie on the homogeneity of darkness just as it had earlier told the lie on the supposed purity of the light? For it is such a form of "light," namely, the shadow or darkness within the night that "reveals" the differential depth of the night, that clearly becomes the focus of "The Sleepwalker Song" and of the mystery of the night. It is the other night, what sleepwalks or wanders within or behind the night, its secret or dorsal inaccessibility— namely, midnight—"the old, the deep deep midnight" (260). Indeed, once there is revealed that deep midnight within the night, Zarathustra can be seen to himself fold back into the night and rejoin his shadow at midnight or in midnight, as if he knew all along that the night would mean not the shadow's disappearance but its very emergence as the shadow in the dark that gives depth to the night. He appears to rejoin his shadow when, by the end of the book's penultimate chapter, according to one reading at least, he progressively metamorphoses from being an observer or medium into being the very sleepwalker that is midnight: from "a midnight lyre, a bell-toad that no one understands, but that *must* speak," which is seemingly differentiated from the drunken and overawake poetess of section 8 (262), to the "drunk" or "midnight bell" of section 10 (263), to the poet who composes "my song" and "my new roundelay" within which deep midnight makes its declaration in section 12. But those voices cannot in fact be consistently distinguished, and what any reunion between Zarathustra and shadow in the deep midnight means in the final analysis is, on the one hand, his becoming impersonal and, on the other hand, an impossibly compounded abyss of shadows whereby the wanderer Zarathustra folds back into his shadow become wanderer and shadow, which has itself folded back into the shadow within the night that is deep midnight.

Or, finally, is the shadow able to live on as what returns? The message of old deep deep midnight is, by the end, explicitly that of the eternal recurrence, of the "rulers of the earth, the least known, strongest, the midnight-souled, who are brighter and deeper than any day" (261), and of the joy beyond suffering and beyond life that "wants itself, wants eternity, wants recurrence, wants everything eternally the same" (262). As shadow that darkens the center of the night, deep midnight sings of a midnight brighter than the "stupid, clumsy, stifling day" (261), hence of a day that illuminates the night by bringing day back to the night, or by inscribing within the night a recurring rhythm of the day. From the depths of the night, and from the woeful depths of life, the day is therefore affirmed, to become joy. And if it is the sun that returns to greet Zarathustra when he jumps from his resting place in the final chapter, if he leaves the higher men still sleeping to join his animals and to be cloaked by the "cloud of love," "swarmed and fluttered around as if by countless birds" (265), if the lion has joined him and scared the obsequious and insecure higher men back into the cave, if by the last line he himself becomes "glowing and strong, like a morning sun that emerges from dark mountains" (266), we nevertheless have to presume, as confidently as we welcome the return of that sun, that the shadow returns with it, and indeed that the shadow is what, inhabiting a space as it were on the other side of the sun and behind whatever stands in its light, allows and affirms the eternal return of the same as difference. It may no longer be mentioned, but that would be because it is speaking in the silence of the dark mountains that are the last words of the text, from where the sun has emerged, out of the shadow of a *Gebirge,* as Heidegger might say, a gathering uttering massively and geologically, signifying topographically in the space on the other side, and behind the end of it.[24]

WHEN ZARATHUSTRA berates the wanderer and shadow for partic- ipating in the "idolatry and popery" of ass worship, the wanderer and shadow replies: "The old God lives again, oh Zarathustra, say what you will. The ugliest human being is to blame for everything; he has awakened him again. And when he says that he once killed him: *death* is always a mere prejudice among gods *[Tod ist bei Göttern immer nur ein Vorurtheil]*" (255; *Werke* 6.1, 387). Before disappearing into the shadow of the text of *Thus Spoke Zarathustra,* the wanderer and shadow thus returns us to the defining context of "The Wanderer and His Shadow" in *Human, All Too Human,* that is to say, the question of credence. Dispute over the con- stative fact of God's (original or continued) existence comes back down to the forms of belief under which his death can operate, the question of whether death is a well-founded belief or simply a "prejudice." Zarathustra can say what he will about God's being dead; the shadow insists that he lives again, that he never died at all, that he was just sleeping, or else has been resurrected.[25] Already, by suggesting those different possibilities, the shadow is saying that it is less a question of fact than of interpretation. But that becomes all the more obvious once it reverts to *reporting* what the ugliest man *claims* (that he once killed him), and once it concludes by advancing a hypothesis that displaces the question from one concern- ing God's existence to one concerning the conception of death. There is a subtlety here that should not be missed: to say that gods never really die, that they cannot be certified dead any more than they can be certi- fied alive, that dispute over their existence is impossible to resolve, is one thing; to say that one can argue God's death only from an ideological per- spective, from the perspective of a "prejudice" that believes what it wants to believe, is still another version of that. However, the claim that, where gods are concerned, *death* is a prejudice is something quite different: to begin, it repeats the idea that if such a thing as a god or immortal being were to exist, then we would have to rethink what we call death; but it also means at the same time that the specific way in which we would have to reconceptualize death would involve understanding it as a performative, as functioning within the structure of credence or faith, as a prejudice or shadow that operates behind what we call faith or belief. Once death itself is a question of credence, a question that is distinct from the extraordinary performative machinery and investment that necessarily accompanies death—heroics/shame, sacrifice/blackmail, expectation/desolation, rebirth/abandonment, inheritance/destitution, and so on—once it is but a putative fact, then death is brought into the realm of Nietzschean value, which allows for its transmutation into an affirmative force beyond that of some purifying destruction, and into a returning that operates as the incursion and recurrence of joy across every border and behind every configuration of life.

The shadow also speaks here in a mode of dissent. Zarathustra berates; the wanderer and shadow excuses itself ("the ugliest human being is to blame for everything") but at the same time mounts a counterargument that shifts the terms of reference in the ways we have just seen. Within the debate with Zarathustra over the merits of worshipping an ass, the wanderer and shadow accepts Zarathustra's reproof ("[I am] wicked enough . . . you're right" [255]), but at the same time it controverts, we might say, or dissents from Zarathustra's presumption that the death of God means no more worship. Yet that dissension of the wanderer and shadow—"death is always a mere prejudice among gods"—reads as an incitement that functions in favor of Zarathustra's cause; it falls within the shadow of his antireligious campaign and, in an important sense, acts to reinforce and even radicalize it. It says that as long as gods are merely prejudicially dead, the death of god and the forms of submission and compliance represented by worship remain the subject of struggle. As if to say there is no discussion, hence no politics, beyond that concerning worship and religion, except for that over whether God is indeed dead. The wanderer and shadow's last exchange with Zarathustra means that if (as I began by arguing) the announcement that God is dead can signify only as a type of shadow for the statement that God lives, within a general performative structure of belief, faith, or promise, then it is no less true that the death of God creates in its turn its own shadow: on the one hand it *controverts* into the conceptual quandary or gray area of a death that is a prejudice, becoming a permanent challenge for thought, and on the other it *dissents* from the idea that God can ever die once and for all time, and lays the foundation for a perpetual resistance to religious forms.

This, then, would be Nietzsche's controversary dissidence, whose structure is introduced once the death of God is uttered, and whose tropological force seems to be traceable all the way into the logic of affirmation and of the eternal return. It contests by turning, controverting rather than simply contradicting, turning behind as much as against, into the shadow that is no longer that of pale imitation or aping, or a sinister and occult system of subversion, but nevertheless a dissidence dogged enough to summon, convoke, and provoke, to challenge or catch off guard the confident presumptions of what is seen and known. It turns and turns, even and especially turning around or upon itself, as is no more clear than in the climactic midnight of *Thus Spoke Zarathustra* as night transmutes or convolutes deeper into night with all the differential force of enfolding shadows, and there is affirmed a type of eternally controverting or recurring joy "deeper still than misery" (262) and "more mysterious *[heimlicher]* than all pain," that "wants *itself* . . . bites into *itself* . . . wants love . . . wants hate . . . bestows, throws away," "longs for failures. . . . wants itself, and therefore it wants all misery too" (263; *Werke* 6.1, 399).

Many commentators have attempted to account for the rhetorical and logical turns made by Nietzsche. Heidegger considers that "as a mere countermovement" Nietzsche's philosophy "remains trapped, like everything anti-, in the essence of what it is challenging," but nevertheless finds that it "is no less rigorously substantial than the thinking of Aristotle."[26] Blanchot reports Jaspers's assertion that "the essential movement of Nietzsche's thought consists in self-contradiction; each time it affirms, the affirmation must be put in relation with the one opposing it. . . . *Everything must at a certain moment turn around.*" He also describes the "logical vertigo" of the thought of the eternal return. But he goes on to distinguish nihilistic turning from a "contestation [that] always keeps on within the horizon of the same interrogation," and to insist that "it is relatively easy to bring Nietzsche's thoughts into a coherency that would justify their contradictions, either by lining them up according to a hierarchy or by making them dialectical."[27] Deleuze, on the other hand, argues from one end of his analysis to the other that Nietzsche's main argument is with dialectics: "Nietzsche's philosophy has a great polemical range; it forms an absolute anti-dialectics and sets out to expose all the mystifications that find a final refuge in the dialectic . . . [whose] idea of a power of the negative as a theoretical principle [is] manifested in opposition and contradiction." For Deleuze, contradiction is absent from Nietzsche's thinking because it does not operate on the basis of the dialectical oppositions that would produce it: "If the speculative element of the dialectic is found in opposition and contradiction this is primarily because it reflects a false image of difference."[28]

Consonance between controversary dissidence and the tenor—if not always the tone—of Nietzschean discourse might be measured vis-à-vis what is perhaps most systematic in his work, namely, the critique of the operations of ressentiment. The most detailed elaboration of that critique is to be found in *The Genealogy of Morals,* but already in "The Wanderer and His Shadow" we find reference to two types of revenge *(Rache):* the first, "a defensive return blow," a "counter-action" designed "to put a stop to [an] injury," an act of "self-preservation *[Selbst-Erhaltung]* . . . without wanting to do harm in return"; and the second, whose "presupposition is a reflection over the other's vulnerability and capacity for suffering," where one "ask[s] oneself how he can be hit at most grievously," where "it is a question of restitution *[Wiederherstellung]*" *(Human,* 316–17; cf. *Werke* 4.3, 202–3]. *The Genealogy of Morals* recasts the contrast as that between proper "reaction *[eigentliche Reaktion]*" and the "imaginary revenge" that constitutes "ressentiment." The first "grows out of a triumphant saying 'yes' to itself"; the second "says 'no' on principle" *(Genealogy of Morality,* 21).[29] Proper reaction constitutes a type of organic instinct or physiological reflex—in a later comparison, Nietzsche will coin the term "reflex movement" *(Reflexbewegung)* *(Genealogy of Morality,* 99; *Werke* 6.2, 392)—whereas ressentiment develops as a whole perverse machinery, culminating in the notion of "bad conscience" that is developed at length in the second essay of the *Genealogy.*

The machinery of bad conscience is defined successively as a mnemotechnics, an economics, and a retroversion. In the first place, "this necessarily forgetful animal . . . has bred for himself a counter-device, memory" (39), whose efficacy is determined by its infliction of pain: "Perhaps there is nothing more terrible and strange in man's pre-history than his *technique of mnemonics [Mnemotechnik].* . . . 'Only something which continues to *hurt* stays in the memory'" (41; cf. *Werke* 6.2, 311). Second, pain finds currency in injury and generates an economics of compensation that derives from "the contractual relationship between *creditor* and *debtor.* . . . A sort of pleasure is given to the creditor as repayment and compensation"

(42–43). Third, in terms that are eerily close to Freud's superego, there thus develops the machinery of bad conscience, what is described in one instance as a "torture-chamber" (62), which becomes internalized, and the instincts that should be discharged outwardly *"turn inwards. . . . All those instincts of the wild, free, roving man [are] turned backwards, against man himself"* (61). Nietzsche thus has recourse to elements of a rather traditional technophobia to describe the sickness of man's bad conscience in terms of "a forcible breach with his animal past," a fall into a type of nonorganic or inanimate prosthetization: "The alteration was not gradual and voluntary and did not represent an organic assimilation into new circumstances but was a breach" (62). Bad conscience is a far cry from the companionable shadow, and the ressentiment that accompanies it is less the organic operation of revenge than a self-generating machine. The instinctual actions of the wild animal have become reactive. Yet if we turn back to the—or one possible—genesis of the concept identified in "The Wanderer and His Shadow," we find that the "defensive return blow" that is distinguished there finds its originating instance in being delivered "even against lifeless objects (moving machinery, for example). . . . The sense of our counter-action is to put a stop to the injury by putting a stop to the machine" (*Human,* 316). At least in that formulation of a primary organic reaction before ressentiment, therefore, Nietzsche will allow an even more primary "action" on the part of a lifeless object *(leblos Gegenstand):* in order for life to act in the simple "revenge" of nonreactive self-affirmation, it has to produce a reflexive movement that is as disinterested—or whose grudge factor is as meaningless—as that involved in a confrontation with a lifeless object. The nonreactive response should be automatic, as mechanistic as the operation of a machine. The only way to conceive of an impulse before conscience—for even insects possess "the cleverness of the lowest rank" (*Genealogy of Morality,* 29)—is by imagining a blow from or toward such an object, that is to say, by means of a type of inanimation, through the operations of a primary technicity. Only such nonconscious physical, prephysiological action can remain without ressentiment and avoid being reaction. Or rather, since we understand the physics of movement as reaction in the purest sense, we would have to imagine and wrestle with the paradoxes of a form of action, and an ethics to shadow it, that was desubjectivized, not to say "dehumanized," to the point of occurring within the structure of the inanimate.[30]

Zarathustra dances through such a structure where "humanity has been overcome," the space of a conceptual umbrality whose every utterance is both followed and overtaken by its shadow, which allows him to be "the most affirmative of all spirits" and to "[contradict] with every word he speaks" (*Ecce Homo,* 129–30). His controversary dissidence accounts for "how someone who to an unprecedented degree says no and *does* no to everything everyone has said yes to so far . . . can nevertheless be the opposite of a no-saying spirit" (131). In order that his "no" be nonreactive, and that his contradiction be affirmative, it must turn through the incompatible coincidence of the figure and its shadow, a shadow conceived of as alien in the sense of being unforeseeable, as the lifelessness of a photophysics, yet credible enough to perform credence itself. The umbrality of controversary dissidence is where utterance in general gains the force of a performance or an action, and where a "no" in particular is turned into affirmation by being engaged outside itself, becoming fiduciary, risked in the structure of belief or promise on the basis of which *one acts,* vis-à-vis the other and vis-à-vis the world. "God is dead" functions as such an utterance, and as we have seen, politics is already there. But the catachrestic or neologistic lexicon of controversary dissidence is pointedly designed to bring politics and rhetoric into a more general focus, and it is to that question that we now return.

FROM THE TIME of "On Truth and Lying in an Extra-moral Sense," Nietzsche insisted on truth as "a mobile army of metaphors, metonyms, anthropomorphisms, in short, a sum of human relations which were poetically and rhetorically heightened, transferred, and adorned," and on the concept, "bony and cube-shaped like a die, and equally rotatable, [as] just what is left over as the *residue of a metaphor*."[31] No nontropological truth, therefore, no concept that does not revolve or devolve into metaphor. From that starting point, he develops a metaphysic—if we continue to accept Heidegger's judgment—that implies a radical ethics and a controversial politics.[32] The emergence of that politics can be traced, on the one hand, through his often problematic analyses of the Greek state and judgments concerning post-Enlightenment politics, as well as through his ideas concerning ressentiment and slave morality, the overman and the will to power. On the other hand, the argument of controversary dissidence means locating the political "moment" in Nietzsche much closer to the rhetorical heightening and transferring of human relations referred to earlier, and to the *rotations* of the concept. It emerges in the specific performative instance exemplified in the claim that God is dead, whereby what appears as a contradiction (of one constative utterance by another) is understood instead as an intervention and a dissension within the structure of competing beliefs. I contend that the performance of that disagreement is what makes politics possible—the opening of the god structure or belief structure as a result of which discourse moves beyond fact or evidence and into opinion and disputation, beyond constatation into performativity— and the particular enactment of it by Nietzsche can be understood to inaugurate a salutary or even revolutionary form of political dissent, a type of nonreactive dissidence that would too easily be dismissed as a surrender to anarchism. Such dissidence would allow for multiple differential resistances within the range of what we normally call strategies of opposition but would differ from the dialectical form of opposition in at least three respects. It would presume in the first place that pure frontal opposition is a logical, rhetorical, and political impossibility, for there is never the stasis of an absolute equilibrium of forces, and every contestation requires the displacement of those forces, some sort of pressure or turn, side step or feint, the deployment of a choreography of actions to match the complex tropology of words. Every contraposition or so-called confrontation is asymmetrical, and it is rendered so precisely by the initial indisposition, nonconcurrence, or refusal, the turning away, dorsal deflection, or *controversion* that constitutes difference from the very beginning.

In the second place, controversary dissidence would presume the originary disequilibrium or asymmetricality of force to have qualitative as well as quantitative effects, such that by turning out of frontal linearity into dorsal space, any movement of contention would operate a displacement of the very terms of the relation involved. On one side and the other there would be an exposure to, or move into, *umbral* space. A shift from frontal to dorsal involves less the opening of another front, the surprise revelation of another face, than the introduction of the shadow, a different form and substance to call into question the form and substance of the supposedly competing powers themselves. Indeed, following Deleuze's analysis of the will to power, we would call our shadow the relation of disequilibrium itself, on the basis of which power takes effect. It comes into play in such a way as to unsettle relations of power by "adding" an element that asks to be contended with on different terms: "We must remember that every force has an essential relation to other forces, that the essence of force is its quantitative difference from other forces and that this difference is expressed as the force's quality. . . . The will to power is, indeed, never separable from particular determined forces, from their quantities, qualities, and directions. It is never superior to the ways that it determines a relation between forces."[33]

Third, the qualitative displacement of relations that comes into operation by means of controversary dissidence necessarily effects the displacement itself, indeed, the dissidence of each side of the relation with respect to itself. What turns back into its shadow never turns once only, for the shadow also turns, and it turns into a new differentiation of light, into another form of shadowing. There is no more a single repositioning to be adopted but instead an open set of tropological shifts, constant change of perspective, exposure of another side, further deviation, and different vantage. Within every shadow there is a deeper unseen, behind every back there is another, what turns necessarily returns. In response to what Nietzsche advocates for philosophy, we would have to recognize in controversary dissidence a consonant propensity for the political dance.

By insisting on tropological necessity or originary metaphoricity, on the structure of rhetoric that renders the concept (and in particular the concept of truth) subject to chance and controversion ("like a die, and equally rotatable"), Nietzsche, in my reading, also renders possible the performative gesture that I am calling dissidence. But we should not presume to amalgamate rhetoricity and performativity, even though, in the final analysis, both refer to a language that is always already turning away from its supposedly constative neutrality. If there is a difference to be preserved between rhetorical divergence (a language of adornment, valuation, persuasion, and so on) and performative dehiscence (a language of action, engagement, legislation, and so on), between figuration and promise, it would perhaps be that between what in the utterance remains linguistic and what becomes extralinguistic; and if there is a point at which utterance crosses over into the political, it would be by means of the same operation: the point at which, for example, speech becomes hate speech, debate becomes legislation, or a dispute becomes a declaration of war.

But a paradox exists there: whereas it is thanks to the performative that rhetoric becomes politics and speech becomes act, that moment or structure nevertheless involves a qualitative transformation of language into a type of automaticity. Language turns away from its supposed literality into figuration, and away from its supposed linguisticity into a different order or reality; and at the very moment or by means of the very structure whereby the subject of discourse is seen to engage itself more authentically in what it utters—promising, believing, legislating—that subject is required to cede a degree of its autonomy. The moment of political engagement at the same time sets in train a type of linguistic machine, not for the first time, but as a significant instance nevertheless. The subject cedes in that moment to a different type of enunciative conventionality, for just as figures of speech operate within certain rhetorical categories, so do performatives evoke certain conventional forms. And it cedes also to the space of a different agency, for although it is in politics that we most explicitly recognize human agency, in acceding to the space of politics—wherever we decide that it begins or is located—one is conceding a type of integrity or integrality by turning to an extrinsic construction of human relations, a particular articulation of the self to what is outside of it. This particular turn, by which one accedes to politics and concedes one's integral autonomy, can be distinguished from the prosthetic articulations of the body, from the one-to-one (or one-to-many) ethical relation, from familial relations, and from various versions of the social. A new form of estrangement takes place by means of this subjection to the mass and to the foreign, which is also, of course, a subjection to a whole new juridical order, beginning with the very conception of the civil and civilian, the frontier and the enemy. We can understand a politics of any consequence to begin once we are dealing with human relations that extend beyond kinship, into more complex forms of the communal, and by extension into the foreign and eventually into the breaking of relations that constitutes enmity. By the same token, in turning into a political being, in controverting rhetoric into the nonlinguistic performance of a dissidence, the subject also falls outside any supposed organic, natural, or immediate relation to its worldly context. This is not just because in general terms one leaves home and family to practice politics, but more specifically because once there is the controversion without which politics could not be practiced, a type of shadow appears or falls: as a result, the first and automatic dissidence is with respect to the self-definition of the subject, turning it outside itself.

I see no reason not to give to that rupture of the integral subject the name of technology. First, precisely because, as I have consistently maintained, it functions within the same prosthetizing structure that defines and inhabits the body and determines the relations of human to other, to other humans, to other animals, and to the inanimate. We saw how Nietzsche, in spite of himself, posited a type of mechanical automaticity for the nonvengeful subject of revenge, how a subject uncorrupted by conscience had as its outside possibility not a lesser animal but the inanimate itself. Technology is the name we give to exteriority once it is seen to be endowed with a systematicity not of our making, some type of mechanicity or automaticity. Second, because, as we have seen more than once, especially in terms of the ethical relation, technology has the dorsal form of a shadow, which—having longer legs than us—consistently catches up with us whenever we seek to outrun it. It catches up with us when we are perplexed by attempts to deal with definitions of life and operations of the cybernetic and biotechnological, and in a more explicitly political context when we struggle to define privacy, individual freedom, and the operations of technologies of information. It hasn't just appeared to interpellate and threaten us; it has been there since the dawn of our existence. We are in it as soon as we give ourselves a new sphere, any new theater of operations, as soon as we turn to acknowledge the shadow that was always there.

It is a shadow, after all, cast by the light and fire of the sun, announcing the Promethean moment. As soon as we step into the sun's light, we have, as it were, stolen its secret, even before we learn to reproduce and rekindle it. We have allowed it to double us and divide us, and to display and deploy our figure on the world outside us, in a space that we consistently conceive of as behind us. We have allowed that figure to operate beyond our control, only intermittently within sight, a body belonging to, yet detached from, our own body; and yet, realizing that concession or devolution, we have consented to have it continue. We have remained content to have constantly before us or behind us an unsettling "exterior" representation of us. I say "we have allowed" and "consented" to draw attention to the extraordinary "decision," massively reinforced by our rhetorical,

mythological, and philosophical regimes, to reject our shadow as something outside ourselves rather than expand our body to encompass it; to
expel it into dorsal space. Not to affirm it as a companionable member,
excrescence of, or appendage to, our body, but to consistently refer to it
as a sinister parody, spectral menace, duplicitous imposture, insubstantial
mirage, or servile parasite. Whereas Nietzsche's relation of wanderer and
shadow is in many ways a notable exception, we have also seen examples
of his recourse to a rhetoric of the photological and his valorization of the
purifying force of light, albeit nuanced enough to differentiate a thinking
of daybreak from a thinking of noon, and a song of twilight from a song
of midnight.

Still, if that massive photological tradition, beginning with Plato's
cave, goes a long way toward explaining why the shadow is much more
consistently disembodied than incorporated, why it more readily rejoins
phenomena connoting absence of light than is celebrated as a corporeal
projection, I would argue that there exists another important reason for
it: the shadow is relegated to dorsal invisibility precisely because of its
technological connotability such as I have just described. By means of the
shadow, we reveal ourselves to be naturally technological; our naturality is
doubled by technology. It operates as our most explicit (because external)
robotic function, a doppelgänger as mechanical as any automaton. Henceforth we are coupled with it in an uncanny dance. We are divided at or in
our very constitutional limit by the Promethean gesture; his flame licks
at our edges. Because of the dorsal shadow—dorsal because it either falls
behind us or is projected to surprise us from behind—we are driven by a
force and a motor that will not let us rest, from which there is no escape
except, abyssally, into the very darkness that constitutes it, into its perpetual and inexhaustible motion.[34]

Dorsality thus affirms the shadow, controversion, and dissidence as a
form of politics. Within that perspective, it begins by affirming the death
of God, as inaugurating instance of dissent. It affirms that death as controversary rather than confrontational with respect to a belief in God;
not because belief in his nonexistence is any less strong or assured, but
because the death of God is simply the beginning of a calling into question
that has no foreseeable end. The death of God is not a counterposition
but a controverting of positionalities in general; affirming it announces

a promise, not an end of anything but the opening to a future. The inaugural controversion that announces the death of God could not install a universal fiat but would, from here, have to begin by controverting the Judeo-Christian God, as promise performed on what is closest, as an act of dissidence vis-à-vis one's own political, cultural, and religious scene. Promising the death of God means turning toward the technological possibility, not simply in order to embrace it, for such an embrace would no more endear us to technology than belief in God would protect us from it. By turning toward technology as structural possibility, as internal necessity, recognizing it as adhering to the very structure of belief, the very transit of utterance, and the very nature of the human, we simply begin to engage in any number of relations of controversion and dissidence with respect to it. But we would begin to be in it from a different perspective, different from a conception of it as outside threat. Therefore, past a dialectical opposition and confrontation between God and technology, past the presumption of a technology that comes to replace God, a technology whose encroachments are mourned like the retreat of the gods, there emerges from the shadow the possibility of another, new or different performative scene, where one can begin to ask what is meant by a promise made to the inanimate, a nonpneumatic belief, saying yes, yes to what, beyond knowing, is still to come.

GIVEN THE TROPOLOGICAL DEPARTURE that constitutes Nietzsche's reasoning, I maintained earlier, there is no longer any pure mountain air such as he finds indispensable for thinking. But seek it he will, to the end. Outside his work into his autobiography (but can we ever determine the status of *Ecce Homo* vis-à-vis his philosophical work in general and his psychological state in particular?) he still insists:

Anyone who knows how to breathe the air of my writings will know that it is the air of high places. . . . The ice is close by, the solitude is tremendous—but how peacefully everything lies in the light! How freely you can breathe! How many things you feel to be beneath you!—Philosophy as I have understood and lived it so far is a life lived freely in ice and high mountains. (*Ecce Homo,* 72)

The eternal recurrence famously occurs at "6,000 feet beyond people and time" (123), but other sections of *Zarathustra* owe as much to Porto Fino (124), Rome (127), and "Nice's halcyon skies" (128). Nice and Porto Fino, and before them "the jumble of rocks near Genoa" that gave birth to *Daybreak* ("round and happy like a sea creature sunning itself" [120–21]), make clear that the mountains often function in association with, or in counterpoint to, the sea, the "horizon of the infinite" and "beautiful monster" of *The Gay Science* (119, 147). The "proud and calm balance" with which the mountains of Porto Fino fall into the sea explicitly recommends them as "masters of the first rank" (160). Indeed, *The Gay Science* contains a highly significant paean to the waves—"This is how the waves live—this is how we live, we who will—I will say no more. . . . You and I are of one kind" (176)—as founding figures of both the will to power and the eternal return. And returning to *Thus Spoke Zarathustra*, let us not forget that, besides the sea opened again by the death of God that was mentioned earlier, practically the entire second book, and up to "On Virtue That Makes Small" of the third, can be presumed to take place on the Blessed Isles to which he "journey[s] over broad seas" in order to answer to the lake inside him, "a hermit-like and self-sufficient lake" that his torrent of love impels "down to the sea" (*Zarathustra*, 64).

Luce Irigaray has elaborated most extensively on Nietzsche's relation to the fluid in her *Marine Lover*. She reproaches him, or Zarathustra, for leaving the sea, for neglecting sea creatures, for not learning to swim as well as he can dance. The sea she has in mind is feminine, a "first nurse" to whom Nietzsche refuses to return, a different, membranous depth from that of hollows and abysses: "For one by one each of her surfaces takes its turn to shimmer. . . . The sea shines with a myriad eyes. And none is given any privilege. Countless and shifting and merging her depths."[35] So we should perhaps not be surprised to find Zarathustra again heading up the mountain. Indeed, "the crucial section that bears the title 'Old and New Tablets' was composed during the most tiring climb from the station up to the glorious Moorish eyrie of Eza" (*Ecce Homo*, 128). Like Moses, Zarathustra heads up the mountain in search of the most weighty writings, for it is the site of the "most perfect vigour and patience" (128), what inspires one to dance.

The path of that climb is today named after Nietzsche (le Chemin Nietzsche). It is indeed a strenuous ascent from the coast up to Èze-Village; one needs to struggle against the heat and concentrate one's energies. One has to leave the sea behind, keep one's back to it. But that sea remains at one's back: it is the point of departure, and the force of it uplifts the climber as he ascends. More than that, the higher one climbs, the more one becomes aware of the sea, whether because one looks behind or because water is accurately felt as the major climatic influence one is inhabiting. The more one climbs, the more the sea grows at one's back, seen or unseen, until it begins to shimmer with the overwhelming immensity of the ocean.

In literal terms, the farther we climb, the more distance we take from it, it cannot overtake us. By the same token, however, it never leaves. It is all around, it does not understand distance in the same way, and it is doubtful that it can tell front from back. There is always more of it than we can imagine, and wherever we are, it keeps coming upon us.

Henceforth, whichever way we walk, we are all on Nietzsche's path.

Notes

1. The Dorsal Turn

1. Cf. Jean-François Lyotard, *The Inhuman*, trans. Geoffrey Bennington and Rachel Bowlby (Cambridge: Polity Press, 1991): "It is perfectly possible to say that the living cell, and the organism with its organs, are already *tekhnai*, that 'life,' as they say, is already technique" (52). Lyotard states earlier: "As anthropologists and biologists admit, even the simplest life forms, infusoria (tiny algae synthesized by light at the edges of tidepools a few million years ago) are already technical devices. Any material system is technological if it filters information useful to its survival, if it memorizes and processes that information and makes inferences based on the regulating effect of behaviour, that is, if it intervenes on and impacts its environment so as to assure its perpetuation at least" (12). Or Jacques Derrida: "Any living being, in fact, undoes the opposition between *physis* and *techne*. As a self-relation, as activity and reactivity, as differential force, and repetition, life is always already inhabited by technicization. . . . A prosthetic strategy of repetition inhabits the very moment of life: life is a process of self-replacement, the handing-down of life is a *mechanike*, a form of technics. . . . At the origin there is technics." "Nietzsche and the Machine," trans. Richard Beardsworth, in *Negotiations: Interventions and Interviews, 1971–2001* (Stanford, Calif.: Stanford University Press, 2002), 244, 248.

2. André Leroi-Gourhan, *Gesture and Speech*, trans. Anna Bostock Berger (Cambridge: MIT Press, 1993), 91, 106. For an extended discussion of Leroi-Gourhan and of the evolutionary process, and a far-ranging analysis of the question of technology in all its aspects, see Bernard Stiegler, *Technics and Time*, vol. 1, *The Fault of Epimetheus*, trans. Richard Beardsworth and George Collins (Stanford, Calif.: Stanford University Press, 1998). Stiegler's work *La technique et le temps* appears in three volumes in French: vol. 1, *La faute d'Epiméthée*, vol. 2, *La désorientation*, vol. 3, *Le temps du cinéma et la question du mal-être* (Paris: Éditions Galilée, 1994, 1996, 2001). I have discussed Stiegler's work at length in "Techneology or the Discourse of Speed," in *The Prosthetic Impulse: From a Posthuman Present to a Biocultural Future*, ed. Marquard Smith and Joanne Morra (Cambridge: MIT Press, 2006). Certain formulations developed there are returned to here. See also my *Prosthesis* (Stanford, Calif.: Stanford University Press, 1995), which serves as "back-ground" for much of what is developed in the present volume.

3. Cf. Heidegger: "What is happening here when, as a result of the abolition of great distances, everything is equally far and equally near? What is this uniformity in which everything is neither far nor near . . . ?" "The Thing," in *Poetry, Language, Thought*, by Martin Heidegger, trans. Albert Hofstadter (New York: Harper and Row, 1971), 164.

4. "*Every . . . technique is a memory support* that 'exteriorizes' a program" (Stiegler, *La*

technique et le temps, 2:16; translation mine). Stiegler devotes an entire section of the second volume (117–216) to the industrialization of memory.

5. The appositeness to what I am arguing here of the ideas of Jean-Luc Nancy, especially as developed in *Corpus* and elsewhere, could not be more obvious. Any number of elements of the conceptual armature of dorsality are represented in his work, from our general interest, "Until one thinks through, without reservations, the ecotechnical creation of bodies as the truth of *our* world, and as a truth that concedes nothing to those that myths, religions, and humanisms have been able to represent, one will not have begun to think this world *here*" (*Corpus* [Paris: Éditions Métailié, 2000], 78); to the body's originary foreignness to itself, "It is *from the perspective of* my body that I have my body as foreign mine *[comme à moi étranger]*, expropriated. The body is the foreigner 'over there' (that's the place of every foreigner) *because it is here*" (19); to the articulation of the body by means of touch, "Perhaps the 'ontological body' can be thought only where thinking *touches* a hard foreignness, at the nonthinking or non-thinkable exteriority of this *body*. But only such a touching, or such a touch *[touche]* can be the condition for a veritable thinking" (18); to language as technological pros-thesis to the body, "Of course, the body also utters in language. . . . All messages are long chains of material clawings and graftings *[griffes et greffes]* (99); to a type of technology of exscription, "The *exscription* of our body, that is what has first to be passed through. Its inscription outside, its placing *outside-text* as the ownmost movement of its text" (14; translations mine). Taking proper account of those resonances would require a chapter, or a book, of its own, as Derrida discovered. See his *On Touching—Jean-Luc Nancy,* trans. Christine Irizarry (Stanford, Calif.: Stanford University Press, 2005). They will be the focus of a future study.

6. See Giorgio Agamben, *Homo Sacer: Sovereign Power and Bare Life,* trans. Daniel Heller-Roazen (Stanford, Calif.: Stanford University Press, 1998).

7. See again my discussion in "Techneology or the Discourse of Speed."

2. Facades of the Other

1. Martin Heidegger, "The Question concerning Technology," in *The Question concerning Technology and Other Essays,*" trans. William Lovitt (New York: Harper and Row, 1977), 10, 13 (hereafter cited in the text). For indispensable insights into the problems of translating Heidegger's text, see Samuel Weber, "Upsetting the Setup: Remarks on Heidegger's 'Questing after Technics,'" in *Mass Mediauras: Form, Technics, Media* (Stanford, Calif.: Stanford University Press, 1966). While acknowledging fully the arguments in favor of the term "technics" as a preferable translation for *Der Technik,* I prefer for consistency's sake to retain "technology" here.

2. Heidegger, "The Turning," in *The Question concerning Technology and Other Essays,* 44.

3. Heidegger, *Introduction to Metaphysics,* trans. Gregory Fried and Richard Polt (New Haven, Conn.: Yale University Press, 2000), 40. One would need to read closely the references in the lectures of 1935, including the infamous bracket/parenthesis relating to National Socialism (213) in the context of the work of 1949–55.

4. Bernard Stiegler, *Technics and Time*, vol. 1, *The Fault of Epimetheus*, trans. Richard Beardsworth and George Collins (Stanford, Calif.: Stanford University Press, 1998), 179 (translation modified).

5. Martin Heidegger, *Being and Time*, trans. John Macquarie and Edward Robinson (New York: Harper and Row, 1962), 41.

6. Stiegler, *Technics and Time*, 1:214 (see also 216).

7. See the tellingly techno-poetic or poetico-technological passage in *Technics and Time* where this process is described (1:231–32) in the context of my analysis in "Techneology or the Discourse of Speed."

8. *Technics and Time*, 1:172.

9. The term is already used in "The Origin of the Work of Art" with a somewhat different sense, which is clarified in an appendix in relation to the later usage. In "Origin," as in "The Age of the World Picture," it already resonates with the poietic setting-forth *(Herstellung)* practiced by the artist-craftsman, and with operations of representation *(Vorstellung)* that go all the way from the self-objectification of beings to scientific experimentation. In all those cases there is raised the question of (the degree of) an instrumentalist positioning structured by technology. See Heidegger, *Off the Beaten Track*, ed. and trans. Julian Young and Kenneth Haynes (Cambridge: Cambridge University Press, 2002), esp. 23–31, 38, 54, 61–71.

10. Heidegger, "The Question concerning Technology," 19–20. On language as "thinking itself" in a context that is contemporaneous with that essay, see also *The Question of Being*, trans. Jean T. Wilde and William Kluback (New Haven, Conn.: Twayne, 1958), 105.

11. Heidegger, "The Thing," in *Poetry, Language, Thought*, trans. Albert Hofstadter (New York: HarperCollins, 1971), 171, 172.

12. Heidegger, "The Way to Language," in *On the Way to Language*, trans. Peter D. Hertz (New York: HarperCollins, 1971), 129n.

13. For further discussion of the instrumentality of the voice, see my "Jasz Annotations: Negotiating a Discursive Limit," *Paragraph* 21, no. 2 (1998): 137–39.

14. Withdrawal itself *(Entziehung, Entzug)* involves a complicated directionality that is beyond the scope of this discussion: that which holds back rather than reveal itself, but leaves a trace in withdrawing; that which, in withdrawing, pulls man back, et cetera. See, for example, *What Is Called Thinking?* trans. J. Glenn Gray (New York: Harper and Row, 1968), 9; and Jacques Derrida, "The *Retrait* of Metaphor," in *Psyche*, vol. 1, ed. Peggy Kamuf (Stanford, Calif.: Stanford University Press, 2007).

15. See again, for example, *The Question of Being*: "I recall our conversation towards the end of last decade. On a walk along a forest road we stopped at a place where a woodland path branches off" (45).

16. Heidegger, *On the Way*, 133 (italics mine). One would need to enfold into this discussion the whole analysis of *Geschick* in the context of adestination that constitutes Derrida's "Envois," in Jacques Derrida, *The Post Card*, trans. Alan Bass (Chicago: University of Chicago Press, 1987).

17. Louis Althusser, "Ideology and Ideological State Apparatuses (Notes towards an Investigation)," in *Lenin and Philosophy and Other Essays*, trans. Ben Brewster (New York: Monthly Review Press, 1971), 174.

18. "Ideology represents the imaginary relationship of individuals to their real conditions of existence" (Althusser, "Ideology," 162).

19. Ibid., 171. Cf. "Ideology has no history. . . . Ideology is eternal, exactly like the unconscious" (161).

20. Michel Pêcheux, "The Mechanism of Ideological (Mis)recognition," in *Mapping Ideology*, ed. Slavoj Žižek (London: Verso, 1994), 148.

21. See, for example, "The Political Technology of Individuals," in *Power: Essential Works of Foucault, 1954–1984*, vol. 3, ed. James D. Faubion (New York: New Press, 2000).

22. Pêcheux, "The Mechanism of Ideological (Mis)recognition," 148.

23. Judith Butler, *The Psychic Life of Power: Theories in Subjection* (Stanford: Stanford University Press), 3–4. Butler is concerned with "thinking the theory of power together with a theory of the psyche" (3) as a means, on the one hand, of addressing the question of agency and, on the other, of relating that to her idea of a constitutive gender melancholy. See also Butler's extensive analysis of the theological overtones in Althusser's argument (109–14).

24. Althusser, "Ideology," 174 (italics mine).

25. Dienst, *Still Live in Real Time: Theory after Television* (Durham, N.C.: Duke University Press, 1994), 141; Keenan, *Fables of Responsibility: Aberrations and Predicaments in Ethics and Politics* (Stanford, Calif.: Stanford University Press, 1997), 26.

26. See again Derrida, *The Post Card*; and my "Matchbook," in *Matchbook: Essays in Deconstruction* (Stanford, Calif.: Stanford University Press, 2005).

27. Derrida, *The Post Card*, 245.

28. Dienst, *Still Life*, 141.

29. Althusser, "Ideology," 174. Cf. "Les appareils idéologiques de l'état," in *Positions (1964–1975)* (Paris: Editions Sociales, 1976), 114.

30. Cited in Sarah Kofman, *Camera Obscura: Of Ideology*, trans. Will Straw (Ithaca, N.Y.: Cornell University Press, 1999), 1.

31. Ibid., 3 (translation modified).

32. Ibid., 7–8, 9–10. See also the extensive discussion of Marx's dancing table in chapter 5 of Jacques Derrida, *Specters of Marx*, trans. Peggy Kamuf (New York: Routledge, 1994).

33. Kofman, *Camera Obscura*, 12–14.

34. Emmanuel Levinas, *Totality and Infinity: An Essay on Exteriority*, trans. Alphonso Lingis (Pittsburgh: Duquesne University Press, 1969), 69 (hereafter cited in the text).

35. "Human nudity interpellates me—it interpellates the self [*moi*] that I am—it interpellates me with its weakness, without protection or defense, with its nudity; but it also interpellates me with a strange, imperative, and disarmed authority, the word of God and the verb of the human face." Emmanuel Levinas, *Totalité et infini: Essai sur l'extériorité* (Paris: Kluwer Academic [Poche], 2001), ii–iii (translation mine).

36. It should again be noted that Levinas makes explicit the problematics involved in his

formulations and the extent to which he seeks to undo any simple opposition of what I am calling here literality and abstraction. Thus, for example: "The face is abstract. . . . Its abstraction is not obtained by a logical process starting from the substance of beings and going from the individual to the general. . . . The face presents itself in its nudity; it is neither a form concealing, but thereby indicating a ground nor a phenomenon that hides, but thereby betrays, a thing itself." "Meaning and Sense," in *Basic Philosophical Writings,* by Emmanuel Levinas, ed. Adriaan T. Peperzak et al. (Bloomington and Indianapolis: Indiana University Press, 1996), 60–61.

37. One can turn to Deleuze and Guattari for a more "frontal" assault on a humanistic facialization, especially for its converse reductive or racist effects: "If the face is in fact Christ, in other words, your average ordinary White Man, then the first deviances, the first divergence-types, are racial: yellow man, black man, men in the second or third category. . . . They must be Christianized, in other words, facialized. European racism as the white man's claim has never operated by exclusion, or by the designation of someone as Other. . . . Racism operates by the determination of degrees of deviance in relation to the White-Man face." Gilles Deleuze and Félix Guattari, *A Thousand Plateaus,* trans. Brian Massumi (Minneapolis: University of Minnesota Press, 1987), 178.

38. As well, by means of a somewhat problematic assimilation, as infant and animal. The caress, Levinas writes, "loses itself in a being that dissipates into . . . an already animal or infantile anonymity" (*Totality and Infinity,* 259), and "the beloved [who] is opposed to me . . . as an irresponsible animality. . . . return[s] to the stage of infancy without responsibility—this coquettish head, this youth, this pure life 'a bit silly' . . . quit[s] her status as a person" (263). Perhaps it is also the particular infantile or animal docility of the eyes that determines the face as nudity of the primary signifier.

39. Emmanuel Levinas, *Otherwise than Being, or Beyond Essence,* trans. Alphonso Lingis (Pittsburgh: Duquesne University Press, 1998), 100 (hereafter cited in the text).

40. Ibid., 104, 112, 116. Cf. *Autrement qu'être ou au-delà de l'essence* (The Hague: Martinus Nijhoff, 1974), 132, 143, 148. Though *acculé* simply means, on the one hand, "backed against the wall" (and in spite of containing the word "ass *[cul]*," hence meaning more literally "backed ass against the wall," it is used noncolloquially), it seems reasonable to draw attention to this particular physical, indeed corporeal, reference that Levinas makes to replace or reinforce other terms such as *récurrence* (recurrence) and *repliement sur soi* (folding back). How far one can take that choice of word in the direction of dorsality is, of course, my whole question.

41. Cf. Levinas, *Otherwise than Being,* 126–27. For extensive discussion of the question of maternity, see Tina Chanter, *Time, Death, and the Feminine: Levinas with Heidegger* (Stanford, Calif.: Stanford University Press, 2001); and Tina Chanter, ed., *Feminist Interpretations of Emmanuel Levinas* (University Park: Pennsylvania State University Press, 2001).

42. Levinas, *Otherwise than Being,* 104, 108, 112 (translation modified). Cf. *Autrement,* 132, 137, 143.

43. Grossman, quoted in "Peace and Proximity," in Levinas, *Basic Philosophical Writings,* 167.

44. See also the "absolute" deterritorialization of the face, or "the abstract machine of facialization" described by Deleuze and Guattari: "The inhuman in human beings: that is what the face is from the start. . . . To the point that if human beings have a destiny, it is rather to escape the face, to dismantle the face and facializations, to become imperceptible, to become clandestine . . . by strange becomings . . . that will in fact make the *traits of faciality* itself finally elude the organization of the face, no longer allow themselves to be subsumed by the face" (*A Thousand Plateaus*, 171; translation modified).

45. *Concrétisation* and *concrètement* are Levinas's words; in French they do not, of course, refer to sand and mortar. Conversely, the translator's choice of English "home" to translate *maison*, which I have not usually modified, introduces a distinction between house and home that does not exist in the French.

46. See Derrida's extensive analysis of the welcome in Levinas, especially in "A World of Welcome," in *Adieu: To Emmanuel Levinas*, by Jacques Derrida, trans. Pascale-Anne Brault and Michael Naas (Stanford, Calif.: Stanford University Press, 1999).

47. For example: "The atheism of the metaphysician means, positively, that our relation with the Metaphysical is an ethical behavior and not theology" (Levinas, *Totality and Infinity*, 78).

48. Jacques Derrida, "Violence and Metaphysics," in *Writing and Difference*, trans. Alan Bass (Chicago: University of Chicago Press, 1978), 312. Cf. also, in relation to the "cracked surface" of philosophy, where "rigidity" is taken for "solidity": "It could doubtless be shown that it is in the nature of Levinas's writing, at its decisive moments, to move along these cracks, masterfully progressing by negations, and by negation against negation" (90). On Levinas's relation to language, see also Derrida, *Monolingualism of the Other* (Stanford, Calif.: Stanford University Press, 1998), 90–92.

3. No One Home

1. Claude Lévi-Strauss, *Structural Anthropology* (London: Penguin Books, 1972), 216.

2. Sigmund Freud, *Civilization and Its Discontents*, trans. James Strachey (New York: W. W. Norton, 1961), 38. See also Sigmund Freud, "The Uncanny," trans. James Strachey, in *Writings on Art and Literature* (Stanford, Calif.: Stanford University Press, 1997), 221–22.

3. Homer, *The Odyssey*, trans. Robert Fagles (London: Penguin, 1996), 77. Hereafter cited in the text by page number, with occasional reference to book and line.

4. Nietzsche will have recourse to this Greek word in his rhetorical dance around the will to truth in *The Gay Science*, trans. Josephine Nauckhoff (Cambridge: Cambridge University Press, 2001), 201.

5. Homer, *The Iliad*, trans. Robert Fagles (London: Penguin, 1996), 531. Hereafter cited in the text by page number, with occasional reference to book and line.

6. See Robert Graves, *The Greek Myths*, vol. 2 (London: Penguin, 1960), 279, 375.

7. Michel Serres, *Genesis*, trans. Geneviève James and James Nielson (Ann Arbor: University of Michigan Press, 1995), 79.

8. Ibid., 25.

9. Steiner, "The Pythagorean Genre," in *Language and Silence* (New York: Atheneum, 1967), 80.

10. James Joyce, *Ulysses* (New York: Random House, 2002), 346.

11. Cf. Exodus 3:14; John 8:3–8.

12. Note that this brief analysis of the overlapping categories of writer and narrator, considered solely from the perspective of Bloom as protagonist, whose "consciousness" gives rise to much of the novel and who writes here in the first person, in no way broaches the question of a relation between a writer or a narrator and an author.

13. At the end of the Lotus-Eaters episode (chapter 5), Bloom tells Bantam Lyons he can keep the newspaper because he was about to throw it away: "Bantam Lyons doubted an instant, leering: then thrust the outspread sheets back on Mr Bloom's arms. —I'll risk it, he said. Here, thanks" (86). The reader doesn't learn the name of the horse until it is first uttered by Lenehan in Cyclops, some 250 pages later (325). The throwaway leaflet is "placed . . . in a hand of Mr Bloom" in a paragraph of third-person narration that is, however, sandwiched between two sections supposedly composed by Bloom's consciousness (151).

14. Hermann Broch, *The Death of Virgil*, trans. Jean Starr Untermeyer (New York: Random House, 1972), 398; cf. *Der Tod des Vergil* (New York: Pantheon Books, 1945), 427: "The manuscript chest . . . was being borne away and actually was a casket, a shell, bearing the remains of a child, of a life [*eigentlich ein Sarg war, ein Kindersarg, ein Lebenssarg*]." Untermeyer's translation is hereafter cited in the text. Where appropriate, a second page number is given from the German original.

15. For a thorough analysis and "deconstruction" of the *Aeneid* as founding narrative of Rome, to which my discussion is greatly indebted, see the remarkable work of Ika Willis, "Discors Machina: Rome and the Teletechnology of History" (Ph.D. thesis, University of Leeds, UK, 2005).

16. Maurice Blanchot, "Orpheus' Gaze," in *The Space of Literature*, trans. Ann Smock (Lincoln: University of Nebraska Press, 1982), 174.

17. See Maurice Blanchot, "Broch," in *The Book to Come*, trans. Charlotte Mandell (Stanford, Calif.: Stanford University Press, 2003), 118.

18. "Leaving" as the originary moment of thinking (and desiring) is a term to which Branka Arsić gives a whole new focus. See her "Thinking Leaving," in *Deleuze and Space*, ed. Ian Buchanan and Gregg Lambert (Edinburgh, UK: University of Edinburgh Press, 2005); "Afterword: On Leaving No Address," in *Book of Addresses*, ed. Peggy Kamuf (Stanford, Calif.: Stanford University Press, 2005); and *On Leaving: A Reading in Emerson* (forthcoming).

4. A Line Drawn in the Ocean

1. An example from the mythology: my maternal grandmother's brother was born on board ship and named "Caris" after the *Carisbrook Castle*, which brought the family to New Zealand in 1875.

2. See Katherine Mansfield's itinerary (leaving New Zealand to embark on a literary career, returning to it in certain of her stories), or an account such as Janet Frame's

The Envoy from Mirror City (Auckland, New Zealand: Random House, 1985), for different versions of such a narrative.

3. The status of commentary is a major question in my *Prosthesis,* and I approach it from
the bias of autobiography, of the commentaries whereby writing is related to the *bios*
and the *autos.*

4. Cf. Gilles Deleuze, in the context of a contrast between continental and oceanic
islands: "That England is populated will always come as a surprise. . . . Islands are
either from before or for after humankind." "Desert Islands," in *Desert Islands and
Other Texts, 1953–1974,* trans. Michael Taormina (New York: Semiotext(e), 2004), 9.

5. For recent discussion of this question, see Étienne Balibar, *We, the People of Europe?*
trans. James Swenson (Princeton, N.J.: Princeton University Press, 2004).

6. Exodus 12:29 (King James Version).

7. See Jacques Derrida, *The Gift of Death (Second Edition); and Literature in Secret,* trans.
David Wills (Chicago: University of Chicago Press, 2008), 3–8, 28–30.

8. Sigmund Freud, *Civilization and Its Discontents,* trans. James Strachey (New York:
W. W. Norton, 1961), 11–12 (hereafter cited in the text).

9. See my *Prosthesis,* 92–104.

10. One should of course examine in this context not only the Oedipal scene but also the
questions of national identity in Freud's *Moses and Monotheism.*

11. Arthur Rimbaud, *Oeuvres,* ed. Suzanne Bernard (Paris: Garnier Frères, 1960), 269.

12. "Le bateau ivre," in Rimbaud, *Oeuvres,* 128–29 (hereafter cited in the text). All trans-
lations are mine. For English versions of this and other poems, see Arthur Rimbaud,
Complete Works, Selected Letters, trans. Wallace Fowlie (Chicago: University of Chicago
Press, 1966).

13. Rimbaud, *Complete Works, Selected Letters,* 119 (italics mine).

14. The 1960 Garnier edition was revised by Suzanne Bernard and André Guyaux in 1981.
Guyaux's presumed authoritative Pléiade edition is currently still in preparation.

15. As a recent biographer quips in response: "One might just as well be amazed that he
managed to write it without having met an inebriated boat." Graham Robb, *Rimbaud*
(New York: W. W. Norton, 2000), 104.

16. René Étiemble, letter to *Le Monde,* February 3, 1962. Cf. Anonymous (Robert Faurisson), "A-t-on lu Rimbaud?" *Bizarre,* numéro spécial, 4e trimestre, 1961.

17. See Jean-François Lyotard's discussion of the Faurisson case in *The Differend,* trans.
George Van Den Abbeele (Minneapolis: University of Minnesota Press, 1988): "His
argument is: in order for a place to be identified as a gas chamber, the only eyewitness
I will accept would be a victim of this gas chamber" (2–3).

18. "Will all great Neptune's ocean wash this blood clean from my hand? No, this my hand
will rather the multitudinous seas incarnadine, Making the green one red." *Macbeth,*
2.2.

5. Friendship in Torsion

1. Carl Schmitt, *The Concept of the Political,* trans. George Schwab (Chicago: University of
Chicago Press, 1996), 26–27.

2. Ibid., 29.

3. Ibid.

4. Ibid.

5. Ibid., 32, 33.

6. See Jacques Derrida, *Politics of Friendship*, trans. George Collins (London: Verso, 1997), 83–89, 121–25; cf. *Politiques de l'amitié* (Paris: Galilée, 1994). The English translation is hereafter cited in the text, in some cases followed by reference to the French original *(Politiques)*.

7. Carl Schmitt, *Theorie des Partisanen: Zwischenbemerkung zum Begriff des Politischen* (Berlin: Duncker and Humblot, 1963).

8. Roland Barthes, *A Lover's Discourse: Fragments*, trans. Richard Howard (New York: Hill and Wang, 1978), 1–2.

9. Jacques Derrida, *The Post Card*, 78, 187, 256. See also "To Give, *Letterally*," in my *Matchbook: Essays in Deconstruction* (Stanford, Calif.: Stanford University Press, 2005), 74, 78.

10. Jean-Luc Nancy, "Borborygmi," trans. Jonathan Derbyshire, in *The Birth to Presence*, ed. Simon Sparks (Stanford, Calif.: Stanford University Press, 1993), 123. See also Nicholas Royle, "Back," *Oxford Literary Review* 18, nos. 1–2 (1996).

11. In French, "Replis."

12. Derrida, *The Post Card*, 4 (italics mine).

13. For the Nietzsche texts, see Friedrich Nietzsche, *Human, All Too Human: A Book for Free Spirits*, trans. R. J. Hollingdale (Cambridge: Cambridge University Press, 2004), 148–49, 274; and *The Gay Science*, 72.

14. "[Convenance, inconvenance. Digression. *Soit dit entre crochets, Montaigne* tire la plus audacieuse et la plus incontestable conséquence . . ." *(Politiques*, 203; italics mine). Inelegantly preserving the French syntax, this would transliterate as "[Suitability, unsuitability. Digression. Said/speaking, as it were, within brackets, Montaigne draws the most audacious and the most uncontestable consequence . . ." Cf. *Politics*, 178: "[A digression here, remaining between square brackets, on suitability, unsuitability. Montaigne draws the most audacious and the most uncontestable consequence . . ."

15. Jacques Derrida, *Of Grammatology*, trans. Gayatri Spivak (Baltimore: Johns Hopkins University Press, 1974), 157–60.

16. See my *Prosthesis*, 286–318.

17. Cf. "Signature Event Context," in *Margins of Philosophy*, trans. Alan Bass (Chicago: University of Chicago Press, 1982), 320–21. For discussion of iterability/undecidability as aesthetics/ethics nexus, see "Lemming," in my *Matchbook*.

18. Schmitt, *Concept of the Political*, 30.

19. Ibid., 31.

6. Revolutions in the Darkroom

1. Béla Balázs, *Theory of the Film: Character and Growth of a New Art*, trans. Edith Bone (New York: Dover Publications, 1970), 56, 60, 63. See also Gilles Deleuze's discussion of Balázs and the close-up in the context of his affection-image in *Cinema 1: The*

Movement-Image, trans. Hugh Tomlinson and Barbara Habberjam (Minneapolis: University of Minnesota Press, 1986), 95–97.

2. Balázs, *Theory of the Film*, 65; on Dreyer, see 74. Cf. Carl Dreyer, *The Passion of Joan of Arc*, 1928.

3. Balázs, *Theory of the Film*, 61. As an example of the paradox, see Balázs's analysis of Hayakawa's face as both revealing nothing to his enemies and at the same time communicating a complex range of messages to his wife (76).

4. Walter Benjamin, "The Work of Art in the Age of Its Technological Reproducibility (Third Version)," trans. Harry Zohn and Edmund Jephcott, in *Selected Writings*, vol. 4, *1938–1940*, ed. Howard Eiland and Michael W. Jennings (Cambridge, Mass.: Harvard University Press, 2003), 258, 265–66.

5. Ibid., 270.

6. Quoted in Samuel Weber, "Art, Aura and Media in the Work of Walter Benjamin," in *Mass Mediauras* (Stanford, Calif.: Stanford University Press, 1996), 102. Cf. Benjamin, "Work of Art," 282 (the Zohn and Jephcott translation has "the masses come face to face with themselves").

7. Philippe Lacoue-Labarthe, *Heidegger, Art, and Politics: The Fiction of the Political*, trans. Chris Turner (Oxford: Basil Blackwell, 1990), 95 (italics mine); Gilles Deleuze and Félix Guattari, *A Thousand Plateaus*, trans. Brian Massumi (Minneapolis: University of Minnesota Press, 1987), 175, 181.

8. Benjamin, "Work of Art," 258.

9. Weber, "Art, Aura and Media," 101, 102.

10. See Jacques Rancière, *The Politics of Aesthetics*, trans. Gabriel Rockhill (New York: Continuum, 2004), 13, 31–34. For Rancière, the political emerges as a function of claims made by those whose sense experience *(le sensible)* is or is not recognized. It is therefore a function of visibility and hence always already aesthetic: "Politics did not have the misfortune of being aestheticized or spectacularized just the other day. . . . There has never been any "aestheticization" of politics in the modern age because politics is aesthetic in principle." Rancière, *Disagreement: Politics and Philosophy*, trans. Julie Rose (Minneapolis: University of Minnesota Press, 1999), 57, 58.

11. Eduardo Cadava, *Words of Light: Theses on the Photography of History* (Princeton: Princeton University Press, 1997), 44.

12. Benjamin, "Work of Art," 282.

13. Walter Benjamin, "On Some Motifs in Baudelaire," trans. Harry Zohn, in *Selected Writings*, vol. 4, *1938–1940*, 338.

14. Cadava, *Words of Light*, 120. Cadava's book offers, in fragmentary—indeed, delicately Benjaminian—form, a comprehensive analysis of the aura. In the passage quoted, he is in fact dealing specifically with the other important aspect of aura, its articulation of distance. See my later comments, as well as *Words of Light*, 153–54.

15. Benjamin, "Motifs in Baudelaire," 338.

16. Ibid., 338, 354. See also "Little History of Photography," trans. Rodney Livingstone, in *Selected Writings*, vol. 2, *1927–1934*, ed. Michael W. Jennings, Howard Eiland, and Gary Smith (Cambridge: Harvard University Press, 1999), 518–19.

17. Benjamin, "Motifs in Baudelaire," 337, 338; cf. 315.
18. Cadava, *Words of Light,* 76, 77. See also 90–97.
19. Benjamin, "Motifs in Baudelaire," 343 (Baudelaire is quoted on 342).
20. Lacoue-Labarthe, *Heidegger, Art, and Politics,* 66.
21. Ibid., 67.
22. Ibid., 78.
23. See my discussion in chapter 1 of Heidegger's analysis of the *physis/techne* relation. Lacoue-Labarthe will here interpret that relation as one of "original supplementarity" (*Heidegger, Art, and Politics,* 83). And again see Cadava regarding Benjamin's distrust of photography as mimetic art, a mimeticism that causes it to be structurally in decline "because it forgets [its] disjunctive power" (*Words of Light,* 14). In the "Little History of Photography" the loss of aura, which Benjamin still discerns in early photographs, is caused precisely by photography's becoming subject to the mimetic imperative ("Little History," 515–17).
24. Liliana Cavani, *The Night Porter,* 1974; Pier Paolo Pasolini, *Saló, or The 120 Days of Sodom,* 1975. We should not forget that the jury is still out on whether Pasolini paid for this particular repoliticization of art with his life in November 1975. The investigation of his murder was reopened in May 2005 following the convicted murderer's recantation of his confession. For a strikingly comprehensive analysis of these two films in the context of cinematic representations of fascism in general, see Kriss Ravetto, *The Unmaking of Fascist Aesthetics* (Minneapolis: University of Minnesota Press, 2002).
25. Michel Foucault, "Sade, Sergeant of Sex," trans. John Johnston, in *Aesthetics, Method, and Epistemology,* vol. 2 of *Essential Works of Foucault,* ed. James D. Faubion (Harmondsworth, UK: Penguin Books, 1998), 227.
26. See, for example, Michel Foucault, *Madness and Civilization,* trans. Richard Howard (New York: Random House, 1965), 208–10, 282–85; *The Order of Things* (New York: Random House, 1970), 209–11.
27. Foucault, "Sergeant of Sex," 226.
28. Ibid., 223.
29. Ibid., 225–26.
30. Lacoste was Sade's family château in the Luberon, the site of certain of his own libertine experiences; the Château de Silling, as discussed later, is the fortress of *The 120 Days of Sodom;* Miolans, Vincennes, La Bastille, and Charenton are the principal places where the writer was incarcerated. For biographies of Sade, see Gilbert Lély, *Vie du Marquis de Sade, avec un examen de ses ouvrages,* in *Oeuvres complètes du Marquis de Sade,* vol. 1–2 (Paris: Cercle du Livre Précieux, 1966); or in English, Maurice Lever, *Sade: A Biography,* trans. Arthur Goldhammer (New York: Farrar, Straus and Giroux, 1993).
31. Pierre Klossowski, *Sade My Neighbor,* trans. Alphonso Lingis (Evanston, Ill.: Northwestern University Press, 1991), 42.
32. Roland Barthes, *Sade, Fourier, Loyola,* trans. Richard Miller (New York: Farrar, Straus and Giroux, 1976), 17.

33. Gilles Deleuze, *Cinema 2: The Time-Image,* trans. Hugh Tomlinson and Robert Galeta (Minneapolis: University of Minnesota Press, 1989), 175.

34. For a discussion of this question in its more complicated form, that which occurs in the case of cinematic representation, see Peter Brunette and David Wills, *Screen/Play: Derrida and Film Theory* (Princeton, N.J.: Princeton University Press, 1989), 77–78. In my *Matchbook: Essays in Deconstruction* (Stanford, Calif.: Stanford University Press, 2005), 163–64, 170–73, I examine further the question of the photographic instant as "technological" law, and as "diagonal" inversion of that law (both invention and contravention of it).

35. Klossowski, *Sade My Neighbor,* 62.

36. Marquis de Sade, *120 Days of Sodom.* In *120 Days of Sodom and Other Writings,* trans. Austryn Wainhouse and Richard Seaver (New York: Grove Press, 1966), 237; cf. Marquis de Sade, *Oeuvres complètes du Marquis de Sade* (Paris: Cercle du Livre Précieux, 1967), 13:46. The English translation is cited hereafter in the text, followed where necessary by reference to the French original *(Oeuvres).* The translation will at times be slightly modified.

37. See Barthes's semiology of the theater of *The 120 Days,* and in particular the relation of mimesis to praxis that I take up, in the context of *Philosophy in the Bedroom,* later (Barthes, *Sade, Fourier, Loyola,* 146–48).

38. Barthes, *Sade, Fourier, Loyola,* 16 (translation modified).

39. Marquis de Sade, *Justine, Philosophy in the Bedroom, and Other Writings* (New York: Grove Press, 1990), 347–48; cf. Marquis de Sade, *Oeuvres complètes du Marquis de Sade* (Paris: Cercle du Livre Précieux, 1966), 3:531–32. The English translation is cited hereafter in the text, in some cases followed by reference to the French original *(Oeuvres).* The translation will at times be slightly modified.

40. Missing from English edition. Cf. Sade, *Oeuvres complètes,* 3:347.

41. Klossowski notes that "it is not by arguments that Sade's character can obtain the assent of his interlocutor but by complicity" (*Sade My Neighbor,* 27).

42. Sade's difficulties with his own accounting point to both the arbitrariness and the stringency of the 150 narrated perversions per month. In his drafts of parts 2 and 3, he arrives at the end of both December (complex passions) and January (criminal passions) with 151 rather than 150 stories and makes a note to himself to "find out why there is one too many," "determine why there is one too many; if one is to be deleted, suppress the last, for I believe I have already used it" (*120 Days,* 595, 623). But then a parsimony of murderous passions brings him, in part 4, to only 148 instead of 150: "But why the last? Where are the other two? They were all there in the original outline" (665). No missing parts, we might therefore suggest, just discrepancies concerning where they were to be fitted, and the possibility of categorical inversions within complexity, criminality, and murder.

43. For Deleuze, reinforcing the relation to Pasolini made earlier, "the Sadean inspiration in *Salo* comes from the fact that, already in Sade, unbearable corporeal figures are strictly subordinated to the progress of a demonstration" (*Cinema 2,* 174).

44. The text is graphically riven, its discourses and its practices subdivided in turn, for example, by the following competing orders of discourse: (1) instructions given by one character commanding others to do this or that to each other (or by appeals to please, help me, do this or that to me); (2) descriptions wherein the characters provide details of what they are doing as they do it; (3) the more or less expletive orgasmic utterances that we should presumably understand to be poetic reductions of the above, progressive disarticulations that go from a request for a particular caress to a "yes" of assent and incitement, to a repetitive obscenity, and finally an inarticulate groan; (4) parenthetical narrative insertions in the guise of stage directions that reduce the action further to some pure diegetic distillation.

45. Klossowski, *Sade My Neighbor*, 41. Klossowski's precise reference is to the "parallelism between the apathetic reiteration of acts and Sade's descriptive reiteration [such that] the act to be done is re-presented each time not only as though it had never been performed but also as though it had never been described."

46. Maurice Blanchot, *The Infinite Conversation*, trans. Susan Hanson (Minneapolis: University of Minnesota Press, 1993), 223–24.

47. Ibid., 220.

48. Thomas Keenan, *Fables of Responsibility: Aberrations and Predicaments in Ethics and Politics* (Stanford, Calif.: Stanford University Press, 1997), 95.

49. As such, it would have lost its aura. But is that logic, or the converse of it, not in fact the means by which history, the singularity of the event, even the revolutionary political event, reinstalls the aura of originality upon the work of art that represents it, endowing it again with a type of cultic value? Is there not that sort of aesthetic overlay superimposed upon the political import of a photograph, say of Prague's residents facing down a Soviet tank, or an Allende at the end, armed and ready for martyrdom, or of any of the countless others we could cite; is there not an aura associated with such photographs that derives precisely from the singular and original moments we call history? On the one hand, the purest political moment, when a program is enacted, relies on a realism of the age of mechanical reproducibility: no aura, an aestheticized politics. On the other hand, that pure political moment gives back to the photographic representation of it the aura that the latter art form had lost. Do we not therefore find some mirroring of the political and the aesthetic whenever, and especially when, we make our realist assumptions? Were those not the assumptions of Jean-Louis David's paintings, and which photography, far from abandoning, was determined precisely to recover and maintain?

50. Blanchot, *Infinite Conversation*, 226. On the relation to nature in Sade, see also Klossowski, *Sade My Neighbor*, 80–84.

51. Blanchot, *Infinite Conversation*, 217–18. Sade's contradictions will not prevent sodomy, for example, from being on the one hand as mimetically natural as the morphological resemblance between penis and anus, and on the other the most blatant transgression of natural propagation that Klossowski has emphasized (*Sade My Neighbor*, 24). See also Foucault's discussion of a nature that, as pastiche of Rousseau, is only a

"first phase of Sade's thought" and later becomes "criminal subjectivity" in the form of the lightning by which it "lacerates" itself in striking Justine (*Madness and Civilization,* 283–84).

52. Barthes, *Sade Fourier, Loyola,* 32 (translation modified).

53. Ibid., 133.

54. Jean-François Lyotard, *The Confession of Augustine,* trans. Richard Beardsworth (Stanford, Calif.: Stanford University Press, 2000), 19. See also 23–24, and Geoffrey Bennington's discussion of this motif in Lyotard in "Behind," in *Afterwords: Essays in Memory of Jean-François Lyotard,* ed. Robert Harvey, Occasional Papers of the Humanities Institute at Stony Brook 1 (Stony Brook, N.Y.: Humanities Institute, 2000).

55. See Foucault, *The Hermeneutics of the Subject,* trans. Graham Burchell (New York: Picador, 2005), 315–27; and Klossowski, *Sade My Neighbor,* 91–98. "Apathy" is Dolmancé's word (342).

56. Klossowski, *Sade My Neighbor,* 23.

57. Barthes, *Sade, Fourier, Loyola,* 30.

58. Ibid., 152–53; see also 125–26.

59. Walter Benjamin, "On the Concept of History," trans. Harry Zohn, in *Selected Writings,* vol. 4, *1938–1940,* 392.

60. Walter Benjamin, "Paralipomena to 'On the Concept of History,'" trans. Edmund Jephcott and Howard Eiland, in *Selected Writings,* vol. 4, *1938–1940,* 405.

61. Walter Benjamin, *The Arcades Project,* trans. Howard Eiland and Kevin McLaughlin (Cambridge, Mass.: Harvard University Press, 1999), 473, 475. See also "On the Concept of History," 390.

62. Benjamin, *Arcades Project,* 463.

63. Benjamin, "Paralipomena," 403.

64. Benjamin, *Arcades Project,* 463.

65. The terms are all Benjamin's, for example in *The Arcades Project,* 473–75. For "revolutionary chance," see "Paralipomena," 402.

7. The Controversy of Dissidence

1. Friedrich Nietzsche, *Thus Spoke Zarathustra,* trans. Adrian Del Caro (Cambridge: Cambridge University Press, 2006), 183. Hereafter cited in the text.

2. Jacques Derrida, *Politics of Friendship,* trans. George Collins (London: Verso, 1997), 29–30.

3. Wills, *Matchbook: Essays in Deconstruction* (Stanford, Calif.: Stanford University Press, 2005), 171; and see again Peter Brunette and David Wills, *Screen/Play: Derrida and Film Theory* (Princeton, N.J.: Princeton University Press, 1989), 77–78.

4. See my "Passionate Secrets and Democratic Dissidence" (*Diacritics,* forthcoming) for an earlier contextualization of these ideas.

5. Derrida, "Nietzsche and the Machine," in *Negotiations: Interventions and Interviews, 1971–2001* (Stanford, Calif.: Stanford University Press, 2002), 218.

6. Nietzsche, *The Gay Science,* trans. Josephine Nauckhoff (Cambridge: Cambridge University Press, 2001), 195, 199. Hereafter cited in the text.

7. Nietzsche, *Human, All Too Human: A Book for Free Spirits,* trans. R. J. Hollingdale (Cambridge: Cambridge University Press, 2004), 79 (hereafter cited in the text); *The Anti-Christ, Ecce Homo, Twilight of the Idols, and Other Writings,* trans. Judith Norman (Cambridge: Cambridge University Press, 2005), 66, 182.

8. See Gilles Deleuze, *Nietzsche and Philosophy,* trans. Hugh Tomlinson (New York: Columbia University Press, 1983), 52–55. Deleuze is exemplary in reading a coherent and rigorous argument, a consistent philosophy throughout Nietzsche's work, to the extent of contradicting what I am maintaining regarding illogicality and lack of systematicity. At the same time, however, his book reads as the elaboration of "properly" Deleuzian concepts and positions that are invented on the basis of, or provoked out of, Nietzsche's writings. Deleuze's interpretation of Nietzsche rightly leads to his own active or activist philosophizing. See hereafter for further discussion of Nietzsche's rhetorical shifts.

9. Thomas Keenan, *Fables of Responsibility: Aberrations and Predicaments in Ethics and Politics* (Stanford, Calif.: Stanford University Press, 1997), 95. See my discussion in chapter 6.

10. Avital Ronell, *The Test Drive* (Urbana: University of Illinois Press, 2005), 164. I note, with gratitude for the inspiration, that this chapter had its beginnings in a response to an address by Ronell ("Nietzsche and Legal Theory" Conference, Cardozo Law School, October 2001), and its inspiration in her theory of testing, leading me to pose the question of the test that will lay all the rest to rest, namely, whether God is really dead.

11. Philippe Lacoue-Labarthe, "The Fable," trans. Hugh J. Silverman, in *The Subject of Philosophy,* ed. Thomas Trezise (Minneapolis: University of Minnesota Press, 1993), 6.

12. See Jacques Derrida on "the appeal to faith that inhabits every act of language and every address to the other" and the alliance between "belief or credit, the fiduciary or the trustworthy" and faith, performativity, and technoscientific or teletechnological performance in "Faith and Knowledge," trans. Samuel Weber, in *Religion,* ed. Jacques Derrida and Gianni Vattimo (Stanford, Calif.: Stanford University Press, 1998), 18–19.

13. Deleuze, *Nietzsche and Philosophy,* 152. He shortly adds: "Nietzsche mistrusts the death of God. With him the age of naive confidence comes to an end, the age which some times acclaims the reconciliation of man and God, at others the replacement of God by man. Nietzsche has no faith in great resounding events" (156). Deleuze's discounting of speculative propositions (such as "God does *or* does not exist insofar as the idea of him does or does not imply a contradiction" [152]) enables him to develop the various ways in which, as he reads Nietzsche, religion (Judaism and Christianity) puts God to death in the service of a reactive life, thus inscribing the event within Nietzsche's antidialectics in a way that again belies its seemingly simple force of emancipation.

14. Such an interpretation, which I am not insisting on, would have to take into account the poem that appears as the epilogue to volume 1 and the volume 2 preface. I prefer to allow the generalized umbrality that I analyze more closely later, in terms of the

shift from prologue to aphorism in volume 2, to reflect back on whatever disjunctions occur between the introduction of the Wanderer and his first conversation with the Shadow.

15. Perhaps even hearing thus comes to be infected with the performative structure of credence, which might help to explain Nietzsche's constant problem with ears.

16. *Zarathustra*, 302. Hollingdale's translation has an exclamation mark and a question mark where the German has two question marks. See Friedrich Nietzsche, *Menschliches, Allzumenschliches II*, in *Werke*, division 4, vol. 3, ed. Giorgio Colli and Mazzino Montinari (Berlin: Walter de Gruyter, 1967), 177.

17. *On the Genealogy of Morality*, trans. Carol Diethe (Cambridge: Cambridge University Press, 2005), 9–10. Hereafter cited in the text (I have retained the traditional English title for this work when referring to it, while using the Cambridge edition for uniformity's sake). See also *Twilight of the Idols:* "I am the first German to have mastered the aphorism. . . . My ambition is to say in ten sentences what other people say in a book,—what other people do *not* say in a book" (*The Anti-Christ, Ecce Homo, Twilight of the Idols, and Other Writings*, 223); and Pierre Klossowski, for whom the form of the aphorism, "rather than pursuing the birth of the concept at the level of the intellect . . . comes to interpret the concept" (*Nietzsche and the Vicious Circle*, trans. Daniel W. Smith [London: Athlone Press, 1997], 255).

18. Cf. Deleuze: "Nietzsche creates his own method: dramatic, typological and differential. He turns philosophy into an art, the art of interpreting and evaluating. In every case he asks the question 'Which one [*qui*, who]?'" (*Nietzsche and Philosophy*, 197; see also 75–79). Deleuze's consistent response, "the one that [*celui qui*] . . . is Dionysus" (ibid.), demonstrates an emphasis different from our own, but its forms, "a mask or a guise of Dionysus, a flash of lightning" ("Preface to the English Translation," ix), share some structural similarities (doubling, surprise) with our sense of the shadow. Regarding the shadow, at least in Zarathustra, see 166, 170, and my discussion hereafter.

19. Blanchot, *The Infinite Conversation*, trans. Susan Hanson (Minneapolis: University of Minnesota Press, 1993), 162–63.

20. Ibid., 162.

21. *The Anti-Christ, Ecce Homo, Twilight of the Idols, and Other Writings*, 125 (hereafter cited in the text); cf. *Ecce Homo* in *Werke* 4.3, 335.

22. Explicit resonances do exist between the two books, beginning with aphorism 638 ("The Wanderer") of *Human, All Too Human* (203), where the central reference to desert experience is echoed in the shadow's wilderness song in *Zarathustra*.

23. Cf. Friedrich Nietzsche, *Also sprach Zarathustra: Ein Buch für Alle und Keinen*, in *Werke* 6.1, 337.

24. See also how *The Gay Science*'s version of "Zarathustra's going under"—the point at which Nietzsche left off writing *The Gay Science* to compose *Zarathustra*—makes the comparison with a sun that steps "into the depths . . . behind the sea" in order to bring "light even to the underworld" (*Gay Science*, 195), that is to say as converse producer of the night as much as of the day, as a type of differential shadow that negates and

affirms at the same time. Note also, therefore, that the geological gathering whence the sun emerges is as much oceanic as it is topographical.

25. Cf. Jean-Luc Nancy: "God died by the death of Nietzsche. And for eleven years, progressive paralysis identified God and he who could write nothing, say nothing anymore. God resuscitated one last time: paralyzed, mad, alienated, so congealed in the anticipated posture of death—preceding death itself, death not ceasing to precede itself—that he could never resuscitate again." Nancy, "Dei Paralysis Progressiva," trans. Thomas Harrison, in *The Birth to Presence* (Stanford, Calif.: Stanford University Press), 48–49.

26. Martin Heidegger, "Nietzsche's Word: 'God Is Dead,'" in *Off the Beaten Track*, ed. and trans. Julian Young and Kenneth Haynes (Cambridge: Cambridge University Press, 2002), 162, 186.

27. Blanchot, *Infinite Conversation*, 140, 148, 150, 151 (italics mine).

28. Deleuze, *Nietzsche and Philosophy*, 195, 196. There would nevertheless be the "Dionysian yes [that] knows how to say no: it is pure affirmation, it has conquered nihilism and divested negation of all autonomous power" (185). We need not restrict ourselves to the examples just quoted. See also Derrida: "The diversity of gestures of thought and writing, the contradictory mobility (without possible synthesis or sublation) of the analytical incursions, the diagnoses, excesses, intuitions, the theater and music of the poetic-philosophical forms, the more-than-tragic play with masks and proper names—these aspects of Nietzsche's work have always appeared to me to defy, from the very beginning to the point of making them look somewhat derisory, all the 'surveys' and accounts of Nietzsche" ("Nietzsche and the Machine," in *Negotiations*, 216); Pierre Klossowski: "Lucid thought, delirium and the conspiracy form an indissoluble whole in Nietzsche. . . . Because his thought was lucid to the extreme, it took on the appearance of a delirious interpretation" (*Nietzsche and the Vicious Circle*, xvi); Sarah Kofman: "The deliberate use of multiple metaphors is . . . the sign of a noble will which, though capable of affirming one perspective for a long stretch of time, is nevertheless at enough of a distance from it to change it and see the world with 'other eyes'" (*Nietzsche and Metaphor*, trans. Duncan Large [Stanford, Calif.: Stanford University Press, 1993], 103); Lacoue-Labarthe: "Nietzsche, of all the philosophers . . . was the one who distinguished himself the most systematically . . . by his contradictory and multifarious, enigmatic and, let us say, disruptive practice of writing" ("Apocryphal Nietzsche," trans. Timothy D. Bent, in *The Subject of Philosophy*, 39); Paul de Man: "As any reader of *The Birth of Tragedy*, *The Genealogy of Morals*, or of that irrepressible orator Zarathustra knows, there hardly is a trick of the oratorical trade which [Nietzsche] is not willing to exploit to the full" (*Allegories of Reading* [New Haven, Conn.: Yale University Press, 1979], 131); J. Hillis Miller: "Much of the time Nietzsche presents figures without the clear and distinct concepts they appear to be in aid of presenting. The reader is given the figurative without the literal, as if what Zarathustra has to say can only be said in figure" (*Topographies* [Stanford, Calif.: Stanford University Press, 1995], 182); see also "Aphorism as Instrument of Political Action in Nietzsche," *Parallax* 10, no: 3

[2004]: "Nietzsche is master . . . of an ironic style that does not so much say one thing and mean another as say two things at once that cancel one another out in a parabasis or suspension of thought and meaning" [74]).

29. Cf. *Zur Genealogie der Moral*, in *Werke* 6.2, 284.

30. In this regard see Nietzsche's difficulty in defining a reaction that is not reactive. In section 10 of the first essay of *The Genealogy of Morals* alone, reaction *[Reaktion]* belongs at the beginning to slave morality (22), and toward the end to the noble man, albeit as his form of ressentiment (23). Similarly, the ressentiment of slave morality is said to need, "physiologically speaking, external stimuli" (22), but by the end the evil enemy of the man of ressentiment resides, albeit as "copy and counterpart," in "himself" (24). A detailed analysis of physical (e.g., machine) versus physiological (e.g., animal) re/action would take us deep into Nietzsche's problematization of cause and effect on the one hand (see *Genealogy of Morality*, 28; and more particularly aphorisms 112, 127, 217, and 360 in *The Gay Science*, 113, 121, 144, 225), and into the question of psychology as physiology, or more particularly as metabolism, such as he expectorates in *Ecce Homo* (81–90). In the latter regard, see Klossowski's analysis of Nietzsche's "tonality of soul" and "valetudinary states," particularly, for our purposes, in the context of how "*meaning* is formed in the upright position, and in accordance with its own criteria: *high, low, before, behind*" (*Nietzsche and the Vicious Circle*, 26; translation modified).

31. Friedrich Nietzsche, "On Truth and Lying in an Extra-moral Sense," trans. David J. Parent, in *Friedrich Nietzsche on Rhetoric and Language*, ed. Sander L. Gilman, Carole Blair, and David J. Parent (New York: Oxford University Press, 1989), 250, 251.

32. See recent assessments and overviews of these questions in Paul Patton, ed., *Nietzsche, Feminism, and Political Theory* (London: Routledge, 1993); Keith Ansell-Pearson, *An Introduction to Nietzsche as Political Thinker: The Perfect Nihilist* (Cambridge: Cambridge University Press, 1994); and Daniel W. Conway, *Nietzsche and the Political* (London: Routledge, 1997).

33. Deleuze, *Nietzsche and Philosophy*, 49–50.

34. For Blanchot, a nonphotological force is what constitutes the Will to Power: "Force escapes light: it is not something that would simply be deprived of light, an obscurity still aspiring to the light of day. Scandal of scandals, it escapes every optical reference" (*Infinite Conversation*, 160).

35. Luce Irigaray, *Marine Lover of Friedrich Nietzsche*, trans. Gillian C. Gill (New York: Columbia University Press, 1991), 47; see also 12–13, 37. See also Cathryn Vasseleu, "Not Drowning, Sailing: Women and the Artist's Craft in Nietzsche," and Frances Oppel, "'Speaking of Immemorial Waters': Irigaray with Nietzsche," in Patton, *Nietzsche, Feminism, and Political Theory*.

Illustration Credits

Index

accident. *See* surprise
Aeneid, The, 88–89, 92–96
Agamben, Giorgio, 13
angel of history, 202–3
Anti-Christ, The, 212
aphorism, 222–24, 260n17
Arcades Project, The, 202
aura, 164–67, 257n49
authorship, 88–95

Barthes, Roland, 141, 171, 175
Being and Time, 27–28, 32
biotechnology, 4, 5–6, 11, 159
Blanchot, Maurice, 142, 187–88, 232

Cadava, Eduardo, 164–66
camera obscura, 41
Capital, 41
Cavani, Liliana, 169, 194
Civilization and Its Discontents, 67–68,
    112–18
close-up, 163–64, 167, 178, 190
commentary, 103–4, 121–27, 155–56
Concept of the Political, The, 133–35
creationism, 5–6
credence/belief. *See* faith

Death of Virgil, The (Der Tod des Vergil), 82,
    88–99
deconstruction, 135, 138, 148–52
Deleuze, Gilles, 164, 232–33, 249n37,
    250n44
departure/detour/deviation/diversion,
    4–5, 27, 40, 44–45, 73, 213; as
    curvature, 45–46; as (Tropo)
    technology, 74–75, 94, 104

Dienst, Richard, 39
Dreyer, Carl, 163
"Drunken Boat, The," 119–23, 125–26

Ecce Homo, 225, 235, 241–42
element: in Levinas, 53–60, 62, 105
eroticism. *See* sexuality
Europe, 103–8, 112, 119–21, 127, 129,
    133–34; Rome, 113–14
exile. *See* home/house
Exodus, 108–11, 133

Fables of Responsibility, 39, 188
faith, 11, 217–18, 220–22, 230–31, 235,
    241
fascism, 164–65, 167–71, 187–88
feminine, 47–48, 51, 53, 67, 185–86,
    249n38; home as, 57–60, 90
Foucault, Michel, 169–170, 194, 196, 198
Future of an Illusion, The, 112, 114

Gay Science, The, 146, 209, 212, 218–19
German Ideology, 41
Gestell, 25–34, 247n9
God, death of, 209–21, 230–32, 240–42
Graves, Robert, 80
Guattari, Félix, 164, 249n37, 250n44

Hephaestus (Vulcan), 69–70, 76
Holocaust, 108, 124–25
home/house, 13–15, 67–68, 70–72, 103,
    238; and Broch, 88–99; and Homer,
    72–75, 78–82; and Joyce, 82–83; and
    Levinas, 53–61
Human, All Too Human, 146, 152, 212,
    219–27, 230, 234

David Wills is professor of Languages, Literatures, and Cultures and of English at the University at Albany, State University of New York. He is the author of several books, including *Prosthesis* and *Matchbook*. His work develops ideas concerning the relation between the human and the technological.